NEWCOMER'S HANDBOOK ®
FOR
Seattle

3000 Market Street N.E., Suite 527
Salem, OR 97301
(503) 588-2224
www.firstbooks.com

FIRST BOOKS

Author: Amy Bellamy
Editor: Bernadette Duperron
Publisher: Jeremy Solomon
Design and production: Erin Johnson
Maps: Scott Lockheed

ISBN: 0-912301-35-X

Manufactured in the United States of America.

Published by First Books, Inc., 3000 Market Street N.E., Suite 527 Salem, OR 97301 • (503) 588-2224

Printed in Canada

CONTENTS

CONTENTS *(continued)*

Welcome to Seattle, one of the most livable urban areas in the world! No doubt you've heard about the rain, but there's a lot more to the "Emerald City" than that. Part of the Pacific Northwest, Seattle is one of the most beautiful and lush regions in the United States. From atop every one of Seattle's many hills, you can view snow-capped mountains, pristine lakes, or the magnificent Puget Sound. Majestic Mount Rainier presides over the city to the southeast, a reminder of the geologic forces at work in shaping the area's majestic landscape. Seattle residents refer to it simply as "the Mountain" and on clear days will excitedly tell you that "the Mountain is out."

Speaking of clear days, don't be daunted by the rumors you've heard about Seattle and rain. While it's certainly true that the city has its share of rainy days, much of Seattle's rains are really a fine mist or "drizzle," and often a day that starts off cloudy becomes bright and sunny by the afternoon. Winters are mild, with infrequent snowfalls in the metropolitan area and summers are comfortably warm, with temperatures hovering in the mid-70s during July and August. Spring and fall are cool but often sunny, and you'll enjoy some of the most spectacular views during these seasons, with snowy mountains set against a backdrop of radiantly clear, sunlit blue sky. Many Seattle residents actually prefer the rainy days, and as summer ends will tell you truthfully that they're relieved to be done with the weeks of "hot" temperatures. Others realize that the rain is an indispensable factor in creating some of the wonderful characteristics of this area, such as the luscious green trees, colorful rhododendrons, and plentiful lakes and waterways.

Situated between two bodies of water and two mountain ranges, Seattle has stunning vistas that can be enjoyed throughout the city. To the west is the Puget Sound, an inland saltwater sea which connects to the Pacific Ocean. The Sound is what makes Washington immediately recognizable on every map of the United States, creating the little hook of land out into the ocean. That piece of land is actually the Olympic Peninsula, west of Seattle across the Puget Sound. The Olympic Mountains, located in the middle of the peninsula, are surrounded by forests and small logging towns. From Seattle, one can see the Olympics clearly and recognize The Brothers, a twin-peaked mountain in the center of the range. East of the city lies Lake Washington, 22 miles long and part of a system of lakes in the Seattle area which were formed by glaciers. Other lakes within the city include Lake Union, just north of Downtown and connected by manmade channels to Lake Washington and the Puget Sound, as well as Green Lake, Haller Lake, and Bitter Lake, all located in the north end of the city. All of these lakes are fed by mountain streams created by melting snow in the Cascades, a volcanic mountain range that runs the length of the state and separates Western and Eastern Washington. Mount Rainier is part of the Cascade Range, as are many smaller mountains that can be seen from vantage points throughout the city.

All of these natural wonders contribute to the abundant recreational opportunities that make Seattle a favorite of outdoor enthusiasts. From early spring to late summer, residents hike and camp in both the Cascades and the Olympics. There is water-skiing in nearby lakes, kayaking on the Sound, and fishing along the many rivers and streams. More intrepid adventurers travel to the eastern side of the Cascades for rock-climbing and bouldering, or head into the mountains for some challenging mountain-climbing on Mount Rainier, Mount Baker, Mount Adams, or The Brothers. In the winter several popular ski resorts open in the Cascades, offering downhill skiing, snowboarding, and cross-country skiing. Those on Snoqualmie Pass are a mere hour-long drive out of Seattle on I-90; others are slightly farther away on Mount Baker, Steven's Pass, and Mount Rainier.

In addition to the mild weather and the natural beauty of the area, Seattle and its surrounding communities also share a thriving economy. Just ten minutes east of Seattle lies the city of Bellevue, home to the world's richest man, Bill Gates, and just ten minutes east of Bellevue lies the town of Redmond, home to Gates' company, Microsoft. In the years since Microsoft began, the greater Seattle area has become a powerhouse in the field of high technology. Other area businesses which have become national successes in recent years, adding fuel to an already strong job market, include: Eddie Bauer, Starbucks, REI, and Cellular One (now AT&T Wireless Services). And then there's Boeing, the world's largest airplane manufacturer.

The combination of good jobs and beautiful surroundings has brought in thousands of newcomers and continues to entice many to the area. Since 1980, the Seattle metropolitan area has grown by 376,000 people, and an additional quarter million new residents are predicted for the area by 2010. Efforts by local governments to limit growth in the region, in particular by instituting an urban growth boundary in 1994, have been largely unsuccessful. Townhouses and condominiums are slowly replacing single-family houses with large yards, and many people are choosing to buy new homes outside of the city limits. While many Seattle homes are still affordable for middle-income and first-time home-buyers, housing prices have continued their relentless upward march and are now climbing at approximately $1,000 a month. With the increased demand for housing, some traditionally overlooked Seattle neighborhoods are now being revitalized with old homes being remodeled and new houses built in these areas.

In the 1990s, Seattle's reputation has been a trend-setting one, making espresso (Starbucks), alternative and "grunge" music (Pearl Jam), microbrews (Red Hook), and software (Microsoft), a daily part of U.S. culture. You'll find that Seattlelites like to go out to coffee, to the movies, or to watch local bands perform — in short, to anyplace where it isn't raining. In addition, Seattle has a thriving and nationally recognized performing arts community, including the Seattle Symphony, the Seattle Opera, and the Pacific Northwest Ballet, as well as several theatrical companies including Intiman, the Seattle Repertory Theater, and A Contemporary Theater.

As newcomers soon learn, conversations here not only revolve around microbrews, coffee, computers and the weather, but also the traffic. Your potential commute is an extremely important factor to consider when choosing a place to live here, especially if your route includes either of the two floating bridges. Highway 520 and I-90 are bridges that span Lake Washington, connecting Seattle with the Eastside communities, which include Bellevue, Kirkland, Issaquah, Renton, Redmond, and Woodinville. Both bridges create traffic bottlenecks during rush hour. On the bright side, however, the views of Lake Washington and Mount Rainier from the bridge decks are unbelievable!

WHAT TO BRING

An umbrella. Although it's easy to find them for sale here, it will probably be raining when you arrive. Also, find a light but warm jacket.

Temperatures in Seattle can vary sharply during the day, going from sunny and warm to cloudy and rainy within a few minutes.

When visiting the city to find your neighborhood, bring or rent a car. Public transportation (buses, monorail, ferries) is available, but it can be a time-consuming task to explore the city without a car. Buses wind through several neighborhoods, stopping at nearly every block. Transferring buses can also cause long delays. If a car is not a possibility, expect to spend the first day getting used to the bus routes and schedules. And don't try to travel around at night by bus without checking the schedule beforehand; many buses stop running or change routes early in the evening. Also, get a detailed map. Although the layout of most of Seattle is on a straightforward grid, many of the major streets are the ones that don't follow the rules.

Finally, bring a good attitude and a smile. While most people in Seattle are friendly and outgoing, you'll notice a layer of reticence when meeting strangers. With a little patience and a calm demeanor you'll be able to get help from just about anybody in Seattle. So stop in, have a café latte, and stay for a while or forever. Welcome to Seattle, a beautiful and friendly place to live!

Seattle was founded on its present site in February 1852, four months after the first party of white settlers landed the schooner *Exact* on Alki Point, in what is now known as West Seattle. The Denny Party included Arthur Denny and his family, his brother David, as well as the Lows, the Bells, the Borens, and the Terrys. Many of the city streets are named after these founders of Seattle. In early 1852 Denny, Low, and Boren set out in a canoe to find a more sheltered area for their settlement. They crossed Elliott Bay and, measuring the depth of the bay using a piece of rope and a horseshoe, chose a harbor for their new city (Seattle) just west of what is now Pioneer Square.

Seattle is named for Chief Sealth, a Salish Indian whose name in his native tongue was too difficult for many early white settlers to pronounce. Dr. David "Doc" Maynard, who arrived in 1852 and started Seattle's first store and hospital, was instrumental in naming the city. Maynard was a friend of Chief Sealth's and suggested Seattle as a more easily pronounced version of the Chief's name. Maynard considered the original name for the settlement, Duwamps, to be unlikely to attract visitors or new settlers to the area. Duwamps was a derivative of the name for one of the Indian tribes who lived around Elliot Bay, the Duwampish or Duwamish. The other nearby tribe, the Salish or Suquampish, lived between the Bay and Lake Duwampish, now Lake Washington. There may have been additional tribes in the Seattle area, but because Native Americans around the Puget Sound were a loose-knit group, it is not apparent how many separate tribes were here originally. What is clear, however, is that all of the area tribes were jointly represented by Chief Sealth. These tribes remained in the area until 1855 when, after some minor skirmishes between the settlers and the Indians, they were relocated to the Suquamish Indian Reservation across Puget Sound. Chief Sealth's farewell speech is a well-known, oft-quoted piece of Seattle history, and an inspiring reminder of the great Native American leader.

Henry Yesler, another of Seattle's most prominent and influential citizens, arrived in the fall of 1852, soon after Doc Maynard. Yesler was a tight-fisted businessman, looking for a site to establish a sawmill. The other claim-holders quickly signed over a piece of the waterfront where, in 1853, Yesler built a sawmill, cookhouse, and a meeting hall, all firsts for the new city. The sawmill initially received its supply of lumber from the heavily wooded hills east of the settlement, which are now a part of the city itself. The trees were pushed to the mill down a slick wooden slipway, built into the side of a hill in Downtown Seattle. The term "skid road" or "skid row," coined for this innovative contrivance, quickly became synonymous with the rowdy behavior of the mill workers who lived in that area.

On June 6, 1889, near what is now 1st Ave. and Madison St., a glue pot caught fire in a carpenter's workshop, starting the Great Seattle Fire. Coming after an unusual early summer drought, the fire quickly burned down every building within a 60 acre area. Soon after the fire, city officials passed an ordinance requiring that any new buildings be constructed of bricks or stone. The buildings destroyed in the fire were swiftly rebuilt under these regulations. Surprisingly, the result of the fire was a strengthened city economy, as the rebuilding projects provided much needed business to local bricklayers and builders. The sawmill was not adversely affected because demand for lumber was still great in California, and most of what was produced at Yesler's mill was shipped to San Francisco. However, the fire and subsequent renovations did have one strange consequence. The city, taking advantage of the opportunity to correct some of the drainage problems that had plagued Downtown, constructed streets at a level 12 feet higher than they had been before the fire, but some business owners, who were not in agreement on this project, rebuilt businesses at their original level, leading to sharp inclines between the city-owned streets and the privately owned sidewalks. Eventually the city put in new sidewalks at the higher street level, and the first floors of these downtown buildings became basements and open spaces. For many years these spaces were used as an underground mall housing legitimate businesses, and later became infamous as opium dens, brothels, and moonshine establishments. Today, the Seattle Underground Tour is a popular tourist attraction that takes visitors through some of the original labyrinthine tunnels under Downtown.

Gold was discovered in several nearby locations during the late 1800s, including the Fraser River in British Columbia, Boise and Coeur d'Alene in Idaho, and the Sultan and Skagit rivers in Washington. Though gold was never present in Seattle itself, the city served many of these locations as a supplier of prospecting goods. As of 1877, the Seattle and Walla Walla Railroad were constructed to transport coal (which had replaced lumber as the city's major export) from Renton to Seattle. Then in 1893, the Great Northern Railroad placed its western terminus in Seattle, the same year the Northern Pacific Railroad Co. bought land in Seattle, extending its western route from Tacoma to Seattle. These events positioned the manufacturers and merchants of Seattle to reap immense profits during the Klondike gold rush, as every prospector headed for Alaska passed through the city. The Klondike gold rush officially began in the summer of 1897 when the steamer *Portland* docked in Seattle carrying "a ton of gold," some of which was quickly spent in Seattle. In addition to the financial prosperity linked to outfitting prospectors bound for Alaska, Seattle also benefited from the gold rush by opening its first assay office, establishing the city as a regional financial center as well a port and manufacturing city.

By the twentieth century, Seattle was a prosperous city with both an expanding population and business community. The need for more space inspired the Denny Regrade project, which began in 1907. Originally, in addition to First Hill, Capitol Hill, and Queen Anne Hill, there was another hill located at the north end of the city center, known as Denny Hill, after Arthur Denny. The hill (actually a bluff overlooking Elliott Bay) prevented easy expansion of the Downtown, standing 190 feet above the level of nearby Pioneer Square. In 1898 some of the western side of the hill had been carted away to fill in around Western Ave. and Alaskan Way. In 1907, the project of regrading the entire hill began in earnest, primarily funded by private property owners. The dirt was hauled away and dumped into Elliott Bay, creating much of the current Seattle waterfront as well as the land that connects Downtown with the Duwamish River neighborhoods. Completed in 1931, the Denny Regrade is now the site of much of Downtown, including the Belltown neighborhood.

The Seattle population has increased steadily since the early 1900s and the city has spread out, enveloping many of the neighborhoods which were originally suburbs to the Downtown area. Seattle hosted the World's Fair in 1962, building what is now the Seattle Center, with the Key Arena, Opera House, and Pacific Science Center, as well as the monorail to Downtown. The Seattle Center marked the city's first venture as a truly major U.S. city, creating a site for civic festivals, sports events, and the performing arts.

Since the 1980s the area has been regularly ranked as one of America's most livable cities, and the resulting influx of newcomers has added to an already growing population. Washington's natural resources have so far provided for such basic needs as water and electricity, and, until recently, the size of the city has provided for plenty of space, housing, as well as a pleasant small-town culture. Today, much of that is changing as Seattle braces for additional population growth, and such matters as adequate public transportation and affordable in-city housing challenge city officials, organizations and individuals. Recently, a plan was approved that will provide additional public transportation between Everett, Seattle, and Tacoma. In addition, low-income housing development has increased, and community groups have received critical financial and planning support from the city government. Prosperity throughout the greater Seattle area, though, is fueling an atmosphere of growth and development, promising the potential of more great changes and challenges to come.

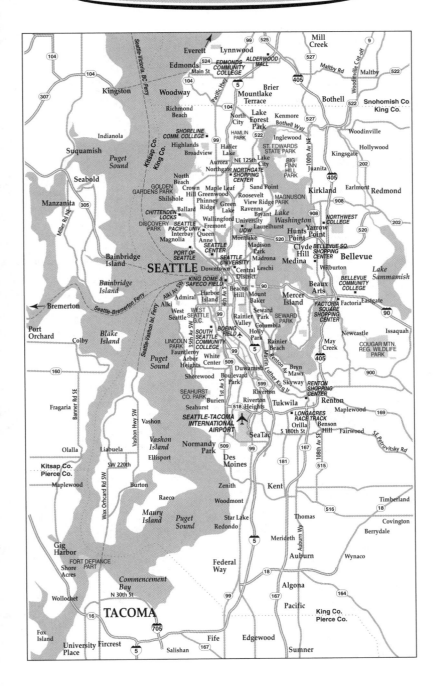

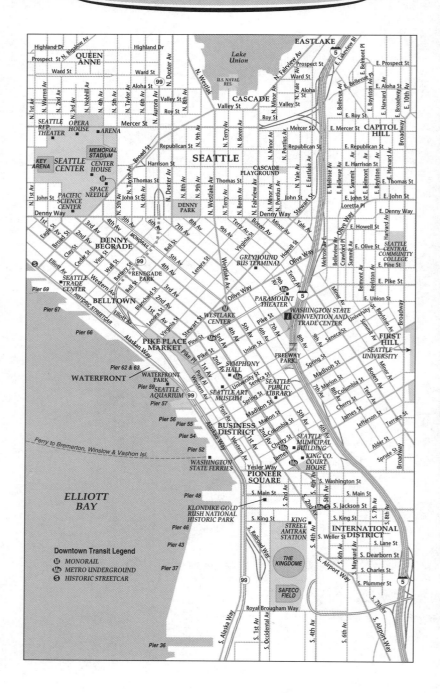

As with many large and growing U.S. cities, most of Seattle's neighborhoods began as small communities located outside the city limits. As Seattle expanded over the years, many of these small mill towns and commerce centers were annexed by Seattle. While the old village names survive as neighborhood monikers, so do the original neighborhood names. A good example of this can be seen in Ballard, where residents may refer to their homes as being in Shilshole, North Beach, Sunset Hill, Blue Ridge, or Crown Hill, all of which are located in the larger neighborhood of Ballard.

As you explore Seattle, you may notice certain repeating housing styles. Most Seattle neighborhoods have only gradually grown denser and more urban, so it is common to see several types of houses on a single residential city block. Victorians dating from the late 1800s, with their turreted front rooms and ornamented roof lines, can be found in most neighborhoods surrounding Downtown, nestled up against Craftsman bungalows, Tudors, Colonials, and Northwest Moderns.

The Northwest Modern or "Classic Box" style of architecture is one of the most plentiful, introduced in Seattle around the turn of the century and instantly popular with local architects and builders. Also know as the "Capitol Hill Box" because of the proliferation of these houses in the Capitol Hill neighborhood, this style was still being built in Seattle as late as the 1940s. Classic Box houses are large two-story, four-square structures with symmetrical windows, front porches, hardwood floors and high ceilings. Unlike the bungalow, another common style in Seattle, the slope of the Classic Box roof starts above the entire square of the second story, so that the upstairs rooms are often the same in size and number as those below. Bungalows were introduced in Seattle in the early 1900s, appearing in the architectural pattern books that were a mainstay of local builders. In particular, the Arts-and-Crafts and Craftsman style bungalows were popular in the city. Characterized by a sloped second story roof, usually with one or two front gables and bracketed roof over-hangs, these homes typically have 3-4 large bedrooms, oak or fir floors, and original built-in cabinetry.

Elaborate and symmetrical Colonials and Dutch Colonials, often referred to as "barn houses" for their distinctive shape, were built throughout Seattle in the decades between the two world wars. Tudors, recognizable for their steep roofs, arched doorways, and leaded win-dows, dot Seattle neighborhoods, as do simple Cape Cod cottages. Some north Seattle neighborhoods contain examples of the ranch house, also called ramblers. Built in the 1940s and 1950s and related to the Prairie school style created by Frank Lloyd Wright, these are sprawl-ing single-story brick houses with giant picture windows. Olympic Manor, in the north end of Ballard, is built almost entirely of this style.

Seattle residents are proud of their neighborhoods, a fact exempli-fied by the number of community centers and neighborhood organiza-tions, both important sources of information for newcomers. Also, many Seattle neighborhoods publish local newspapers, usually available free of charge, which provide valuable information about community issues and activities. Every neighborhood in Seattle has at least one coffee-house or espresso stand, always a good place for information as you begin exploring the area.

In the past several years, Seattle's crime rates have remained level or have declined, due in part to strong community involvement. However, as in any major city, be sure to take reasonable precautions when in unfa-miliar surroundings. Keep money and other possessions out of sight, and avoid exploring new neighborhoods after dark. One current concern for area residents is "road rage." Though by no means a common occur-rence, rush hour traffic in and around Seattle can cause tempers to flare and tension to rise. When leaving for an appointment, give yourself plen-ty of time and avoid drivers who seem reckless or confrontational.

Unlike many other major cities, Seattle's neighborhoods do not have official borders. Those listed in this book reflect the most widely accepted neighborhood boundaries, many of which are guided by simple geogra-phy. For instance, many of Seattle's neighborhoods sit atop a single hill, separated by a miniature "valley" from the next neighborhood. Additionally, the neighborhoods listed in this book are only those located within the city limits. Other communities, which are not formally a part of the city, may be of interest to newcomers. Some of these towns and cities are described briefly at the end of the neighborhood profiles, along with suggestions as to where to find more information about these areas.

DOWNTOWN

Pioneer Square
Pike Place Market
Belltown (Denny Regrade)
Waterfront
Cascade

Boundaries: North: Denny Way, Mercer St.; **West:** Elliott Bay; **South:** S. Royal Brougham Way, S. Jackson St.; **East:** I-5

Pioneer Square is perhaps the most historic and well-known of all districts in the Downtown area. Located near the site of Henry Yesler's saw mill and the original "skid road" (now Yesler Way), Pioneer Square was quickly rebuilt after the Great Seattle Fire of 1889 destroyed the wooden buildings of early Seattle. The Pioneer Building at 1st Ave. and James St. is one of the oldest buildings in Seattle, designed in 1889 by architect Elmer H. Fisher, at the request of Henry Yesler. Today, the brothels and gambling dens are long gone and Pioneer Square is a flourishing business and retail district. Small business offices are located in the upper floors of most of the old stone buildings. Oriental rug sellers, kite shops, sporting goods stores, bookstores, cafes, and art galleries fill the ground floor spaces.

Also home to a dynamic music scene, Pioneer Square's bars fill nightly with music-lovers and party-goers. Many of Seattle's influential bands have played in area clubs such as the OK Hotel, Central Saloon, and Colourbox. Both the New Orleans and Larry's feature fine Blues and Jazz musicians; the Fenix Underground hosts rock and alternative bands. Joint cover is offered on the weekends for those who want to visit several bars in one evening. Fat Tuesday, Seattle's Mardi Gras celebration, fills the district with revelers each spring for a week of music and festivities. Pioneer Square is also a popular meeting place before Seattle Mariners and Seattle Seahawks home games.

There are several apartment buildings in Pioneer Square near the Kingdome, most of which are converted warehouses. While this is a busy, exciting part of the city, it may be most appropriate for those prospective residents who want to live in a fast-paced urban environment. Prior to the erection of the new sports stadia, this area was quite affordable and as a result several homeless shelters were located here. Today, intermingled with the expensive new developments, these residences for the down and out remain.

Established in 1907, the **Pike Place Market** is Seattle's most beloved

Downtown landmark. City dwellers come here first with their out-of-town guests to see the fish-throwers at the seafood stands, sample teas at Market Spice, or listen to talented street musicians. Many Seattle residents frequent Pike Place weekly for fresh fruits and vegetables, fish and shellfish, teas and coffees, and baked goods. Originally the market was organized by local farmers who wanted to sell their produce without the involvement of middlemen. Gradually fish and meat were added to the available goods, then bakeries and cafes moved in, soon followed by folks selling jewelry, pottery, honey, flowers, kites, and coffees. Today, you can find just about anything at the Market, from the best local tomatoes and homemade jams to kitchen wares and furniture. Many of these products are sold in shops in the blocks around the market itself, or in the Corner Market Building, designed in 1912, and located at the corner of 1st Ave. and Pike St. A few blocks south of Pike Place, you'll find the magnificent new Seattle Art Museum with its notable "A Hammering Man" sculpture facing the waterfront.

Located north of the Pike Place Market and centered around 2nd Ave. and Bell St., **Belltown** is a part of the Denny Regrade, a section of Downtown created when Denny Hill was flattened in the early 1900s. Actually the dirt of the original steep bluff that stood in this area of Downtown was carted off and dumped into Elliott Bay, creating part of today's Waterfront area. Like Pioneer Square, the Belltown district is a hub for Seattle's nightlife and music scene. The Crocodile Cafe on 2nd Ave. is a great club for new and local bands; the Moore Theater, also on 2nd Ave., is an historic concert hall designed in 1907 by Seattle architect Edwin W. Houghton.

South of Pike Place Market on 1st Ave., many high-rise condominiums face Elliott Bay and the Olympic Mountains. While these are often quite expensive, only a few blocks east there are more affordable studios and one-bedrooms in buildings from the early 1900s. Just north of Pike Place, the Belltown neighborhood has an assortment of apartments and low-income housing units. As in the Pioneer Square area, home and personal security issues may make Belltown an unsuitable choice for some newcomers to the city. People interested in living Downtown should become familiar with the area before choosing a home here.

The Seattle **Waterfront**, facing Elliott Bay and the craggy snow-capped Olympic Mountains, is another lively and exciting part of Downtown. Though one of the few truly touristy areas of Seattle, the Waterfront has many attractions for city residents. Restaurants featuring fresh local seafood and superior views line the piers, as do many more casual eateries and several ice cream stands. A short walk from Pike Place down the market steps ends at Pier 62/63, where the "Summer Nights at the Pier" series combines delightful musicians such as Lyle Lovett, Indigo Girls, and Johnny Mathis, with incredible summer sunsets over the Olympics. Lucky Seattle residents tie up their boats next to the pier to listen to the concerts for free.

In the past few years the city's retail district has expanded, adding new stores and enticing shoppers back from the area malls. Seattle-based Nordstrom, still the dominant player in the Downtown shopping scene, will be moving soon to the spacious and newly-remodeled Frederick & Nelson building. Planet Hollywood, Nike Town, and FAO Schwartz have all added stores on 6th Ave., and trendy designer clothes can be found in the nearby City Center Building. The Four Seasons Olympic Hotel, on the site of the original University of Washington, offers visitors lavish accommodations close to the City Center and Rainier Square shops.

Finally, northeast of the Downtown corridor at the south end of Lake Union, the **Cascade** neighborhood is experiencing a revival. Although efforts to create a "Seattle Commons" in this area have met with voter resistance, new apartments and low-income housing units have been built in the blocks east of Fairview Ave. Sophisticated Federal style brick buildings on Eastlake Ave. also offer affordable apartments and low-income housing opportunities, and the REI flagship store near I-5 has increased commercial interest in the neighborhood.

Area Code: 206

Zip Codes: 98121, 98101, 98104, 98109, 98134

Post Office: Main Office Station, 301 Union St., 800-275-8777

Library: Central Library, 1000 4th Ave., 206-486-4636

Police: West Precinct, 610 3rd Ave., 206-684-8917

Emergency Hospital: Harborview Medical Center, 325 9th Ave., 206-731-3074

Public Transportation:
1: Downtown/Belltown/Queen Anne
2: First Hill/Central District/First Hill/Downtown/Belltown/Queen Anne
3: Madrona/Central District/First Hill/Downtown/Queen Anne
4: Judkins Park/Central District/First Hill/Downtown/Queen Anne

5: Downtown/Fremont/Greenwood/Northgate
6: Downtown/Green Lake/Bitter Lake/Shoreline
7: University District/Capitol Hill/Downtown/International
   District/Rainier Valley/Columbia City/Rainier Beach
9: University District/Capitol Hill/First Hill/Rainier Valley/Columbia
   City/Rainier Beach
10: Capitol Hill/Downtown
11: Madison Park/First Hill/Downtown/Waterfront
12: Capitol Hill/First Hill/Downtown
13: Downtown/Queen Anne
14: Downtown/Pioneer Square/International District/Central
    District/Mount Baker
15: Downtown/Queen Anne/Ballard/Crown Hill
16: Downtown/Queen Anne/Wallingford/Green Lake/Northgate
17: Downtown/North Queen Anne/Ballard/North Beach
18: Downtown/Ballard/North Beach
19: Downtown/Belltown/Magnolia
21: Downtown/SoDo/West Seattle
22: Downtown/West Seattle
24: Downtown/Belltown/Magnolia
25: Downtown/Eastlake/Montlake/University District/Wedgwood/
    Lake City
26: Downtown/Fremont/Wallingford/Green Lake
27: Downtown/Central District/Leschi
28: Downtown/Fremont/Ballard/Broadview
32: Downtown/University District/Laurelhurst
33: Downtown/Magnolia
36: Downtown/Beacon Hill/Rainier Beach
39: Downtown/SoDo/Beacon Hill/Seward Park/Rainier Beach
42: Downtown/Rainier Beach
43: Downtown/Capitol Hill/Montlake/University District
56: Downtown/Admiral/Alki/West Seattle Junction
65: Downtown/Montlake/University District/Wedgwood/Lake City
70: Downtown/Eastlake/University District
71: Downtown/Eastlake/University   District/Ravenna/View
    Ridge/Wedgwood/Lake City
72: Downtown/Eastlake/University District/Maple Leaf/Lake City
73: Downtown/Eastlake/University District/Maple Leaf/Jackson Park
74: Downtown/University District/Ravenna/Sand Point
76: Downtown/Ravenna/Wedgwood
79: Downtown/University District/Maple Leaf/Lake City

83: Downtown/Eastlake/University District/Maple Leaf/Ravenna

Neighborhood Organizations:
Downtown Neighborhood Service Center, 1825 Jackson St. Suite 103, 206-233-8560

Downtown Seattle Association, 500 Union St., 206-623-0340

INTERNATIONAL DISTRICT

(formerly known as Chinatown)

Boundaries: North: S. Jackson St.; **West:** 4th Ave. S.; **South:** S. Dearborn St.; **East:** Rainier Ave. S.

The International District, known as Chinatown until the early 1960s, was originally home to the scores of immigrant Chinese men who, in the late 1800s, provided an inexpensive source of labor for the railroad, fish and lumber industries. In the early 1900s, the center of the neighborhood shifted from the waterfront to its present location, just east of the Kingdome. By then, Japanese immigrants had also moved to the area and Filipino families soon followed. Today the International District continues to have strong Asian ties, with residents of Chinese, Japanese, Filipino, and Vietnamese descent.

Located close to Downtown Seattle, Pioneer Square, and the Central District, and with I-5 rumbling through the middle of the neighborhood, the International District strives to maintain and improve its tourist appeal, while still taking care of local issues and interests. Visitors frequent the area for its historic hotels and ground-floor retail shops and restaurants, many with signs in several languages. With many second, third, and fourth generation Asian-Americans relocating to the suburbs and to the Eastside, old hotels in the International District are now being converted into affordable apartments for local senior citizens. Others have been converted into low-income housing. There are also apartments and condominiums available for middle-income families.

Historic designations and joint ownership of many buildings have contributed to limited growth in the district. The construction of the new baseball stadium south of the Kingdome and the renovation of Union Station herald some much needed economic development for the neighborhood. Unfortunately, the median income remains low as many of the area's property owners no longer live in the district.

The heart of the International District is the site of the old Chinatown, which lies between the Kingdome and I-5. The main thoroughfare is Jackson St., although many of the historic buildings and businesses are a few blocks off Jackson St. On the east side of I-5, a stretch of the International District known as "Little Vietnam" or "Little Saigon" is centered around the intersection of 12th Ave. and Jackson St. This area is closely associated with the more recent influx of southeast Asian immigrants which began in the 1960s, and has many small Vietnamese groceries and tasty take-out restaurants.

While the majority of residents in the International District are Asian- or Pacific-Americans, there are some whites and African-Americans living here as well. An interest in Downtown living seems to be attracting younger residents to a community that in recent decades has had a median age in the mid-50s. The neighborhood is conveniently located near Downtown, and you'd be hard pressed to find another Seattle neighborhood with as much cultural history. Security continues to be a concern for residents, but crime rates are equivalent to the rest of Downtown.

Area Code: 206

Zip Codes: 98134, 98144, 98104

Post Office: International Station, 414 6th Ave. S, 800-275-8777

Library: Central Library, 1000 4th Ave., 206-486-4636

Police: West Precinct, 610 3rd Ave., 206-684-8917

Emergency Hospital: Harborview Medical Center, 325 9th Ave., 206-731-3074

Public Transportation:
7: University District/Capitol Hill/Downtown/International District/Rainier Valley/Columbia City/Rainier Beach
14: Downtown/Pioneer Square/International District/Central District/Mount Baker

Neighborhood Organization:
Downtown Neighborhood Service Center, 1825 Jackson St. Suite 103, 206-233-8560

FIRST HILL

Boundaries: North: E. Pike St.; **West:** I-5; **South:** Yesler Way; **East:** 12th Ave. E.

First Hill, commonly referred to as "Pill Hill" because of the concentration of hospitals, clinics, and medical offices in the area, lies directly east of Downtown. First Hill was originally settled in the mid-1800s by Seattle's elite as the city expanded beyond the Downtown boundary. Later many affluent First Hill residents moved to more distant neighborhoods such as Madison Park and Laurelhurst. Only a few of the early homes remain, including the Tudoresque Stimson-Green Mansion built in 1898. Other remaining structures not supplanted by medical office buildings, schools, hospitals and hotels, serve as private clubs and reception halls.

The main commercial street on First Hill is Madison St., along which there are an assortment of cafes, delis, hotels, and pharmacies that serve hospital and office personnel, patients, and nearby residents. The Sorrento Hotel on Madison St. is an exquisite brick building, constructed in 1907 and designed by well-known Seattle architect Harlan Thomas, designer of the 1929 Harborview Medical Center. Harborview, a few blocks south of Madison St. on First Hill, serves as the premier emergency care center in the Seattle area.

There are few single family houses on First Hill except for those in the area south of Harborview, which tends to be noisy due to ambulance sirens and the nearby freeway. Most First Hill residents live in apartments or condominiums facing Downtown to the west or Capitol Hill to the north. On the west side of First Hill, an assortment of apartment buildings border I-5, offering views of Downtown and Elliott Bay. Although freeway noise can be distracting in these residences as well, there is a nice mix of high- and low-end apartments, and many Downtown professionals and doctors choose to live in the area for convenience. Elegant brick apartment buildings from the early 1900s are tucked along side streets, offering secured entrances and pleasant surroundings. These buildings are only a few minutes walk from Downtown. Also, check the north end of First Hill for a selection of brick or stucco apartment buildings which date from the late 1920s.

As with nearby Capitol Hill, First Hill plays an important role in Seattle's Catholic community. Two influential Catholic schools are located here: Seattle University, a private Jesuit college on Broadway, and

O'Dea Catholic High School near Madison St.

Area Code: 206

Zip Codes: 98101, 98104

Post Office: Main Office Station, 301 Union St., 800-275-8777

Library: Central Library, 1000 4th Ave., 206-486-4636

Police: East Precinct, 1519 12th Ave., 206-684-4300

Emergency Hospital: Harborview Medical Center, 325 9th Ave., 206-731-3074

Public Transportation:
2: First Hill/Central District/First Hill/Downtown/Belltown/Queen Anne
3: Madrona/Central District/First Hill/Downtown/Queen Anne
4: Judkins Park/Central District/First Hill/Downtown/Queen Anne
9: University District/Capitol Hill/First Hill/Rainier Valley/Columbia City/Rainier Beach
11: Madison Park/First Hill/Downtown/Waterfront
12: Capitol Hill/First Hill/Downtown
60: Capitol Hill/First Hill/Beacon Hill/Georgetown

Neighborhood Organization:
Yesler Community Center, 835 E Yesler Way, 206-386-1245

CAPITOL HILL

Boundaries: North: Fuhrman Ave. E.; **West:** I-5; **South:** E. Pike St.; **East:** 23rd/24th Ave. E.

Capitol Hill is a vibrant urban neighborhood that is simultaneously quaint, upscale, retro, staid and notorious. It is both the center of Seattle's large gay community and a neighborhood of traditional Catholic families. At the north end, there is St. Mark's Cathedral and the Episcopal Archdiocese; at the south end is Neighbor's, a cavernous gay dance club.

Well known throughout Seattle, Broadway is the main street of Capitol Hill. It runs the length of the hill, and is the center of the community's commercial district. Broadway is the place to go for lively dining or take-out. Boisterous, young residents fill innumerable restaurants and bars nightly, and on summer evenings the street rings with voices late into the night. There are many businesses on Broadway that cater to a youthful and bohemian clientele, including tattoo and body piercing shops, second-hand clothing and record stores, costume jewelers, bead shops, head shops, and gay/lesbian bookstores.

East Pike St. and E Pine St., south of Broadway's retail core, are the center of Capitol Hill's nightlife. The area has the usual assortment of smoky bars, pool halls, dance clubs, and restaurants, though lately this slightly seedy district has become a bit more refined. On E Pike St., a collection of trendy boutiques has sprung up, and a large grocery and shopping complex was completed in 1997 at the corner of E Pike St. and Broadway.

Fifteenth Ave. E, five blocks east of Broadway, is another Capitol Hill retail district. This area is understated and stylish but also funky and quaint, with mod boutiques, swank eateries, and cozy pubs. Fifteenth Ave. E caters to a slightly older generation, attracting hip baby boomers and comfortably domestic gays and lesbians. The mood on this street is laid-back and placid, an agreeable alternative to the constant bustle of Broadway.

The north end of Capitol Hill is filled with lovely, albeit expensive, houses, most with enchanting views. To get a look at the stunning vistas, climb to the top of the old water tower in Volunteer Park, several blocks north of the 15th Ave. E shopping district. Homes on the eastern slope of Capitol Hill have views of the Cascades or Lake Washington; a few may even offer a glimpse of Mount Rainier from a top story window. On the west side, residences look out over Lake Union, the Fremont Bridge, and the Olympic Mountains. Homes in Capitol Hill, particularly at the north end, are large and fashionable. While many are Colonials, Dutch Colonials, Victorian or Federal style houses, the most common type of home in this area is the Northwest Modern, often referred to as the "Capitol Hill Box House." This style of house is generally two or three stories, with a roof that starts above the entire second story, a wide front porch, and large symmetrical windows.

In addition to the water tower, Volunteer Park features the Seattle Asian Art Museum, a charming old water reservoir, a delightful glass conservatory, and an outdoor amphitheater for summer concerts. Homes around Volunteer Park include some of the most formal and ornate mansions in Seattle. Many are old Victorian or Federal style houses, while others are stately versions of the Northwest Modern style.

While a few homes have become unobtrusive bed and breakfasts, most are still occupied by wealthy Seattle families. Many of Capitol Hill's afflu-ent Catholic residents live in the area and attend church at the beautiful St. Joseph's Catholic Church. Others attend St. Patrick's, at the far north end of Capitol Hill, near Roanoke Park.

South of E Aloha St., apartments become more common and hous-es are smaller. Federal style brick buildings abound in this area, subdivid-ed into small but classic apartments, with hardwood floors and coved ceilings. Most people who live near Broadway are renters, although there are houses tucked away on the side streets that lead back toward Volunteer Park. West of Broadway, almost all of the available residences are apartments or condominiums, with many large modern apartment complexes built over I-5 and offering views of Downtown and the Olympic Mountains. Rents are relatively expensive in this area, although many studio apartments are available. Despite its dense population, the charm of this neighborhood is that it is one of the few Seattle areas where you can walk anywhere you might need to go. In fact, having a car can be a disadvantage here because parking is a challenge on Capitol Hill. In addition, several bus routes connect Capitol Hill with Downtown and the University District, the major hubs of the Metro bus system.

East of Broadway, residences are a haphazard mix of houses, duplexes, and apartment buildings. Homes tend to be smaller and less ornate than those on north Capitol Hill but the styles are similar, primar-ily Northwest Moderns, Colonials, and Victorians. Many houses here are available as single-family or multiple tenant rentals. Apartments in this area are generally less expensive than those on the west side of the hill, depending on the building and location. East of 15th Ave. E and south of E John St., houses and apartments are even less expensive, particularly south of the radio towers and close to the Central District. Residents here tend toward the bohemian, consisting of a mix of college students from Seattle Central Community College or Seattle University, artists, and musicians.

Area Code: 206

Zip Codes: 98102, 98112, 98122

Post Office: Broadway Station, 101 Broadway E, 800-275-8777

Library: Henry Library, 425 Harvard Ave. E, 206-684-4715

Police: East Precinct, 1519 12th Ave., 206-684-4300

Emergency Hospital: Swedish Medical Center, 747 Broadway, 206-386-2573

Public Transportation:
7: University District/Capitol Hill/Downtown/International District/Rainier Valley/Columbia City/Rainier Beach
8: Rainier Valley/Capitol Hill/Lower Queen Anne
9: University District/Capitol Hill/First Hill
10: Capitol Hill/Downtown
12: Capitol Hill/First Hill/Downtown
43: Downtown/Capitol Hill/Montlake/University District

Neighborhood Organizations:
Capitol Hill Neighborhood Service Center, 501 19th Ave. E, 206-684-4574

Miller Community Center, 330 19th Ave. E, 206-684-4753

EASTLAKE

Boundaries: North: Lake Washington Ship Canal; **West:** Lake Union; **South:** E. Galer St.; **East:** I-5

Just north of Downtown, on the east side of Lake Union, lies the aptly named Eastlake neighborhood. Long thought of as simply an easy shortcut to Downtown, Eastlake has recently blossomed into a charming close-knit community. Along Eastlake Ave. E are most of the retail shops and restaurants of the neighborhood, including the original Red Robin Burger & Spirits Emporium, the first of a successful local restaurant chain. Rows of houseboats share the shore of Lake Union with marine repair shops, dry docks, and National Oceanic and Atmospheric Administration (NOAA) ships. To explore the appealing houseboats in Eastlake begin at Pete's Grocery, located at the base of E Lynn St. then work north or south along the shore. While the houseboats vary widely in size and luxury, all share in the daily spectacle of sailboats and seaplanes on Lake Union, the sensational Independence Day fireworks display, and the annual Christmas Ship Parade.

More traditional housing is abundant in Eastlake as well. The neighborhood has an interesting mix of apartments, condominiums, duplexes, and single-family homes. Large 1970s style apartment buildings dot the area and offer fairly inexpensive rentals, many with views of Lake Union. More traditional brick Federal style buildings offer both apartments and condominiums. Homes in Eastlake range from turn-of-the-century Victorians to simple Northwest Moderns. Eastlake has boomed in recent years as both a commercial and residential area, and the result has been extensive new construction throughout the area. New town-houses and apartments can be found in the few blocks between Eastlake Ave. and the lake and along Franklin Ave. E.

At the north end of Fairview Ave., along the edge of Lake Union, are the last vestiges of the old Eastlake community. Here quaint and slightly run-down summer cottages face the lake shore. This is the site of the Eastlake P-Patch community garden; like the community gardens in the International District and on Capitol Hill this garden is a quiet treasure for those who live here. Unfortunately what makes this area quaint — the small number of houses — also makes it difficult to find a place to live. However, it's a great place to visit.

Eastlake is an accessible neighborhood with a growing community and spirit to match. It is also nicely located with easy access to Downtown and the 520 bridge. Prospective neighbors might include university students who rent apartments and houses along busy Boylston Ave. E; young professionals who rent and buy homes and con-dominiums along Franklin Ave. E, E Roanoke St. and E Lynn St.; and well-to-do baby boomers residing west of Eastlake Ave. E, close to Lake Union. In addition, many older lifelong Eastlake residents still live in this community, providing a strong backbone to the neighborhood. Rents are on the rise in this area, as they are throughout Seattle, but Eastlake is still affordable for most middle-income families.

Area Code: 206

Zip Codes: 98102

Post Office: Broadway Station, 101 Broadway E, 800-275-8777

Library: Henry Library, 425 Harvard Ave. E, 206-684-4715

Police: West Precinct, 610 3rd Ave., 206-684-8917

Emergency Hospital: Harborview Medical Center, 325 9th Ave., 206-731-3074

Public Transportation:
25: Downtown/Eastlake/Montlake/University District/Wedgwood/ Lake City
70: Downtown/Eastlake/University District
71: Downtown/Eastlake/University District/Ravenna/ViewRidge/

Wedgwood/Lake City
72: Downtown/Eastlake/University District/Maple Leaf/Lake City
73: Downtown/Eastlake/University District/Maple Leaf/Jackson Park
83: Downtown/Eastlake/University District/Maple Leaf/Ravenna

Neighborhood Organization:
Montlake Community Center, 1618 E Calhoun St., 206-684-4736

QUEEN ANNE

Interbay
Lower Queen Anne
Westlake

Boundaries: North: Lake Washington Ship Canal; **West:** 15th Ave. W., Elliott Ave. W.; **South:** Denny Way; **East:** Lake Union, Aurora Ave. N. (Hwy. 99)

Situated on a hill towering 457 feet over Downtown and Elliott Bay, Queen Anne is one of the oldest and loveliest residential areas in the city. In the 1890s, streetcar lines from Downtown brought affluent residents up the south slope of the hill to their grand mansions. Since its origin, the neighborhood of Queen Anne has flourished, remaining an idyllic residential area located only minutes from Downtown. Queen Anne Ave. N is the main commercial street on the hill, where residents gather for morning coffee and brunch in picturesque cafes, meet for lunch or dinner at quaint local pubs and restaurants, or shop in upscale boutiques, specialty bakeries, ethnic delis, and small bookstores.

Surrounding the shopping district, modest Colonials and simple bungalows are owned and/or rented by a mix of students, artists, professionals, and families. In addition, formal Northwest Moderns and Tudors are home to retired folks who have lived on the hill for many years. The most affordable houses and apartments on Queen Anne are those without a view, and there are many such residences on the top of the hill. This is a very pleasant area, with well-maintained houses surrounded by lovely lawns and beautiful nearby parks. A local grade school playground east of Queen Anne Ave. N is the site of weekend basketball games on summer weekends; a block west of this main thoroughfare, city ball-parks host softball games on lazy summer afternoons.

The southwest corner of Queen Anne remains an enclave for affluent and longtime residents. The homes in this area are extremely lavish; many can only be glimpsed briefly through breaks in landscaped hedges.

W Highland Drive, offering unbelievable views of Downtown, Elliott Bay, Mount Rainier and the Olympic Mountains, is lined with many of the hill's original Queen Anne style houses. In the blocks north of W Highland Drive, homes are less expensive but still immaculately maintained. Most are modest Four Square or Queen Anne style houses; a few are Craftsman style bungalows. For a first-hand experience of the merits of this neighborhood, walk or drive to Kerry Park, located on the south side of W Highland Dr. From this vantage point, the Downtown cityscape and the shipping activities of Elliott Bay seem an arm's length away, and in the distance, Mount Rainier towers over the city. The park is a favorite of nearby residents, who come after dark to admire the brilliant lights of Downtown or to watch fireworks over the bay on Independence Day.

East of Queen Anne Ave. N, a variety of large and expensive homes share the lovely view of Downtown and Mount Rainier. Many are elaborate Elizabethans and Colonials; others are large unadorned contemporary homes. Residents include a mix of wealthy entrepreneurs, foreign diplomats, and affluent professionals. In addition to breathtaking glimpses of Mount Rainier and Downtown, the east side of the hill offers views of azure Lake Union and Capitol Hill. Many 1950s apartment buildings cling to this side of the hill, offering affordable rentals for young professionals. In addition, several houses and apartment buildings in the area have been recently remodeled into modern condominiums. Many of the people living in this corner of Queen Anne are middle-income professionals who work Downtown. A word of advice: this is not the neighborhood to live in if your job is on the Eastside. Commuting from Queen Anne to the Eastside can easily take an hour during peak travel times.

The north and west sides of Queen Anne Hill are the best locations for reasonably-priced rentals in the neighborhood. The west side of Queen Anne, including **Interbay**, a light industrial strip between Queen Anne and Magnolia, offers affordable rental apartments in modest brick and large contemporary buildings as well as rental houses and duplexes, mostly converted bungalows. Many students and faculty live in Queen Anne because Seattle Pacific University (SPU) is located at the base of the hill to the north. Around the SPU campus are numerous rentals, including unpretentious apartment buildings, modest houses, tiny houseboats, and renovated storefronts.

Apartments are also plentiful in the **Lower Queen Anne** area, which surrounds the Seattle Center, site of the Space Needle. Built for the 1962 World's Fair, the 74-acre Seattle Center is a combination amusement park and community center. Among its many attractions are the Pacific

Science Center, Opera House, Pacific Northwest Ballet, Seattle Repertory Theater, Intiman Theater, and Key Arena, where the Seattle Sonics play. Every summer, Seattle Center is the site for Bumbershoot, a music and arts festival, as well as the Northwest Folk Life Festival and the Bite of Seattle. The Lower Queen Anne area includes retail and residential districts to the north and west. Small ethnic restaurants are located along Roy St. north of the Seattle Center; aromatic cafes, scrumptious bakeries, old-fashioned diners, and upscale restaurants cluster around Queen Anne Ave N. Apartment buildings of all styles fill this area, from small brick buildings on Roy St. to enormous contemporary buildings along Queen Anne Ave. N.

Finally, the **Westlake** area, located at the eastern base of the hill, is a commercial district that runs along the west side of Lake Union. Westlake Ave. is lined with upscale view restaurants, private marinas, and boating goods retailers, a combination common on Seattle's waterfront areas. A few houseboats, including the one featured in the movie "Sleepless in Seattle," are moored here.

Area Code: 206

Zip Codes: 98109, 98119

Post Office: Queen Anne Station, 415 1st Ave. N, 800-275-8777

Library: Queen Anne Library, 400 W Garfield St., 206-386-4227

Police: West Precinct, 610 3rd Ave., 206-684-8917

Emergency Hospital: Harborview Medical Center, 325 9th Ave., 206-731-3074

Public Transportation:
1: Downtown/Belltown/Queen Anne
2: First Hill/Central District/First Hill/Downtown/Belltown/Queen Anne
3: Madrona/Central District/First Hill/Downtown/Queen Anne
4: Judkins Park/Central District/First Hill/Downtown/Queen Anne
8: Rainier Valley/Capitol Hill/Lower Queen Anne
13: Downtown/Queen Anne
15: Downtown/Queen Anne/Ballard/Crown Hill
16: Downtown/Queen Anne/Wallingford/Green Lake/Northgate
17: Downtown/North Queen Anne/Ballard/North Beach

Neighborhood Organizations:
Queen Anne/Magnolia Neighborhood Service Center, 908 N 34th St.,
206-684-4812 Queen Anne Community Center, 1901 1st Ave. W, 206-
386-4240

MAGNOLIA

Boundaries: North: Lake Washington Ship Canal; **West:** Puget Sound;
South: Elliott Bay; **East:** 15th Ave. W.

Just west of Queen Anne is the neighborhood of Magnolia. Like Queen
Anne, Magnolia is both a landmark Seattle hill and a community. Rumor
has it that the hill was originally named for the distinctive Madrona trees
which line the bluff, and which a visiting sailor mistakenly identified as
magnolias. In any case, the name stuck and now designates a charming
neighborhood.

Despite its proximity to Downtown, Magnolia is a truly residential
community. It has an eclectic mix of homes, mainly Northwest Moderns,
Craftsman bungalows, and brick Tudors, most with views of the beautiful Puget Sound and craggy Olympic Mountains to the west, or of the
Downtown skyline and busy Elliott Bay to the southeast. There are a few
commercial junctions on the hill, including elegant cafes and boutiques,
and a marina at the south end is home to several popular restaurants,
which share a spectacular panorama of Elliott Bay and Downtown.

Because of the extraordinary views, the sheltered nature of the community, and the easy commute to Downtown, homes in Magnolia are
fairly expensive. Along the bluff, at the south end of Magnolia, are especially lavish homes. There are more modestly sized and priced homes
located at the north end of the hill and in the middle of the hill where
there is little or no view. Here homeowners tend to be a mix of young
families, affluent professionals or senior citizens; many are longtime residents. A unique neighborhood organization called Magnolia's Ageless
Maternity Association (MAMA) provides networking support for new
mothers, particularly those in their thirties and forties.

Renters in Magnolia represent all levels of income and occupations.
Because Magnolia is not conveniently located to I-5, apartments here rent
for slightly less than the Seattle average, even those with water or city
views. This is particularly true for the larger, two-bedroom apartments;
studio rents are comparable to other neighborhoods. You'll find many
apartment buildings located at the north end of the hill, facing Ballard.

Nearby on the Lake Washington Ship Canal, the Fisherman's Terminal is an energetic hub, with constant activity from the fishing vessels that dock there. In addition, part of the Fisherman's Terminal recently was transformed into a small shopping and dining destination, located just off W Emerson St. Continue on this route and you'll find Discovery Park and the Hiram Chittenden Locks. The locks, which separate the Lake Washington Ship Canal from the Puget Sound, offer an easy route for foot and bicycle traffic between Magnolia and Ballard. Discovery Park, in the northwest corner of Magnolia, is Seattle's largest and most verdant park, consisting of 534 acres of meadows, forest, and beach, with clay cliffs and seven miles of nature trails. The nearby West Point Lighthouse was built on the northwest point of the beach in 1881 and is still a popular attraction, although it is now somewhat diminished by the close proximity of the West Point Sewage Treatment Plant.

Although Magnolia does not technically qualify as a peninsula, access to the hill is limited to Dravus St., Nickerson St., and the Magnolia Bridge. Interbay, the semi-industrial area between Magnolia and Queen Anne, effectively cuts Magnolia off from the main thoroughfare of 15th Ave. W (Elliott Ave.) with only those three streets as overpasses into the neighborhood. In reality, Magnolia is actually quite convenient to Downtown and the surrounding neighborhoods, although getting to I-5 can be difficult.

Area Code: 206

Zip Codes: 98199

Post Office: Magnolia Station, 3211 W McGraw St., 800-275-8777

Library: Magnolia Library, 2801 34th Ave. W, 206-386-4225

Police: West Precinct, 610 3rd Ave., 206-684-8917

Emergency Hospital: Swedish Medical Center — Ballard, 5300 Tallman Ave. NW, 206-781-6341

Public Transportation:
19: Downtown/Belltown/Magnolia
24: Downtown/Belltown/Magnolia
30: Laurelhurst/University District/Wallingford/Fremont/Magnolia
62: Magnolia/Ballard/Northgate

Neighborhood Organizations:
Queen Anne/Magnolia Neighborhood Service Center, 908 N 34th St.,

206-684-4812

Magnolia Community Center, 2550-34th Ave. NW, 206-386-4235

BALLARD

North Beach
Shilshole

Boundaries: North: N.W. 110th St.; **West:** Puget Sound; **South:** Lake Washington Ship Canal; **East:** 3rd Ave. N.W.

Ballard is a quaint and delightful neighborhood located just 15 minutes north of Downtown. Originally a town of workers for the local Stimson Mill, it was annexed by Seattle in 1906 after a dead horse in the town's drinking water forced residents to turn to the city for a new water supply. In the early 1900s Scandinavian immigrants settled in Ballard, attracted to the abundant fish in the Puget Sound. Although currently commercial salmon fishing in the Sound is restricted to local Native American tribes, Ballard remains home to many professional fishermen who catch pollack, halibut, cod, and salmon along the coast of Alaska. From the Ballard Bridge, and from homes in the south end of the neighborhood, one can enjoy the colorful sight of off-season fishing vessels harbored at Fisherman's Terminal and along the Lake Washington Ship Canal. For a first-hand experience of the boating and fishing history of Ballard, visit the Hiram Chittenden Locks and Fish Ladder, located at the west end of NW Market St. (just as the street becomes Seaview Ave. NW).

Ballard is well-known as a tight-knit Scandinavian community, celebrating its heritage by hosting yearly festivals for Santa Lucia (a Swedish saint honored during the Christmas Season), and for Siettende Mai (Norwegian Independence Day). During these celebrations, Ballard's main street, NW Market St., is roped off from traffic and gaily decorated, and everyone is welcome to attend the festivities. NW Market St. is the retail section of the original town, lined with quaint Scandinavian bakeries, delis, and restaurants, as well as modern hobby shops, record stores, and ethnic eateries. The Nordic Heritage Museum, several blocks northwest of NW Market St., offers a fascinating glimpse at the Scandinavian culture that pervades the neighborhood. In contrast, one very un-Scandinavian restaurant on NW Market St. is the popular Lombardi's, famous for good Italian food, and host of an annual garlic festival. Samples from this lively event include such delicacies as garlic ice cream and garlic martinis.

Another major street in Ballard is 15th Ave. NW, which begins at the Ballard Bridge and runs north through the neighborhood. Fifteenth Ave. NW is lined with a variety of small businesses, appliance and auto repair shops, fast-food restaurants, dry cleaners, pet shops, and antique malls. The streets beyond this main thoroughfare, however, are largely residential. Typically you'll find modest 1950s bungalows, brick Tudors, and simple wood-frame houses lining quiet streets. Many of these homes have views of the Olympic Mountains to the west; others overlook the boating activity along the Lake Washington Ship Canal. All homes in Ballard have easy access to Downtown but, because of the longer distance to I-5, they are often less expensive than comparable houses elsewhere in the city.

Elegant homes with views of the Puget Sound and the Olympic Mountains are situated on the northern and western hillsides of Ballard. Many of the homes in the **North Beach** area, north of NW 85th St., are sprawling 1950s ranch houses with exquisitely landscaped yards. Other more recent additions to the neighborhood include elaborate colonials, immaculate brick Tudor cottages, and contemporary designs from the 1960s and 1970s. Homes in this area have a front-row seat for breathtaking sunsets over the Olympic Mountains. In the summer months, residents can watch weekend sailboat races on the sound; during the winter holidays, colorfully lighted ships follow the shoreline as part of the annual Christmas Ship Parade. East of 32nd Ave. NW, the **Shilshole** neighborhood offers modest brick Tudors and Arts-and-Crafts style homes with a panorama of Bainbridge Island, Puget Sound, and the Olympics. Shilshole is best known throughout the city for the seafood restaurants that line Seaview Ave. NW, and for Golden Gardens Park. On summer evenings visitors to the park watch in awe as the sun dips behind the Olympic Mountains. The park also attracts Seattle residents for summer picnics, swimming, and volley ball, as well as the occasional after-dark campfire.

Rental homes are available throughout Ballard, particularly south of NW 65th St. Apartment buildings line 24th Ave. NW, offering reasonable rents for studios and one- or two-bedroom units. Extremely modest condominiums are available near NW Market St.; more plush condominiums can be found in the Shilshole area along the waterfront. Public transportation is readily available in Ballard. Several bus routes run to Downtown along 15th Ave. NW and 24th Ave. NW, and there are regular routes to Wallingford and the University District that run along NW

Market St. and NW 85th St.

While Ballard is known for blond, Nordic-looking residents, people of many cultural backgrounds live happily in this neighborhood. In addition to fishermen, Ballard is home to local merchants, teachers, public servants, and a flourishing senior citizen community. Shilshole and North Beach attract affluent professionals and wealthy retirees. Despite its proximity to Downtown, Ballard has retained its village appeal and offers residents a mixture of close community and convenient location.

Area Code: 206

Zip Codes: 98107, 98117, 98103

Post Office: Ballard Station, 5706 17th Ave. NW, 800-275-8777

Library: Ballard Library, 5711 24th Ave. NW, 206-684-4089

Police: North Precinct, 10049 College Way N, 206-684-0850

Emergency Hospital: Swedish Medical Center - Ballard, 5300 Tallman Ave. NW, 206-781-6341

Public Transportation:
15: Downtown/Queen Anne/Ballard/Crown Hill
17: Downtown/North Queen Anne/Ballard/North Beach
44: Ballard/Wallingford/University District/Montlake
46: Shilshole/Ballard/Fremont/University District
62: Magnolia/Ballard/Northgate

Neighborhood Organizations:
Ballard Neighborhood Service Center, 2305 NW Market St., 206-684-4060

Ballard Community Center, 6020 28th Ave. NW, 206-684-4093

Loyal Heights Community Center, 2101 NW 77th St., 206-684-4052

PHINNEY RIDGE/GREENWOOD

Boundaries: North: Holman Rd. N.W., N 105th St.; **West:** 8th Ave. N.W., 3rd Ave. N.W.; **South:** N. 50th St.; **East:** Aurora Ave N. (Hwy. 99)

The Phinney Ridge and Greenwood neighborhoods are located north of

Fremont, between Ballard and Green Lake. The central feature of Phinney Ridge is the Woodland Park Zoo, located southwest of Green Lake across Aurora Ave. N. If visiting, be sure to walk through the fabulous rose garden at its 50th St. entrance. Phinney Ridge, a neighborhood known for its ever-present population of young families, is a perennial favorite of lower-middle-income, white collar professionals — teachers, public servants, non-profit organization employees, etc., creating a neighborhood reputation of liberal political views and strong community involvement. In recent years, the neighborhood has become popular with more affluent professionals, and unfortunately housing prices have risen accordingly.

Most Phinney Ridge residents live in Northwest Moderns or Craftsman bungalows on the west side of the hill, sharing lovely views of Ballard, the Puget sound and the Olympic Mountains. Apartment buildings line Phinney Ave. N along the ridge of the hill, although they taper off north of the zoo as retail shops and restaurants become more prevalent. Just north of NW 65th St. the main street jogs over to become a stretch of Greenwood Ave. N and the true commercial district begins. Here the Red Mill Burger Company serves delicious burgers to people from all over Seattle; on summer evenings the line to the counter commonly stretches out the door and along the sidewalk. A popular destination on Sunday mornings is Mae's Phinney Ridge Café at 65th St., where hungry Seattle residents also fill the sidewalk, waiting to be seated for brunch. To join the brunch bunch, just look for the large Holsteins painted on the bright green walls of the café. This area also offers a fun selection of ethnic and vegetarian restaurants, cozy pubs, funky coffeehouses, card and gift shops.

The main intersection of the Greenwood neighborhood is NW 85th St. and Greenwood Ave. NW. Commercial buildings include banks, antique stores, old-fashioned diners, and well-stocked pubs, as well as the Greenwood Senior Center and the Greenwood Library. Heavy traffic on NW 85th St. keeps this from being the modern shopping district that the community had hoped it would be, but it is a comfortable and pleasant area. South of NW 85th St. the Phinney Ridge and Greenwood neighborhoods are almost identical, with roomy bungalows and Northwest Modern homes on either side of the Greenwood Ave. NW retail core. North of NW 85th St., however, Greenwood has a collection of more modest homes primarily belonging to blue-collar workers and their families. Along NW 85th St., there are many new apartment buildings, particularly in the few blocks just west of Aurora. Apartments built in the 1970s line Greenwood Ave. NW, north of NW 90th St. Affordable cottages, modern split-level homes, and duplexes can be found tucked away from the main streets both east of Greenwood Ave. N and north along 8th Ave. NW. Both Greenwood and Phinney Ridge are comfortable middle-class neighborhoods and many of the residents here are young professionals and their families.

Several blocks of both Greenwood and Phinney Ridge are situated close to Aurora Ave. N, a busy state highway and commercial district. Prospective residents may want to consider the highway when evaluating home security in the few blocks closest to Aurora Ave. N.

Area Code: 206

Zip Codes: 98103, 98107, 98117

Post Office: Greenwood Station, 8306 Greenwood Ave. N, 800-275-8777

Library: Greenwood Library, 8016 Greenwood Ave. N, 206-684-4086

Police: North Precinct, 10049 College Way N, 206-684-0850

Emergency Hospital: Swedish Medical Center — Ballard, 5300 Tallman Ave. NW, 206-781-6341

Public Transportation:
5: Downtown/Fremont/Greenwood/Northgate
28: Downtown/Fremont/Ballard/Broadview
44: Ballard/Wallingford/University District/Montlake

Neighborhood Organizations:
Greenwood Neighborhood Service Center, 8505 Greenwood Ave. N, 206-684-4096

Phinney Neighborhood Association, 6532 Phinney Ave. N, 206-783-2244

FREMONT

Boundaries: North: N. 46th St./N. Market St.; **East:** Stone Way N.; **West:** 8th Ave. N.W.; **South:** Lake Washington Ship Canal and Fremont Bridge

Ten minutes north of Downtown and across from the Lake Washington Ship Canal lies the picturesque Fremont district. A small Seattle neighborhood with its central core at the intersection of Fremont Ave. N, N 35th St., and Fremont Pl. N, one block north of the Fremont Bridge. From here it is less than a five minute walk to two of Seattle's most beloved sculptures, "Waiting for the Interurban" and the "Fremont Troll," as well as Seattle's most controversial statue, Emil Venkov's "Lenin," which was originally displayed in communist Slovakia in 1988.

Fremont charms even the most cynical of Seattle residents with its mixture of inviting shops and events. It is the home of the original Red Hook Brewery, as well as several other microbreweries and pubs. There are art galleries galore, vintage clothing and "junk" stores, barber shops and tattoo parlors. On the weekends, Seattle residents flock to the district for brunch and shopping, or for coffee and dessert at The Still Life Coffeehouse on N 35th St. At night, Fremont's pubs overflow with a friendly and diverse crowd of locals. This area is still miraculously free of tourists, despite its proximity to Downtown.

During the summer, the neighborhood hosts the Fremont Market each Sunday where residents and visitors can buy goods from local artists and artisans. Throughout the week, many residents shop for groceries at the Puget Consumers Co-op on N 34th St., a refreshing alternative to the corporate mega grocers. One weekend in June is devoted to the summer solstice, and includes the annual Solstice Parade and the Fremont Fair. On summer Saturday evenings, a parking lot doubles as the site for the Fremont Outdoor Cinema. Movie-goers bring their own chairs and join in the theme of the double feature, which is projected on the wall of a building bordering the lot. Costume and talent contests are held during intermission.

Residents of Fremont are primarily artists, students, and young professionals. The last five years have seen rapid commercial growth in the area, but the neighborhood has maintained its delicate balance of bohemian culture and middle class comfort. It is a close-knit community, popular among low and middle-income families and fortunately still affordable for first-time homeowners.

If you'd like to live in Fremont, your best bet is to drive, bicycle, or walk through the area looking for "For Rent" signs in windows. There is plentiful rental property here, both apartments and houses, but potential rentals are generally snapped up before being advertised in the local newspapers. The shopping district of Fremont contains some rental space, especially in the few blocks north of Fremont Pl. N, but don't limit your search to that area. To the east of Fremont Ave., and across or under Aurora Ave., there are many affordable housing opportunities.

Aurora can be fairly noisy during high traffic times, so if you're sensitive to that, try to visit nearby rentals around 5 p.m. on a weekday to experience the noise level first hand.

A few blocks north of Fremont's shopping district is NW 39th Ave, which is lined with large apartment buildings built in the 1950s and 1960s. This area can also be a little noisy during high traffic times, since this is one of the main routes between Ballard, Downtown and the University District. You'll find a more traditional residential area of 1920s Craftsman style bungalows between NW 39th and NW 46th and east of Fremont Ave N. As with most Seattle neighborhoods near a university or college, the best time for renting is late April through early June, when students are making plans to head home for the summer. Fremont is 20-25 minutes by car or bus from the University of Washington. It is a 5-15 minute walk from Seattle Pacific University, which is just across the Fremont Bridge on the north side of the Queen Anne neighborhood.

Area Code: 206

Zip Codes: 98103, 98107

Post Office: Wallingford Station, 1329 N 47th St., 206-632-6366

Library: Fremont Library, 731 N 35th St., 206-684-4084

Police: North Precinct, 10049 College Way N, 206-684-0850

Emergency Hospital: Swedish Medical Center — Ballard, 5300 Tallman Ave. NW, 206-781-6341

Public Transportation:
5: Downtown/Fremont/Greenwood/Northgate
26: Downtown/Fremont/Wallingford/Green Lake
28: Downtown/Fremont/Ballard/Broadview
30: Laurelhurst/University District/Wallingford/Fremont/Magnolia
46: Shilshole/Ballard/Fremont/University District

Neighborhood Organizations:
Fremont Neighborhood Service Center, 908 N 34th St., 206-684-4054

Fremont Public Association, 215 W Harrison St., 206-286-0115

Fremont Neighborhood Council, 206-781-6624

WALLINGFORD

Boundaries: North: N.E. 50th St.; **West:** Aurora Ave. N. (Hwy. 99); **South:** Lake Washington Ship Canal; **East:** I-5

A symbol of a bygone era, the old gasworks at the north end of Lake Union marks the tip of the Wallingford neighborhood. In the early 1900s, when the plant was still operational, Wallingford was a hub of industrial activity. Now the neighborhood is predominantly residential, and the old plant is a beloved Seattle landmark and popular public park. Gasworks Park is a favorite for kite-flying enthusiasts because of steady winds off the lake, and for bicyclists who meet to ride the Burke-Gilman trail along Lake Union and Lake Washington. In addition, Gasworks Park is the site of one of Seattle's annual Independence Day fireworks displays. Although the fireworks can be seen from anywhere around the lake, attendees at the park enjoy watching the fireworks to the accompaniment of the Seattle Symphony.

Despite its proximity to Downtown, Wallingford exudes a quiet charm. On summer evenings, couples stroll down tree-lined streets and visit with neighbors. On Sundays, people crowd into local restaurants for brunch or catch a matinee at the Guild 45th Theater. Like nearby Fremont, Wallingford has retained an aesthetic appeal and artistic temperament that nicely complements its unified community spirit. Elegant Wallingford Center, an old school that was remodeled in the 1980s to become an upscale condominium and retail shopping center, is considered the crown jewel of the area. Nearby, the 45th St. Community Clinic shares a remodeled fire station with the Wallingford branch of the Seattle Public Library. Northeast 45th St., connecting Fremont and Ballard to the University District, offers a pleasant assortment of ethnic restaurants, travel and used bookstores, and funky boutiques.

North of Gasworks Park, on the south slope of the hill, beautifully restored view homes look out over the park and the Downtown skyline. Many of the Victorian and Colonial houses here were built in the early 1900s. Northwest Moderns and Craftsman bungalows were added during the 1920s. Homeowners in this area tend to be young professionals, although rental opportunities attract students from the nearby UW and Seattle Pacific University. Streets here are quiet; churches and old schools dot the area, as do corner grocery stores and coffeehouses. Spectacular views of Lake Union and Downtown, as well as modestly sized homes, have attracted many middle-income families to this area. That trend is changing slowly, however, as higher real estate prices throughout Seattle have made this neighborhood less affordable for single-income families.

North of 45th St. and close to I-5, modest and more affordable homes can be found. Most are bungalows similar to those in the south end of the neighborhood, without the panoramic views of Lake Union and Downtown but occasionally with views of the tips of the Cascades to the east. The area population includes many young professionals and students, residing in a mix of rentals and owner-occupied houses. There are few true apartment buildings in the blocks between 45th St. and Green Lake, but they become more common as one heads toward I-5 and the University District.

Wallingford is surprisingly well located for those commuting to either Downtown or the Eastside. Aurora Ave. N (Hwy. 99) runs parallel to Stone Way, just a few blocks into the Fremont neighborhood. This is generally an excellent route into Downtown, and even to West Seattle or the Sea-Tac Airport. Savvy Eastside commuters take a shortcut along Lake Union to bypass I-5 and catch up with Hwy. 520 at the Montlake entrance.

Area Code: 206

Zip Codes: 98103, 98105

Post Office: Wallingford Station, 1329 N 47th St., 800-275-8777

Library: Wallingford-Wilmot Library, 4423 Densmore Ave. N, 206-684-4088

Police: North Precinct, 10049 College Way N, 206-684-0850

Emergency Hospital: University of Washington Medical Center, 1959 NE Pacific St., 206-548-4000

Public Transportation:
26: Downtown/Fremont/Wallingford/Green Lake
30: Laurelhurst/University District/Wallingford/Fremont/Magnolia
44: Ballard/Wallingford/University District/Montlake
45: Queen Anne/Wallingford/University District

Neighborhood Organization:
Wallingford Community Council, 4649 Sunnyside Ave. N, 206-632-4759

GREEN LAKE

Maple Leaf

Boundaries: North: N.E. 110th St.; **West:** Aurora Ave. N. (Hwy. 99);
South: N. 50th St.; **East:** I-5

In the late 1800s trolleys connected Green Lake to Downtown, creating a popular recreation spot for Seattle residents. An amusement park was opened on the west side of the lake and Woodland Park Zoo was developed at the south end. In the early 1900s, the city of Seattle annexed Green Lake and its surrounding lands, designating them a public space. Today, Green Lake is one of Seattle's most popular public parks. It is surrounded by a three mile paved walkway, attracting bicyclists, in-line skaters, runners, and strolling couples. During the summer, fields at the east side of the lake fill with volleyball teams; basketball courts offer informal but competitive pick-up games; and in-line skaters play hockey in a drained wading pool. At the south end of the lake, Woodland Park has baseball and soccer fields, lighted tennis courts, and a running track.

North and east of Green Lake, cozy coffee shops, fragrant bakeries, sporting goods and bike shops provide services for visitors and residents. Most are located near the intersection of Ravenna Ave. and Green Lake Way, or a few minutes north at Green Lake Way and 80th St. Beautiful Northwest Modern and Tudor style homes line Green Lake Way, facing the lake. Even though there is heavy traffic along this main thoroughfare, the view of the lake and the popularity of the area keep up the value of these homes. Original neighborhood houses still exist, although the distance from these houses to the lake shore increased when the lake was partially drained in the early 1900s.

The neighborhood's charm and immediate accessibility to the park makes Green Lake a high demand area, which is reflected in its real estate prices. Homes just off the lake are the most expensive; many are elegant Colonial style mansions with views of the lake and even of the Olympic Mountains. Recent construction has increased the number of condominiums and townhouses that are available east of the lake, although the area remains primarily a mix of detached houses and apartments. More modest Northwest Modern and Craftsman style homes line idyllic residential streets in the blocks southeast of Green Lake, bordering the Wallingford neighborhood. These homes have the advantage of proximity to Green Lake without the inconvenience of heavy traffic or summer parking problems. Northwest and west of the lake, particularly across Aurora Ave. N near the Phinney Ridge neighborhood, modest and affordable Craftsman style bungalows and Cape Cod style cottages line steep, quiet streets. There are few rentals available in this area, but prices for home buyers are often much lower than those closer in to the lake. Unpretentious yet comfortable homes may also to be found north of 80th St. While many of these areas seem far from the lake, most are merely a few minutes walk away. Green Lake is one of the few Seattle neighborhoods where many residents walk to do their errands. The area around the lake is flat rather than hilly and the heavy traffic in the area makes walking a pleasant alternative to driving.

While the majority of houses around Green Lake are detached bungalows, ramblers, or duplexes, there are many options for those who would like to rent in the Green Lake area. On the southeast and east sides of the lake, particularly near Ravenna Blvd. there are a several apartment buildings and condominiums. Most are contemporary high-rise complexes; others are smaller Federal or 1950s style apartment buildings. Many are a few blocks off the lake, surrounded by houses or other similar apartment buildings. In the smaller buildings, apartments are often not advertised in local newspapers, so prospective tenants should visit the area periodically looking for rental signs. For the best deals, try the area in the spring when University of Washington students vacate for the summer.

The Green Lake neighborhood is primarily white and middle-income. Southeast of the lake and across Aurora Ave. (Hwy. 99) to the west, couples and young families keep that part of the neighborhood hopping. These two areas have been growing rapidly as housing prices increase in the more affluent blocks north and east of Green Lake.

Just north of Green Lake is the **Maple Leaf** neighborhood, recognizable for its blue water tower decorated with enormous white maple leaves. It is a neighborhood of quiet streets and modest but immaculately maintained homes. Most houses in the area are brick Tudors or contemporary split-levels, with small landscaped yards. Perched on a hill over I-5, many homes have views of the Olympics or Mount Rainier. Housing prices in Maple Leaf are surprisingly affordable considering the neighborhood's proximity to Green Lake and I-5.

Area Code: 206

Zip Codes: 98103

Post Office: Wedgwood Station, 6801 35th Ave. NE, 800-275-8777

Library: Green Lake Library, 7364 E Green Lake Dr. N, 206-684-7547

Police: North Precinct, 10049 College Way N, 206-684-0850

Emergency Hospital: Northwest Hospital, 1550 N 115th St., 206-364-0500

Public Transportation:
6: Downtown/Green Lake/Bitter Lake/Shoreline
16: Downtown/Queen Anne/Wallingford/Green Lake/Northgate
26: Downtown/Fremont/Wallingford/Green Lake
40: Wedgwood/Green Lake/University District/Georgetown/ Duwamish
67: University District/Maple Leaf/Northgate
72: Downtown/Eastlake/University District/Maple Leaf/Lake City
73: Downtown/Eastlake/University District/Maple Leaf/Jackson Park
78: University District/Maple Leaf/Lake City/Jackson Park
79: Downtown/University District/Maple Leaf/Lake City
83: Downtown/Eastlake/University District/Maple Leaf/Ravenna
Neighborhood Organization:
Green Lake Community Center, 7201 E Green Lake Drive N, 206-684-0780

UNIVERSITY DISTRICT

Roosevelt
Ravenna
Bryant

Boundaries: North: N.E. 75th St.; **West:** I-5; **South:** Lake Washington Ship Canal; **East:** N.E. 35th St, Union Bay

In 1861, the University of Washington was founded on the present-day site of the Four Seasons Olympic Hotel in Downtown Seattle. Four Grecian pillars, all that remain of the original building, can now be seen on a small piece of land near the Paramount Theater (at the intersection of Pike St. and Boren Ave. The university moved to its present location near Union Bay in 1895, intent upon shaking off its reputation as an elementary and high school. The UW graduated its first university student in 1876, but continued accepting pre-college students as late as 1897. Two influential Seattle citizens, Arthur Denny and Daniel Bagley, were instrumental in bringing the college to Seattle. Denny persuaded the legislature to grant Seattle the rights to the territorial university and donated 10 acres of his own property as the original site. Bagley had convinced Denny that the college would be more of an asset to the city than the other available alternatives: the state capitol, prison, or customs house. Asa Mercer, the university's first president and teacher, is best known today as the man who went east and recruited single women to move to Seattle when it was still a primarily male logging community. His substantial contributions to the fledgling college are largely overlooked.

The University District is known for its young inhabitants and unique culture. You'll find the many coffee-houses in the area filled with students and faculty, often deeply involved in philosophical debate. On campus, be sure to visit the Burke Museum for, among other attractions, its marvelous exhibits on local Native American tribes, and the Graduate Reading Room, a beautiful cathedral shaped room in the Suzzallo Library. For a look at one of Seattle's natural wonders, stop at "Frosh Pond" for a fabulous view of Mount Rainier over the Guggenheim Fountain. Also worth a visit is the "Wall of Death," located under the north end of the University Bridge. The bright orange sculpture was inspired by the circus tradition of riding motorcycles at high speeds around a nearly vertical wall.

In 1909, the Alaska-Yukon-Pacific Exposition was held on campus, marking a publicity turning point for the young university. Originally intended to celebrate the 10th anniversary of the Klondike Gold Rush, the event was held two years late but drew nearly four million visitors to the area. As a result of the exposition, the university received several new permanent buildings and gained national attention. Since then, annual enrollment has reached the 35,000 mark and the university has gained a reputation as a premier medical research institution. While some critics claim that the university gives special preference to its graduate and research programs, particularly the sciences over the humanities, it remains an affordable way to receive a high quality undergraduate education.

In addition to its solid academic reputation, the University of Washington is nationally recognized for its football program. The Huskies routinely attract sold-out crowds for home games, even during disastrous seasons. Wealthy UW graduates and football fans are generous supporters of the program, and in fact regularly generate more interest in the team than the university students. The UW crew and basketball teams (particularly the women's) also receive local attention, although they are overshadowed by the fervent devotion of Husky football fans. All of the UW sports facilities are on the shore of Union Bay, an inlet of Lake Washington, along Montlake Ave. Parking is scarce and traffic problems are common on football Saturdays; at other times two large parking lots north of the stadium are sufficient. Traffic is generally heavy before and after games and parking in the area can be tricky for non-residents; city regulations have benefited those who live near the stadium by assigning parking stickers and limiting parking on most streets to neighborhood residents. Some lucky football fans come to the games by boat, tying up at the east side of the UW stadium. Others take advantage of the additional buses that are added to local routes on game days. For the fitness and environmentally-minded, you can bike or walk to the games via the Burke-Gilman trail.

Locals and students refer to the university as the UW (pronounced "U-Dub") and to the area around it as the "U-District." Although the campus is the geographic focal point of the area, the center of the community is "the Ave.," which is really University Way, a street just a block west of the campus. It's a great place to see movies, buy books and CDs, play video games, or eat at a variety of ethnic restaurants. The Ave. is also a central location for bus service to the University District and other parts of the city, with routes to neighborhoods throughout the north end of Seattle and to Downtown and Capitol Hill. Just south of NE 45th St. on the Ave., the University Bookstore carries an array of books, gifts, and art supplies, as well as required materials for UW classes. During the school year, the Ave. draws university students to some of their favorite hangouts, and in the summer it is the site for the University District Street Fair, which takes over several blocks of the street for an entire weekend.

The University District is primarily a neighborhood of young people (the median age is 22). Residents include undergraduate and graduate students and university faculty members, as well as young professionals, scholars and artists. Some families own homes in the northeast corner of the district near Ravenna Blvd., but over 90 percent of U-District residents are renters. Just north of campus, 17th Ave. NE, a tree-lined avenue known informally as "Greek Row," is bordered by beautiful colonial-style mansions. Many of these buildings, as well as those in the blocks east of 17th Ave NE, have been converted into fraternities, sororities, and rooming houses. The north end of this area is popular with graduate students and visiting faculty, as well as long-time neighborhood residents.

West of campus there are many apartment buildings and shared houses. Close to the campus there are several brick apartment buildings, offering small studios or one-bedrooms with hardwood floors and occasional views. Many large modern buildings, built in 1980s, are located near I-5 and offer multiple bedroom apartments. Other rental opportunities are available near the University Village mall, at the northeast corner of the UW campus. The mall has been recently remodeled to include a Starbucks and national chain stores such as The Gap, Eddie Bauer, Banana Republic, and Pottery Barn. Though many feel these changes have given the area a much-needed face-lift, they have also pushed out smaller local businesses which couldn't afford the higher rents. Apartment buildings and townhouses line NE 22nd St., and other rentals are tucked into the base of the hill behind the retail stores and strip malls that line NE 25th St. The most affordable options are rooms for rent in group houses — these are often listed in local papers such as *The Stranger* and *The Seattle Weekly*, and in the UW student paper *The Daily*. Rental houses are also readily available, particularly north of 50th Ave. NE. The best time for finding rentals of any kind is at the end of the school year when students head home for the summer. Many rentals are not listed in local papers, so it is generally a good idea to roam the neighborhood looking for "For Rent" signs.

The Roosevelt and Ravenna neighborhoods, located north of the University District, traditionally attract UW graduate students, faculty, and staff. In recent decades, professionals willing to commute to Downtown or the Eastside have also moved to these areas. The center of the **Roosevelt** neighborhood is a small retail district around the intersection of Roosevelt Ave. NE and NE 65th St., which boasts several small ethnic restaurants, coffee shops, and bookstores. One unique event occurs on the first Wednesday of every month, as motorcycle enthusiasts flock to Teddy's Bar, lining the street with bikes of all makes and models. Despite this "biker bar" tradition, the Roosevelt neighborhood is a tranquil residential community. Most houses in the Roosevelt District are Arts-and-Crafts style bungalows and Tudor-style cottages. There are few apartment buildings and condominiums in the neighborhoods, mostly near I-5 and Ravenna Blvd.

The **Ravenna** neighborhood is named for the ravine which runs through the area, at one time connecting Green Lake with Union Bay and Lake Washington. Water still flows in the ravine, now fed by underground streams and Seattle's ubiquitous rain. Ravenna Park follows the ravine, winding northwest toward the Green Lake area. It is a beautiful and lush city park with trails, tennis courts, and picnic areas. There are a variety of architectural styles in Ravenna, including modest Tudors, roomy Arts-and-Crafts homes, and 1960s bungalows. There are occasional opportunities for renting houses here, and a few apartments and townhouses line 25th Ave. E.

The **Bryant** neighborhood, east of University Village, has much in common with Ravenna. Houses here are mainly modest bungalows and Tudors, with a few scattered brick ranch houses. Ravenna and Bryant attract families, UW faculty and staff members, and professionals who work Downtown or on the Eastside. Commuters to the Eastside have few choices on their route to the 520 bridge from here, so the drive at rush hour can be time-consuming. Beyond that, you can't beat its offer of quiet streets and friendly neighbors.

Area Code: 206

Zip Codes: 98105, 98115

Post Office: University Station, 4244 University Way NE, 800-275-8777

Library: University Library, 5009 Roosevelt Way NE, 206-684-4063

Police: North Precinct, 10049 College Way N, 206-684-0850

Emergency Hospital: University of Washington Medical Center, 1959 NE Pacific St., 206-548-4000

Public Transportation:
7: University District/Capitol Hill/Downtown/International District/Rainier Valley/Columbia City/Rainier Beach
9: University District/Capitol Hill/First Hill/Rainier Valley/Columbia City/Rainier Beach
25: Downtown/Eastlake/Montlake/University District/Wedgwood/Lake City
30: Laurelhurst/University District/Wallingford/Fremont/Magnolia
32: Downtown/University District/Laurelhurst
40: Wedgwood/Green Lake/University District/Georgetown/Duwamish
43: Downtown/Capitol Hill/Montlake/University District
44: Ballard/Wallingford/University District/Montlake
45: Queen Anne/Wallingford/University District
46: Shilshole/Ballard/Fremont/University District
48: Ballard/Greenwood/Ravenna/University District/Montlake/Central District/Columbia City/Rainier Beach

65: Downtown/Montlake/University District/Wedgwood/Lake City
66: Waterfront/Downtown/University District/Northgate
67: University District/Maple Leaf/Northgate
68: University District/Ravenna/Wedgwood/Northgate
70: Downtown/Eastlake/University District
71: Downtown/Eastlake/University District/Ravenna/View Ridge/Wedgwood/Lake City
72: Downtown/Eastlake/University District/Maple Leaf/Lake City
73: Downtown/Eastlake/University District/Maple Leaf/Jackson Park
74: Downtown/University District/Ravenna/Sand Point
75: University District/Sand Point/Lake City/Northgate
78: University District/Maple Leaf/Lake City/Jackson Park
79: Downtown/University District/Maple Leaf/Lake City
83: Downtown/Eastlake/University District/Maple Leaf/Ravenna
205: University District/Montlake/First Hill/Mercer Island
243: Jackson Park/Lake City/Ravenna/Montlake/Bellevue

Neighborhood Organizations:
University Neighborhood Service Center, 4534 University Way NE, 206-684-7542 Ravenna Eckstein Community Center, 6535 Ravenna Ave. NE, 206-684-7534

LAKE CITY

Boundaries: North: N.E. 145th St.; **West:** 5th Ave. N.E.; **South:** N.E. 95th St.; **East:** Lake Washington

Lake City is located near the north end of Lake Washington, just inside the city limits. When Seattle annexed Lake City in 1957, it was a quiet lakefront suburb with a small retail core along Lake City Way, a branch of the state highway system. Much of that small town character remains in Lake City, which attracts a mix of low- and middle-income families and professionals. The residential streets of Lake City are sheltered from the busy traffic of the highway, giving each a feeling of seclusion with a friendly small-town atmosphere.

Those looking to live in Lake City will find affordable homes and ample rental apartments. Homes in Lake City are predominantly modest bungalows or modern split-levels. Many have unusually large lots with private backyards. Those east of Lake City Way may have views of Lake Washington and the Cascades. The Lake Washington waterfront in Lake City used to be lined with small weekend cottages, but as property values have soared many of those have been replaced with large, contemporary homes. Real estate prices and rents are generally lower here than in other residential neighborhoods in Seattle, because of the distance from Downtown and the Eastside. However, living in Lake City makes for an easy commute to the north end of Lake Washington, Bothell, and Kenmore. Most apartment buildings are located in the few blocks to either side of Lake City Way and along NE 125th St. Nearly half of the residents of Lake City rent apartments or houses, and the number of apartments in the area has increased by about 30 percent since 1980.

Lake City Way has also changed significantly since 1957, and is now crowded with strip malls, gas stations, second-hand and antique stores, and a variety of small locally owned retail businesses. Adult bookstores and strip clubs have given Lake City Way a slightly seedy reputation, although the businesses have had little impact on the residential areas of the neighborhood. The community has experienced some problems with criminal activity near the highway, but community watch groups and patrols have substantially reduced crime along Lake City Way and throughout the neighborhood.

While the majority of Lake City's residents are white, recent Asian and Hispanic immigrants to Seattle have begun to settle here. This infusion of diverse cultures is reflected in the assortment of new businesses in operation along Lake City Way, including ethnic art shops and restaurants. Because of the affordable rents and homes, residents are primarily blue-collar workers and their families, many with school-aged children. More recently, the area has begun to attract artists and college-educated professionals, as well as retirees with modest incomes.

Area Code: 206

Zip Codes: 98125

Post Office: Lake City Station, 3019 NE 127th St., 800-275-8777

Library: Lake City Library, 12501 28th Ave. NE, 206-684-7518

Police: North Precinct, 10049 College Way N, 206-684-0850

Emergency Hospital: Northwest Hospital, 1550 N 115th St., 206-364-0500

Public Transportation:
25: Downtown/Eastlake/Montlake/University District/Wedgwood/ Lake City
65: Downtown/Montlake/University District/Wedgwood/Lake City

71: Downtown/Eastlake/University District/Ravenna/View Ridge/Wedgwood/Lake City
72: Downtown/Eastlake/University District/Maple Leaf/Lake City
78: University District/Maple Leaf/Lake City/Jackson Park
79: Downtown/University District/Maple Leaf/Lake City
243: Jackson Park/Lake City/Ravenna/Montlake/Bellevue

Neighborhood Organizations:
Lake City Community Center, 12531 28th Ave. NE, 206-362-4378

Lake City Neighborhood Service Center, 12707 30th Ave. NE, 206-684-7526

NORTHGATE

Jackson Park
Oak Tree
Aurora

Boundaries: North: N. 145th St.; **West:** Aurora Ave. N. (Hwy. 99); **South:** N.E. 92nd St.; **East:** 5th Ave. N.E.

Northgate is a large neighborhood centered around the Northgate Mall, which opened in 1950 and claims to be the oldest shopping mall in North America. The mall itself is rather small by current standards, and the businesses located there tend to be scaled-down versions of their Downtown or Bellevue Square counterparts. Nevertheless, ample parking around the mall as well as its close proximity to I-5 make it a popular shopping destination. A recent construction project corrected some nasty traffic patterns near the highway, and the mall has just been remodeled, making it more attractive to shoppers.

The immediate area around the Northgate Mall is filled with small retail businesses which benefit from the mall traffic. Restaurants, drug stores, banks, and sporting goods stores line Northgate Way at the north end of the mall. Many contemporary apartment and condominiums are just off the main streets in this area.

The heart of the Northgate residential community is north of the mall, stretching as far as the **Jackson Park** neighborhood at the city boundary. Houses in this area are 1950s brick ranch houses or modest split-levels on large lots. There are also a number of duplexes, town-houses, apartment buildings and condominiums, as well as an increasing number of senior citizen residences. While real estate and rental prices are lower here than in other parts of the city, there is a strong sense of community among residents, with well-kept lawns, freshly-painted houses, and friendly neighbors. If chosen wisely, a house in this neighborhood would be an excellent spot for first-time home buyers. West of I-5, the **Oak Tree** area runs along Aurora Ave., north of Green Lake. Located in Oak Tree is a cultural center, formerly a public school, as well as a collection of modest homes and brightly painted townhouses. The Oak Tree Shopping Center, which gave this area its name, has a Starbucks, several good restaurants, a large multiplex theater, and Larry's Market, a gourmet supermarket. Nearby North Seattle Community College, an imposing concrete structure which resembles a small penitentiary, has a solid reputation, attracting students of all ages. The area around the college includes several small government agencies as well as the North Precinct for the Seattle Police Department.

North of the Oak Tree area is **Aurora**, which includes the area north of Northgate Way (105th St.) between Aurora Ave. N (Hwy. 99) and I-5. Aurora Ave. N is a major business district, with a seemingly endless series of strip malls, car dealerships, small hotels, taverns, and appliance stores. While Aurora Ave. N has a reputation for petty crime and prostitution, residents who live even a few blocks off this main street rarely encounter any problems. A block or two east of Aurora Ave. N there are many modest split-level and contemporary brick homes. Real estate and rental prices in this area tend to be slightly lower than in those neighborhoods closer to Downtown.

Area Code: 206

Zip Codes: 98133, 98125

Post Office: Northgate Station, 11036 8th Ave. NE, 800-275-8777

Library: Lake City Library, 12501 28th Ave. NE, 206-684-7518

Police: North Precinct, 10049 College Way N, 206-684-0850

Emergency Hospital: Northwest Hospital, 1550 N 115th St., 206-364-0500

Public Transportation:
5: Downtown/Fremont/Greenwood/Northgate
6: Downtown/Green Lake/Bitter Lake/Shoreline
16: Downtown/Queen Anne/Wallingford/Green Lake/Northgate
25: Downtown/Eastlake/Montlake/University District/Wedgwood/

Lake City
65: Downtown/Montlake/University District/Wedgwood/Lake City
73: Downtown/Eastlake/University District/Maple Leaf/Jackson Park
75: University District/Sand Point/Lake City/Northgate
243: Jackson Park/Lake City/Ravenna/Montlake/Bellevue

Neighborhood Organization:
Bitter Lake Community Center, 13035 Linden Ave. N, 206-684-7524

BROADVIEW

Boundaries: North: N.W. 145th St.; **West:** Puget Sound; **South:** N.W. 110th St.; **East:** Aurora Ave. N. (Hwy. 99)

Located in the northwest corner of Seattle, Broadview is really more of a suburban community than an urban neighborhood, with quiet residential streets and an unremarkable commercial district. Most of the area bears a close similarity to the suburban Shoreline community located just north of the city.

Greenwood Ave. N is the commercial street in this neighborhood and is lined with a variety of retail businesses, restaurants, and several small strip malls. Greenwood Ave. N also serves as a dividing line down the center of the neighborhood, with affluent and white collar residents to the west, young families and blue-collar workers to the east. Bitter Lake, just northeast of the intersection of 130th and Greenwood, is surrounded by single-family homes that attract middle-income professionals. There are some apartments and condominium complexes between Greenwood Ave. and Aurora Ave. N, particularly south of 130th St. These generally rent for slightly less than comparable in-city units, because this area is not as close to Downtown or I-5.

Houses in the Broadview neighborhood are mainly modern bungalows, ramblers, and split-levels, although the homes grow more grand as you progress north along 3rd Ave. NW, especially on the west side of the street. Many of these homes have splendid views of the Puget Sound and the Olympic Mountains, similar to the more expensive homes just south in the North Beach area. At the far north end of 3rd Ave. NW, the Seattle Golf Club and the entrance to The Highlands present a glimpse of one of the most exclusive developments in Seattle. **The Highlands,** designed in 1909 by the Olmsteds (who also designed Seattle's park system), remains an exclusive and private enclave for the very wealthy.

Although the lots are smaller now than the original minimum of five acres, the winding wooded roads and gated entrance have preserved the quiet seclusion of this community. While Broadview residents are primarily white, middle-income professionals, the neighborhood is open to all ethnic groups and income levels. Houses and apartments close to Aurora Ave. N offer the least expensive prices and rents, while still providing the comforts of a close-knit residential community. Between 3rd Ave. NW and Greenwood Ave. NW and north of 130th St., and in the vicinity of Carkeek Park, there are a variety of modest and affordable houses for young families and middle-income professionals. While this neighborhood does not attract tourists nor does it promise adventurous living, it will satisfy those looking for a stable suburban-style city community.

Area Code: 206

Zip Codes: 98177

Post Office: Greenwood Station, 8306 Greenwood Ave. N, 800-275-8777

Library: Broadview Library, 12755 Greenwood Ave. N, 206-684-7519

Police: North Precinct, 10049 College Way N, 206-684-0850

Emergency Hospital: Northwest Hospital, 1550 N 115th St., 206-364-0500

Public Transportation:
6: Downtown/Green Lake/Bitter Lake/Shoreline
28: Downtown/Fremont/Ballard/Broadview

Neighborhood Organization:
Bitter Lake Community Center, 13035 Linden Ave. N, 206-684-7524

SAND POINT

Laurelhurst
View Ridge
Wedgwood

Boundaries: North: N.E. 95th St.; **West:** 35th Ave. N.E., Lake City Way; **South:** Union Bay; **East:** Lake Washington

On the shore of Lake Washington, the Sand Point neighborhood (which includes Laurelhurst, View Ridge, and Wedgwood) is best known as the location of the National Oceanic and Atmospheric Administration (NOAA) and Children's Orthopedic Hospital. NOAA, a federal research facility that studies the weather and its impact upon the ocean and coastlines, shares a base with the Sand Point Naval Station on Lake Washington. Children's Orthopedic Hospital, located on Sand Point Way, is a nationally recognized private hospital that specializes in treating terminally ill children.

Sand Point also features two public parks, both with access to the Lake Washington waterfront. Matthews Beach, located north of NOAA, is a summer favorite of sunbathers, picnickers and swimmers. The Burke-Gilman trail stops off at Matthews Beach as it follows the edge of Lake Washington, giving bicyclists and in-line skaters easy access to the park. South of NOAA, Magnuson Park offers visitors the use of several softball fields and a boat launch. Magnuson Park is also the home of the Soundgarden, a wind chime sculpture which inspired the name of the now-famous local band.

Laurelhurst, on the southern hill of the Sand Point neighborhood, is a quiet and determinedly private neighborhood. Residents of Laurelhurst are affluent professionals and retirees living in homes overlooking the boats and water-skiers on Lake Washington and Union Bay. Views from these homes are incredible with Mount Rainier and the snow-capped Cascades providing a stunning backdrop. This is a neighborhood of manicured lawns and private waterfront access; thus homes here are correspondingly expensive. Most Laurelhurst houses are single-family residences, ranging from modest brick Tudors to palatial Georgian and Colonial style homes. The border of Laurelhurst, along Sand Point Way, includes a thriving upscale retail district, as well as Children's Orthopedic Hospital and other clinics. At the top of the hill, the Laurelhurst park and community center serves as a hub for neighborhood activities, including softball games, summer picnics, aerobics and pottery classes. There are very few opportunities to rent in this neighborhood, with only a handful of apartment buildings located along Sand Point Way.

View Ridge, north of Laurelhurst, tends to attract wealthy professionals, affluent retirees, and tenured UW professors. Homes in this area are modest brick Tudors and 1950s ranch houses with immaculately kept lawns. Most residences have panoramic views of the sun rising over Lake Washington and the Cascades each morning. Near Matthews Beach, many of the houses are renovated beach cottages, a reminder of an earlier time when this area was an out-of-town destination for Seattle residents. There are several newer "view" condominiums in this area as well. As with Laurelhurst, most rentals are limited to apartment buildings on busy Sand Point Way. Located between Sand Point Way and a small retail district at the intersection of NE 75th St. and 35th Ave. NE, **Wedgwood** offers a mix of affordable single-family homes, duplexes, townhouses and apartment buildings with occasional views of the Cascade Mountains. Homes are less expensive here than elsewhere in the Sand Point area, with most Wedgwood homes being Cape Cod and Saltbox style cottages, as well as some Craftsman-style bungalows. Residents are middle-income professionals and young families, as well as UW faculty and staff. In addition, Wedgwood has a strong and active Jewish community, with three synagogues located in the neighborhood.

Area Code: 206

Zip Codes: 98105, 98115

Post Office: Wedgwood Station, 6801 35th Ave. NE, 800-275-8777

Library: North East Library, 6801 35th Ave. NE, 206-684-7539

Police: North Precinct, 10049 College Way N, 206-684-0850

Emergency Hospital: University of Washington Medical Center, 1959 NE Pacific St., 206-548-4000

Public Transportation:
25: Downtown/Eastlake/Montlake/University District/Wedgwood/ Lake City
32: Downtown/University District/Laurelhurst
65: Downtown/Montlake/University District/Wedgwood/Lake City
68: University District/Ravenna/Wedgwood/Northgate
71: Downtown/Eastlake/University District/Ravenna/View Ridge/Wedgwood/Lake City
74: Downtown/University District/Ravenna/Sand Point
76: Downtown/Ravenna/Wedgwood

Neighborhood Organizations:
Laurelhurst Community Center, 4554 NE 41st St., 206-684-7529

Sand Point Community Housing Association, 7400 Sand Point Way NE, 206-517-5499

MADISON PARK

Washington Park
Denny Blaine
Broadmoor

Boundaries: North: Union Bay; **West:** Lake Washington Blvd.; **South:** Lake Washington Blvd.; **East:** Lake Washington

On the shore of Lake Washington, the community of Madison Park lies just south of Union Bay and the 520 Floating Bridge. During the late 1800s, Madison Park was a beach-front resort town frequented by early Seattle residents. People took the cable car from downtown Seattle out to the shore to spend the day or they rented a nearby cottage for the week. During the summer there was a carnival at Madison Park with food and games and a Ferris wheel. Today, Madison Park is an affluent community with a small town feel. Shop owners know the names of their local customers, traffic is slow and leisurely, people stroll the sidewalks and smile at one another. It's one of the few Seattle neighborhoods that is not a shortcut route to other parts of the city, and so it is spared the traffic problems of other less fortunate neighborhoods.

Unique restaurants and cafes, fashionable boutiques, and fragrant bakeries offering scrumptious goodies line E Madison St., Madison Park's main thoroughfare. Businesses here are small and charming; nowhere will you find sprawling supermarkets, warehouse stores, chain restaurants or fast food joints. Although First Hill and Capitol Hill, with their mainstream business districts, are only a ten minute drive away, many Madison Park residents do their shopping locally.

Near the east end of E Madison St., Colonial and Northwest Modern homes intermingle with modest Cape Cods, reminiscent of the beach cottages that lined the beach in early Madison Park. Two traditionally expensive and fashionable Madison Park neighborhoods, **Washington Park** and **Denny Blaine**, lie further south along the shore of Lake Washington and on the hill facing the lake. Homes in these areas are an eclectic mix of styles, primarily Colonials and Northwest Moderns, as well as a few Elizabethan or Tudor homes. Many of the stately homes here were built when Seattle's most wealthy citizens migrated to this area and other posh neighborhoods, such as Queen Anne and Capitol Hill, away from Downtown and First Hill. Finally, **Broadmoor** offers a variety of elegant homes in an ultra-exclusive golf and country club setting, tucked between Lake Washington and the Arboretum. Just south of E Madison St., high-rise condominiums face Lake Washington. Since these were completed local zoning restrictions have changed, preventing other similar buildings from crowding out the homes that are the core of Madison Park. Nevertheless, these have attracted a variety of wealthy professionals and retirees, offering the neighborly appeal of Madison Park and spectacular views of Lake Washington, the Cascades and imposing Mount Rainier. In particular, these condominiums might interest those looking to live in a less urban environment without the responsibilities of owning a home and a yard . . . . On the north shore of the Madison Park peninsula, other contemporary and Colonial style condominiums offer views of Lake Washington and the 520 bridge.

Madison Park continues to be a neighborhood of wealthy and influential Seattle citizens. Residents are affluent professionals and entrepreneurs; the community as a whole has a median income more than twice that of the rest of the city. Madison Park homes are correspondingly some of the more expensive homes in Seattle, with even modest Cape Cod cottages running in the several hundred thousand dollar range. The grand residences in Broadmoor and Denny Blaine are generally even more expensive.

Area Code: 206

Zip Codes: 98112, 98122

Post Office: East Union Station, 1110 23rd Ave., 800-275-8777

Library: Montlake Library, 2300 24th Ave. E, 206-684-4720

Police: East Precinct, 1519 12th Ave., 206-684-4300

Emergency Hospital: Swedish Medical Center, 747 Broadway, 206-386-2573

Public Transportation:
11: Madison Park/First Hill/Downtown/Waterfront

Neighborhood Organization:
Madison Park Community Council, 206-689-6218

MONTLAKE

Portage Bay

Boundaries: North: Lake Washington Ship Canal; **West:** Fuhrman Ave. E.; **South:** Boyer Ave. E.; **East:** Lake Washington Blvd.

The Montlake Cut is a small man-made waterway which connects Lake Union and Lake Washington. Each year, the annual Opening Day celebration of boating season is celebrated here. Just south of the UW Husky Stadium, the Montlake Bridge crosses the cut, connecting Montlake Ave. to 24th Ave. E. The Montlake neighborhood includes all of the homes to the south side of this bridge and to either side of 24th Ave. E, which dissects the community into east and west sides. Hwy. 520 splits the area again into north and south halves. Being at the crossroads of two major thoroughfares both increases Montlake's accessibility and its traffic. Despite these busy streets and the overwhelming rush hour traffic, the Montlake neighborhood seems tucked away from the cares of the city.

Homes in Montlake are an exclusive mélange of imposing mansions, exquisite cottages, brick Tudors and elaborate colonials. Winding streets and faux cul-de-sacs add to the feeling of privacy in the neighborhood, though it makes navigating the area confusing. With the Montlake Cut to the north and the Arboretum to the east, Montlake's only close neighbor is **Portage Bay**, itself a tiny residential offshoot of the Eastlake and Capitol Hill neighborhoods. There are no shopping centers or malls, only a couple of small corner grocers and the requisite freeway on-ramp gas station. University Village, a shopping center located just north of Montlake on 25th Ave. NE, offers everything from Banana Republic and Eddie Bauer to a huge QFC (a local grocery store chain). The neighborhood is home to two of Seattle's premier yacht clubs, the Seattle Yacht Club and Queen City Yacht Club, giving members easy access to both Lake Union and Lake Washington. Also, the Museum of History and Industry is here as well as beautiful Foster Island Park. One can rent canoes, rowboats or sailboats from the UW waterfront activities center and paddle/sail through the arboretum for a leisurely outing.

On the south side of Hwy. 520 and west of 24th Ave. E, the Montlake Park is a center of activity for the neighborhood, with quiet tennis courts and a popular activity center. Just across 24th Ave. E, Montlake homes brush up against the Washington Park Arboretum, a 200-acre public park with 5,500 different trees and shrubs and the

University of Washington's Japanese Gardens. A quick drive through the Arboretum brings you to the edge of the Madison Park neighborhood, and provides access to the heavenly bakeries, elegant salons, and excellent restaurants that line Madison St.

Most Montlake residents are middle- or high-income professionals who work Downtown or on the Eastside. As lucrative high-tech jobs, including those at Microsoft, have increased in number on the Eastside, Montlake has become a popular neighborhood for successful software engineers and other technical workers. More traditional Montlake residents include current and retired UW professors and UW Medical Center doctors. The convenient access to I-5 and the Hwy. 520 bridge, as well as the secluded and quiet nature of the residential area of Montlake make this an attractive and sought-after location for affluent professionals.

Area Code: 206

Zip Codes: 98112

Post Office: East Union Station, 1110 23rd Ave., 800-275-8777

Library: Montlake Library, 2300 24th Ave. E, 206-684-4720

Police: East Precinct, 1519 12th Ave., 206-684-4300

Emergency Hospital: University of Washington Medical Center, 1959 NE Pacific St., 206-548-4000

Public Transportation:
25: Downtown/Eastlake/Montlake/University District/Wedgwood/ Lake City
43: Downtown/Capitol Hill/Montlake/University District
44: Ballard/Wallingford/University District/Montlake
48: Ballard/Greenwood/Ravenna/University District/Montlake/ Central District/Columbia City/Rainier Beach
65: Downtown/Montlake/University District/Wedgwood/Lake City
205: University District/Montlake/First Hill/Mercer Island
243: Jackson Park/Lake City/Ravenna/Montlake/Bellevue

Neighborhood Organization:
Montlake Community Center, 1618 E Calhoun St., 206-684-4736

CENTRAL DISTRICT

Boundaries: North: E. Madison St., **West:** 12th Ave. E., 23rd Ave. E.; **South:** I-90; **East:** Martin Luther King Way

Driving east on E Madison St. from First Hill, one sees a characteristic example of Seattle's neighborhood distinctions. North of E Madison St. is the wealthy, primarily white neighborhood of Capitol Hill, to the south is the Central District; a neighborhood generally comprised of African-American families in the low-to-middle income bracket. The Central District or Central Area, referred to as "the CD" by most Seattle residents, cuts a long narrow swath through the center of Seattle. Most retail enterprises in the CD are located along 12th Ave. E and on 23rd Ave. E. Many are (great) family-owned restaurants and shops, and small African- or Asian-American groceries.

Sandwiched between Capitol Hill, First Hill, and the International District to the west, Madison Park, Madrona, and Leschi to the east, the CD has long had an uneasy relationship with the rest of Seattle. Homes in the Central District are not all that different from those at this end of Capitol Hill — most are charming turn-of-the-century Victorians, 1920s Colonials, and Craftsman bungalows, which were built in times of prosperity. Nevertheless, housing prices in the Central District, especially the eastern portion, have generally lagged behind prices in the rest of Seattle as many homes in the area were neglected or even abandoned.

Recently, housing prices in the CD have risen as more affluent residents of various ethnic backgrounds have moved to the area. This is particularly true in the north end of the neighborhood, with it taking on the appearance of nearby Capitol Hill and Madison Park. The city has begun to funnel much needed financial support to this community. Although many houses in the north end of the CD are still run-down from years of neglect and poverty, some are being refurbished by newcomers and longtime residents. Crime rates here are actually lower here than in other parts of the city; still, home and car security remain an issue for those living in the CD.

Area Code: 206

Zip Codes: 98122, 98144

Post Office: East Union Station, 1110 23rd Ave., 800-275-8777

Library: Douglass-Truth Library, 2300 E Yesler Way, 206-684-4704

Police: East Precinct, 1519 12th Ave., 206-684-4300

Emergency Hospital: Swedish Medical Center, 747 Broadway, 206-386-2573

Public Transportation:
2: First Hill/Central District/First Hill/Downtown/Belltown/Queen Anne
3: Madrona/Central District/First Hill/Downtown/Queen Anne
4: Judkins Park/Central District/First Hill/Downtown/Queen Anne
14: Downtown/Pioneer Square/International District/Central District/Mount Baker
27: Downtown/Central District/Leschi
48: Ballard/Greenwood/Ravenna/University District/Montlake/Central District/Columbia City/Rainier Beach

Neighborhood Organizations:
Central Area Motivation Program, 722 18th Ave., 206-329-4111

Central Area Youth Association, 119 23rd Ave., 206-322-6640

Central Neighborhood Service Center, 1825 S Jackson St. Suite 101, 206-684-4767

Garfield Community Center, 2323 E Cherry St., 206-684-4788

Langston Hughes Cultural Arts Center, 104 17th Ave. S, 206-684-4757

Meadowbrook Community Center, 330 19th Ave. E, 206-684-7522

Yesler Community Center, 835 E Yesler Way, 206-386-1245

MADRONA/LESCHI

Boundaries: North: Denny Way; **West:** Martin Luther King Way; **South:** I-90; **East:** Lake Washington

The Madrona and Leschi neighborhoods lie along Lake Washington, east of the Central District and the International District. While Madrona sits atop the hill facing west, Leschi, named for a Nisqually Indian who was executed for resisting the whites, faces east toward Lake Washington. Some consider Madrona and Leschi part of the Central District, but both neighborhoods are quite different from the CD. Both Madrona and Leschi were affluent neighborhoods that declined in prestige after the 1960s, when many wealthy residents moved to other areas of Seattle. Fortunately for many, this shift made the area more affordable, and allowed for an influx of people from a wide variety of racial and cultural backgrounds. Today, though primarily white, both neighborhoods offer a blend of ethnic groups and income levels, made up of longtime residents as well as newcomers.

Central to the Madrona neighborhood is the intersection of 34th Ave. E and E Union St. Clustered here are the popular cafes and trendy shops of Madrona. The few blocks around this intersection create an idyllic urban village, with people sitting on storefront steps and at restaurant tables along the sidewalks. There are several small eateries here that cater to a lively Sunday brunch crowd. In Leschi, most businesses are located on the lake, and are primarily view-restaurants and boat related ventures, including the Corinthian Yacht Club. In addition, the newly constructed condominium and retail complex, Lakeside at Leschi, is located on the shore of Lake Washington. To the south, Leschi Park features Victorian-style grounds, towering sequoias, and colorful tulip trees. Atop the hill, Frink Park offers lovely walking trails under grand maples.

Many of the residents of Madrona and Leschi are artists and artisans, young professionals, retired entrepreneurs, and families with young children. Incomes in these neighborhoods vary widely, with wealthy residents living around the corner from low- or middle-income families. Homes also run the gamut in size and style, from opulent turn-of-the-century Victorians and Colonials to remodeled corner groceries. Many of the splendid homes in Leschi have spectacular views of Lake Washington, the Cascade Mountains, and Mount Rainier. Other homes in both Madrona and Leschi share a view of Downtown and the distant Olympics to the west.

Concerns about home and personal security are reflected in the bars on the windows of some businesses and homes in these neighborhoods. While there is a strong community spirit among residents, close proximity to higher crime neighborhoods such as Rainier Valley and the Central District make both Madrona and Leschi more vulnerable than other more isolated Seattle neighborhoods. However, the crime rates are trending down in these areas and local neighborhood watch groups are organized and effective.

Area Code: 206

Zip Codes: 98122, 98144

Post Office: East Union Station, 1110 23rd Ave., 800-275-8777

Libraries:
Douglass-Truth Library, 2300 E Yesler Way, 206-684-4704

Madrona Sally Goldmark Library, 1134 33rd Ave., 206-684-4705

Police: East Precinct, 1519 12th Ave., 206-684-4300

Emergency Hospital: Harborview Medical Center, 325 9th Ave., 206-731-3074

Public Transportation:
3: Madrona/Central District/First Hill/Downtown/Queen Anne
27: Downtown/Central District/Leschi

Neighborhood Organizations:
Central Area Motivation Program, 722 18th Ave., 206-329-4111

Garfield Community Center, 2323 E Cherry St., 206-684-4788

BEACON HILL

South Beacon Hill
Holly Park
Mount Baker

Boundaries: North: I-90 **West:** I-5; **South:** S. Ryan St. (to Martin Luther King Way S.), S. Genesee St.; **East:** Lake Washington

At night, the Pacific Medical Center on Beacon Hill looms over the city like a huge gothic castle. Designed by architects Bebb & Gould, the building may be the most recognized structure in the Beacon Hill neighborhood. Like many south Seattle communities, Beacon Hill tends to be overlooked by prospective home-owners or tenants, who generally prefer to set up house in a neighborhood north of Downtown. Nevertheless, it is a flour-ishing neighborhood with a strong community spirit and comfortable, affordable homes. In addition, the Beacon Hill community is diverse, with many Asian-American, African-American and white residents.
North of S Spokane St., quiet streets are lined with 1940s tract houses and modest bungalows on small but well-kept lots. This area typ-

ically attracts middle-income families and young or retired couples. On the busier streets, brick Federal style apartment buildings offer studios and one-bedrooms for rents slightly below the city average. Some houses on the hill have pleasant views of Downtown, the Cascades, or the Olympic Mountains.

South of S Spokane St., small bungalows and contemporary split-levels sell for slightly less than comparable homes at the north end of the hill. This area has a mixed population of African-Americans and Asian- and Pacific-Americans and a slightly lower median income. Small family businesses such as Asian delis and groceries dot the neighborhood, and the Jefferson Public Golf Course is located here. Further south, the **South Beacon Hill** and **Holly Park** areas also offer modest yet affordable bungalows and simple tract houses.

The **Mount Baker** neighborhood, which clings to the east slope of Beacon Hill, is the most affluent section of Beacon Hill. Most homes here have spectacular views of the south end of Lake Washington and the Cascades; some may have views of the majestic Mount Rainier to the southeast. Many wealthy professionals live in this area, and it is certainly one of the most racially diverse of Seattle's affluent neighborhoods.

Violent crime may be a concern in some parts of the Beacon Hill area. While most Beacon Hill residents are hard-working blue-collar individuals and families, gang-related activities occasionally spill into the Beacon Hill neighborhoods from nearby Rainier Valley, particularly in the southwest sections. Local crime prevention groups have been increasingly successful in holding the community together, but newcomers may find it advisable to become familiar with the district before choosing a home here.

Area Code: 206

Zip Codes: 98118, 98144

Post Offices:
Columbia Station, 3727 S Alaska St., 800-275-8777

International Station, 4141 6th Ave. S, 800-275-8777

Library: Beacon Hill Library, 2519 15th Ave. S, 206-684-4711

Police: South Precinct, 3001 S Myrtle St., 206-386-1850

Emergency Hospital: Harborview Medical Center, 325 9th Ave., 206-731-3074

Public Transportation:
14: Downtown/Pioneer Square/International District/Central
District/Mount Baker
36: Downtown/Beacon Hill/Rainier Beach
38: Beacon Hill/Rainier Valley
39: Downtown/SoDo/Beacon Hill/Seward Park/Rainier Beach
50: Columbia City/Beacon Hill/SoDo/West Seattle
60: Capitol Hill/First Hill/Beacon Hill/Georgetown

Neighborhood Organizations:
Greater Duwamish Neighborhood Service Center, 3801 Beacon
Ave. S, 206-233-2044

Jefferson Community Center, 3801 Beacon Ave. S, 206-684-7481

RAINIER VALLEY

Columbia City
Rainier Beach
Dunlap

Boundaries: North: S. Genesee St.; **West:** Martin Luther King Way S.;
South: S. Juniper St., S. 116th St.; **East:** 48th Ave. S., Lake Washington

Originally the Rainier Valley neighborhood, located just south of the CD,
was basically an extension of the Central District, until I-90 created a bar-
rier between the two neighborhoods. Today, Rainier Valley is an ethnical-
ly diverse neighborhood with a large minority and immigrant population.
Unfortunately, it has a high percentage of residents living in poverty and
more problems with crime than many other areas of the city. Perhaps
because of its physical isolation from the rest of Seattle, Rainier Valley has
not received the attention that might have prevented or lessened many
of its current socioeconomic problems.

The retail district of Rainier Valley is located along Rainier Ave. S, the
main thoroughfare of the neighborhood, and is home to small locally
owned shops, delis, bakeries, and take-out restaurants. The renowned
Borracchini's Bakery has been in the neighborhood for over 70 years,
and attracts people from all over Seattle for its delicious decorated-
while-you-wait sheet cakes. It's one of the few reminders of Rainier
Valley's Italian heritage when, almost a century ago, the area was settled
by Italian immigrants and was referred to as "Garlic Gulch." Once the

exclusive province of ethnic shops and eateries, the area has gained national chain retailers as well, permitting residents to shop for nearly everything in the neighborhood. For the alternative-minded, the neighborhood offers a Puget Sound Consumers Co-op (bordering the Seward Park neighborhood). Overall, Rainier Valley seems to be benefiting from both the hard work of committed community groups and the increased prosperity of the greater Seattle area.

Columbia City, a neighborhood situated in the heart of Rainier Valley, is also experiencing a revival because of its supportive and loyal residents. The quaint commercial district of Columbia City along 47th Ave. S contains many of the original historic buildings of the neighborhood. Homes in Columbia City range from turn-of-the-century Victorians to modest bungalows. While homes here are slightly more expensive than those in the rest of Rainier Valley, the prices are still well below the city average.

Rainier Beach and **Dunlap**, located on the Lake Washington waterfront, offer lovely old homes, ranging from modest 1920s bungalows to stately turn-of-the-century mansions, most with spectacular views of Lake Washington and the Cascades. Crime rates in this part of the Rainier Valley are at or below the Seattle average, and recently the city has taken steps toward creating more affordable and pleasant low-income housing units. Nevertheless, real estate prices in this neighborhood remain slightly lower than those for comparable view homes in other parts of the city.

Newcomers to Seattle should use caution when visiting Rainier Valley and considering potential housing opportunities here. Gang-related activities and violent crimes may be more common here than elsewhere in the city. Although the vast majority of residents are respectable hard-working folks, and there are many wonderful streets in Rainier Valley, pockets of criminal activity may be only a block or two away. However, those familiar with dynamic urban neighborhoods will find affordable homes in this area; apartments also rent for less than the city average.

Area Code: 206

Zip Codes: 98118, 98178

Post Office: Columbia Station, 3727 S Alaska St., 800-275-8777

Libraries:
Columbia Library, 4721 Rainier Ave. S, 206-386-1908

Holly Park Library, 6805 32nd Ave. S, 206-386-1905

Rainier Beach Library, 9125 Rainier Ave. S, 206-386-1906

Police: South Precinct, 3001 S Myrtle St., 206-386-1850

Emergency Hospital: Harborview Medical Center, 325 9th Ave., 206-731-3074

Public Transportation:
7: University District/Capitol Hill/Downtown/International District/Rainier Valley/Columbia City/Rainier Beach
8: Rainier Valley/Capitol Hill/Lower Queen Anne
9: University District/Capitol Hill/First Hill/Rainier Valley/Columbia City/Rainier Beach
36: Downtown/Beacon Hill/Rainier Beach
39: Downtown/SoDo/Beacon Hill/Seward Park/Rainier Beach
42: Downtown/Rainier Beach
48: Ballard/Greenwood/Ravenna/University District/Montlake/Central District/Columbia City/Rainier Beach

Neighborhood Organizations:
Central Area Motivation Program, 77919 Rainier Ave. S, 206-722-2417

Southeast Neighborhood Service Center, 4859 Rainier Ave. S, 206-386-1931

Rainier Community Center, 4600 38th Ave. S, 206-386-1919

Rainier Beach Community Center, 8825 Rainier Ave. S, 206-386-1925

South Park Community Center, 8319 8th Ave. S, 206-684-7451

VanAsselt Community Center 2820 S Myrtle St., 206-386-1921

SEWARD PARK

Boundaries: North: S. Genesee St.; **West:** 48th Ave. S.; **South:** S. Holly St.; **East:** Lake Washington

The Seward Park neighborhood is located just south of Mount Baker, on Lake Washington. The park from which this community takes its name is a 277-acre peninsula filled with lush vegetation, including cherry trees, lofty Douglas firs, and silvery Madrona trees. Seward Park is always worth a visit; in addition to nature trails and the lake, it is one of the best places in the city to savor breathtaking views of Mount Rainier. During the summer, the park hosts jazz concerts, the Seafair celebration, and the annual

Danskin triathlon. The Seward Park Art Studio, located in the original 1927 bathhouse, offers pottery classes for all levels of students and serves as a workshop for several professional artists.

Residents of Seward Park are affluent professionals, including local politicians and judges, as well as senior citizens who reside in the Kline Galland nursing home. While nearly half of Seward Park residents are Asian-American or African-American, the neighborhood is best known for its strong Jewish community. Most of Seattle's Orthodox Jews live in or near Seward Park, attending one of the many synagogues located here. Bikur Cholim-Machzikay, the oldest synagogue in Washington, is located in the neighborhood.

Homes in Seward Park range from 1950s brick ranch houses to stately modern mansions. Most have views of Lake Washington and Mount Rainier; many have waterfront access. While homes here are expensive due to the panoramic views, the neighborhood's proximity to Rainier Valley has kept real estate prices slightly lower than those for comparable homes elsewhere.

Area Code: 206

Zip Codes: 98178

Post Office: Columbia Station, 3727 S Alaska St., 800-275-8777

Library: Rainier Beach Library, 9125 Rainier Ave. S, 206-386-1906

Police: South Precinct, 3001 S Myrtle St., 206-386-1850

Emergency Hospital: Harborview Medical Center, 325 9th Ave., 206-731-3074

Public Transportation:
39: Downtown/SoDo/Beacon Hill/Seward Park/Rainier Beach

Neighborhood Organizations:
Southeast Neighborhood Service Center, 4859 Rainier Ave. S, 206-386-1931

Rainier Beach Community Center, 8825 Rainier Ave. S, 206-386-1925

DUWAMISH DISTRICT

South Park
Georgetown
SoDo

Boundaries: North: S. Royal Brougham Way, S. Dearborn St.; **West:** Duwamish Waterway, Hwy. 509; **South:** S. Barton St.; **East:** I-5

The Duwamish District is a primarily industrial area that starts just south of the Kingdome and follows the Duwamish River south to the city limits. Originally the land on either side of the river was fertile farmland, but eventually the farms were displaced by industries which used the river for shipping and, unfortunately, dumping. Today, most of the district remains strictly industrial, although there are pockets of residential and retail activity in the South Park and Georgetown areas. Boeing Field is located in the vicinity, but most employees commute to the area rather than live here. People from other parts of the city visit the Gai's Bakery outlet store and the nearby Museum of Flight at Boeing Field, or use the through streets in this neighborhood as a shortcut to the SeaTac Airport, Burien, and West Seattle.

South Park is a small community at the south end of this district, near the Duwamish River. This is a neighborhood of extremely modest bungalows, many of which are rented, and a tiny core of commercial businesses and restaurants near 14th Ave. S. The **Georgetown** neighborhood, in the area around S Michigan St., is an eclectic assortment of simple frame houses, breakfast cafes, warehouses, and other industrial buildings. Residents of Georgetown tend to be blue-collar workers and a handful of artists who appreciate the lower housing prices. The **SoDo** (South of the Dome) area borders Downtown at Royal Brougham St., south of the Kingdome. SoDo is an industrial neighborhood, filled with warehouses and small manufacturing plants. The historic Sears building, now headquarters to Starbucks Coffee, is located here.

Area Code: 206

Zip Codes: 98108, 98168, 98106

Post Office: Georgetown Station, 620 S Orcas St., 800-275-8777

Library: Delridge Library, 4555 Delridge Way SW , 206-937-7680

Police: West Precinct, 610 3rd Ave., 206-684-8917

Emergency Hospital: Harborview Medical Center, 325 9th Ave., 206-731-3074

Public Transportation:
21: Downtown/SoDo/West Seattle
39: Downtown/SoDo/Beacon Hill/Seward Park/Rainier Beach
40:         Wedgwood/Green   Lake/University
    District/Georgetown/Duwamish
50: Columbia City/Beacon Hill/SoDo/West Seattle
60: Capitol Hill/First Hill/Beacon Hill/Georgetown

Neighborhood Organizations:
Greater Duwamish Neighborhood Service Center, 3801 Beacon Ave. S, 206-233-2044

Southwest Neighborhood Service Center, 9407 16th Ave. SW, 206-684-7416

WEST SEATTLE

Admiral
Alki
Delridge
Fauntleroy

Boundaries: North: Puget Sound, Elliott Bay; **West:** Puget Sound; **South:** Seola Beach Dr. S.W., S.W. Roxbury St.; **East:** Duwamish Waterway, Hwy. 509

In 1851, the schooner Exact landed on Alki Beach in what is now West Seattle, bringing the Denny party to the Puget Sound. Charles Terry, one of the original party, remained behind while the rest of the group moved on to what is now the Seattle waterfront. By 1897, the peninsula had a large enough population to merit a ferry between Downtown and West Seattle. Today, West Seattle is a comfortable residential hill connected to the rest of the city by the West Seattle Freeway, which bridges the Duwamish Waterway and the man-made Harbor Island.

Atop the hill, the West Seattle Junction at SW Alaska St. and California Ave. SW is a commercial center for West Seattle. Clothing boutiques, bookstores, small diners, and drug stores fill the ground floor retail space around "the Junction." Young couples and single residents rent the quaint apartments above the storefronts. East of the Junction,

auto dealerships and ethnic take-out restaurants cluster around the inter-
section of SW Alaska St. and Fauntleroy Way SW. The intersection of SW
Admiral Way and California Ave. SW is the second retail core on the hill.
Here, the historic Admiral Theater presides over the intersection which is
lined with small shops, espresso joints, and funky restaurants. The
Admiral district, which surrounds this intersection, is one of the more
affluent areas in West Seattle. Homes at the top of the hill, mainly
Craftsman bungalows and Northwest Moderns, have views of
Downtown to the northeast or of the Olympics to the west. Residents of
the Admiral area tend to be middle- to upper-income professionals and
their families.

Alki is a long, narrow beach neighborhood which stretches along
the north and west sides of the peninsula and offers the atmosphere of
an ocean resort town. In the summer, the beach is crowded with sunbathers, in-line skaters, bicyclists, and volleyball players. In the spring
and fall, residents meet for coffee and dessert at the Alki Bakery, or stop
for dinner at Spuds Fish & Chips or Pegasus Pizza. Although development has begun to change the face of this area, many 1960s condominiums and beach cottages are still located just a short walk or bicycle
ride from the beach. Residents are generally middle-income service professionals, many of whom are longtime West Seattle residents. Alki has
extraordinary views of downtown Seattle or the Olympic peninsula; you
can catch the most spectacular view of the Olympics from here during
early spring or late fall, when the sun is bright and the snow has not yet
melted in the mountains. The Alki beachhead is a popular destination for
couples watching the sunset over the Olympic Mountains. Also, many
intrepid Seattle residents brave inclement weather to watch the waves
crash against the shore during the winter months.

The **Fauntleroy** neighborhood lies along the southwest slope of the
hill of West Seattle, facing the Puget Sound. Though Fauntleroy is best-
known throughout the rest of Seattle for its ferry dock, with services to
Vashon Island and the Olympic Peninsula, it is also a comfortable, secluded neighborhood. Beautiful brick Tudors, classic Northwest Modern
homes, and modest bungalows line winding streets and quiet cul-de-
sacs. Homes here have unparalleled views of the Puget Sound, Vashon
Island, and the Olympics. Lincoln Park, located here, has barbecues for
summer fun and a heated salt water pool (Olympic size) right on the
edge of the sound for spectacular summer swimming. As Fauntleroy's
popularity grows, low- and middle-income families living in modest
homes are being supplanted by wealthy retirees and professionals.

In the southeast quarter of West Seattle, **Delridge** is a neighborhood of simple 1950s ramblers, contemporary split-levels, and tract houses owned or rented by people in the low- to middle-income range. On its eastern edge near W Marginal Way, Delridge is primarily industrial. To the west, residential areas offer modest homes and modern apartment complexes. The median income in this neighborhood is lower than that in most of West Seattle; rents and real estate prices tend to be much lower as well. Community groups in Delridge are working to improve the quality of life here. Home and car security is an issue in some areas of Delridge, and newcomers are advised to explore this neighborhood carefully when considering housing opportunities here.

For nature lovers, West Seattle's Schmitz Park, with its tremendous old growth Douglas Fir, offers a glimpse of what the area looked like before the arrival of the white man.

Though West Seattle is only a 20 minute drive from Downtown, the neighborhood will not be convenient for those people working on the Eastside. The commute would cover the West Seattle Freeway, I-5, and I-90, all of which have heavy traffic during rush hour. However, for people working Downtown who would like to live in a neighborhood that feels utterly removed from the city, West Seattle is a great place to live.

Area Code: 206

Zip Codes: 98106, 98116, 98126, 98136

Post Office: West Seattle Station, 4412 California Ave. SW, 800-275-8777

Libraries:

Delridge Library, 4555 Delridge Way SW , 206-937-7680

High Point Library, 6338 32nd Ave. SW, 206-684-7454

Southwest Library, 9010 35th Ave. SW, 206-684-7455

West Seattle Library, 2306 42nd Ave. SW, 206-684-7444

Police: South Precinct, 3001 S Myrtle St., 206-386-1850

Emergency Hospital: Harborview Medical Center, 325 9th Ave., 206-731-3074

Public Transportation:
21: Downtown/SoDo/West Seattle

22: Downtown/West Seattle
37: Downtown/Harbor Island/Alki/West Seattle Junction/Admiral District
50: Columbia City/Beacon Hill/SoDo/West Seattle
55: Downtown/West Seattle Junction/Admiral District
56: Downtown/Admiral/Alki/West Seattle Junction

Neighborhood Organizations:
West Seattle Neighborhood Service Center, 4750 California Ave. SW, 206-684-7495

Alki Community Center, 5817 SW Stevens St., 206-684-7430

Delridge Community Center, 4501 Delridge Way SW, 206-684-7423

Hiawatha Community Center, 2700 California Ave. SW, 206-684-7441

High Point Community Center, 6920 34th Ave. SW, 206-684-7422

Southwest Community Center, 2801 SW Thistle St., 206-684-7438

SURROUNDING COMMUNITIES

Today Seattle is composed of much more than simply the metropolitan area. Beyond the city limits, many lovely and thriving communities benefit from and contribute to Seattle's economy. A good number of Seattle residents commute to work on the Eastside, to communities such as Bellevue, Kirkland, or Redmond (where Microsoft is based). Both Seattle and Eastside residents commute to jobs in Seattle, Tacoma, or Everett. Many catch a ferry each day heading to or from Vashon Island near West Seattle, Bainbridge Island west of Downtown or from towns and cities on the Olympic Peninsula. Rising real estate and rental prices in the city and immediate suburbs have persuaded many people to make their homes in traditionally rural communities, beyond the suburbs, including Duvall, Carnation, and Bothell. At the same time, exclusive neighborhoods in some of the Eastside suburbs, particularly those with views of Lake Washington or Lake Sammamish, attract affluent Seattle residents looking for a more suburban lifestyle.

The following numbers and web pages are provided as resources for information on the surrounding communities. Generally the phone numbers provided are for city offices or chambers of commerce in the community.

EASTERN COMMUNITIES
(KNOWN COLLECTIVELY AS "THE EASTSIDE")

Bellevue is a small city best known to most Seattle residents as home to Bellevue Square, an upscale mall. The area has a reputation of being home to wealthy residents, but you'll find people of various incomes living in Bellevue. Suburban housing developments filled with modest split-level and contemporary homes dot the area. Homes close to Lake Washington to the west or Lake Sammamish to the east, are more elegant and expensive. Most houses on the Eastside are of contemporary styles, from traditional brick ranch houses to angular art deco homes. **Issaquah** and **Newport Hills**, two communities south of Bellevue, offer large contemporary homes in quiet developments.

> **Bellevue**, 425-452-7810, www.ci.bellevue.wa.us/bellevue/
>
> **Issaquah**, 425-837-3000, www.ci.issaquah.wa.us/
>
> **Newport Hills**, 425-746-5354, www.scn.org/neighbors/nwprthls /organiza.htm

Kirkland is a small town on the shore of Lake Washington, just north of Hwy. 520. The downtown area is a quaint shopping district with a colorful marina, cozy cafes, trendy boutiques, and unique gift shops. Homes near the lake are a mix of contemporary condominiums, townhouses, and apartments. Real estate prices here are expensive, as most homes have spectacular views of the lake. East of Kirkland, more modest and affordable homes without views are available. **Juanita**, just north of Kirkland, has an assortment of modern condominiums and contemporary ramblers.

> **Kirkland**, 425-828-1127, www.ci.kirkland.wa.us/

Once a sleepy farming community, **Redmond** is now best known as the home of Microsoft. The downtown area was still a tiny and unremarkable shopping district until recently, when the new Redmond Town Center mall was constructed. Residents of Redmond tend to be middle-income families and young Microsoft or Nintendo employees. There are many condominium complexes and apartments near Marymoor Park in Redmond. Modest developments of contemporary homes dot the hills around the town.

Redmond, 425-556-2150, www.ci.redmond.wa.us/

Woodinville is a close neighbor of Redmond, attracting many Microsoft employees and their families. Most homes in Woodinville are large contemporary structures in suburban developments or modest farmhouses on acreage. The city is also home to two wineries, Chateau St. Michelle and Columbia, and the Redhook Brewery's new restaurant and bottling facility.

Woodinville, 425-489-2700

Mercer Island, in the south end of Lake Washington, is a pleasant community with beautiful view homes. Residents are mostly affluent professionals and entrepreneurs living in sprawling modern mansions on large landscaped estates. Most homes on the island have views of Lake Washington or Mount Rainier; many also have waterfront access. I-90 provides the only bridge access to and from Mercer Island, but special designations for island residents in the carpool lanes provide a shortcut around the worst traffic.

Mercer Island, 206-236-5300, www.halcyon.com/mmatt/mihome.htm

Monroe, Duvall, and **Carnation** are farming communities nestled in the valley east of Redmond and Bothell. While Monroe is still a little too far from the urban core for most commuters, Duvall and Carnation attract professionals and families looking for a country home and a half-hour commute to Redmond or Bellevue. Homes here are hidden on wooded hills or have views of the Snoqualmie River, lush farmland, and the Cascades.

Monroe, 360-794-7400
Duvall, 425-788-1185
Carnation, 425-333-4192

WESTERN COMMUNITIES

Vashon Island is a small triangular island west of the West Seattle penin-sula. With winding roads and towering evergreens, Vashon is a peaceful haven for artists, artisans, and entrepreneurs. Ferry service makes commuting to and from Seattle or Tacoma simple.

Vashon Island, 206-463-9602, www.vashonisland.com/

Bainbridge Island becomes more popular every year, as Seattle residents search out alternatives to the bustle of the city. A 30 minute ferry ride from the Seattle waterfront, Bainbridge Island is a community of lawyers, doctors and other successful ex-Seattle denizens. Many homes on the island have stunning views of the Puget Sound or the distant Seattle skyline.

Bainbridge Island, 206-842-7633, www.ci.bainbridge-isl.wa.us/

Though a little too distant for an easy commute to Seattle, **Whidbey Island** is home to many affluent retirees, writers, and artists. Several towns are located on the island, each with a few restaurants and inns that fill quickly during the summer tourist season. Many homes on Whidbey look out over Puget Sound and either the Cascade or Olympic Mountains.

Whidbey Island, 360-678-5434, www.whidbey.net/islandco/

NORTHERN COMMUNITIES

Bothell, **Kenmore**, **Mountlake Terrace** and **Lake Forest Park** are communities near the north end of Lake Washington which are also rising in popularity as real estate prices escalate around the Puget Sound. Kenmore located near Seattle's Lake City neighborhood, and has spacious homes overlooking the lake and more modest homes on partially forested hills. Mountlake Terrace and Lake Forest Park have a mix of contemporary single-family homes on large lots. Bothell is slowly becoming a more established suburb, particularly with the recent construction of large office buildings by Seattle and Eastside companies.

Bothell, 425-489-3392, www.bothell.com/

Kenmore, 206/728-3924, www.kenmore.mpl.net/

Mountlake Terrace, 425-776-1161

Lake Forest Park, 206-364-7711

Edmonds, overlooking the Puget Sound just north of Seattle, is a peaceful village with a quaint shopping district. The Edmonds-Kingston ferry terminal, once the central attraction of the city, is now overshadowed by the popular downtown waterfront amenities, including restaurants, chic clothing boutiques, and funky gift shops. Affordable split-level homes on quiet streets abound, while attractive sprawling homes in new developments are being built on the hills overlooking the city and Puget Sound. **Richmond Beach**, at the south end of Edmonds, is a neighborhood of view homes on quiet winding streets attracting affluent professionals and retirees. **Shoreline**, inland from Edmonds and Richmond Beach, offers affordable contemporary homes and is a favorite with young families.

Edmonds, 425-775-2525

Shoreline, 206-546-1700

Everett is a large city about an hour north of Seattle which was originally established to support the infamous Monte Cristo gold mines. Although the mines never produced the amount of gold expected, the city continues to thrive as an industrial center. Boeing is one of the primary employers in Everett, although many other companies, including a saw mill, are also located here. As with Seattle, many distinct neighborhoods exist in Everett, each worth exploring if you are considering making your home here.

Everett, 425-257-8700, www.halcyon.com/everett/

If you can get beyond the sprawling Alderwood Mall and surrounding strip malls, you may find a gem of a home in the residential areas of **Lynnwood**. Tranquil suburban streets with modest affordable homes make Lynnwood the choice of many middle-income families and first-time home buyers.

Lynnwood, 425-775-1971

SOUTHERN COMMUNITIES

At the south end of Lake Washington is the city of **Renton**, which many consider the odd-ball of the Eastside communities. Traditionally home to middle-income Boeing employees and low-income blue-collar workers,

Renton is slowly attracting a crowd of young professionals and first-time home buyers. For the price of a small Seattle home on a tiny lot, prospective homeowners can buy a large, new home in Renton.

Renton, 425-235-2553, www.ci.renton.wa.us/

Located just south of West Seattle, the towns of **Burien** and **White Center** offer modest homes. While both offer pleasant and affordable housing options, home and personal security may be a concern in some areas of White Center.

Burien, 206-241-4647, www.ci.burien.wa.us/

White Center, 206-763-4196

Federal Way, **Kent**, **Auburn**, and **SeaTac** (named for the Seattle Tacoma International Airport) are modest middle-class suburbs with pleasant and inexpensive (compared to Seattle) contemporary homes. Airline and Boeing employees live in these areas, but other local businesses employ many residents as well. Recently, Kent and Auburn have attracted warehouse stores and outlet malls, improving the overall economy of the area.

Federal Way, 253-661-4000

Kent, 425-859-3370

As the second largest city in Western Washington, **Tacoma** doesn't quite count as a suburb, although some residents do commute to Seattle for work. An industrial and port city, Tacoma remains a less expensive alternative to Seattle. There are many distinct neighborhoods in Tacoma, each of which should be considered when contemplating making a home there. A few years back, parts of Tacoma were reputed to be gang-infested, but efforts by the city and local community action groups have done much to contain and improve the situation. Today, home and personal security concerns for Tacoma residents are comparable to those in Seattle.

Tacoma, 206-591-5171, www.ci.tacoma.wa.us/

SEATTLE ADDRESS LOCATOR

While most Seattle streets stick to a standard grid pattern, running east-west or north-south, others meander aimlessly through several neighborhoods. The information included here will give you a good starting point for finding your way around the city, but a map or street atlas is highly recommended. Likewise, the guidelines below apply only to streets within Seattle proper or immediately north and south of the city limits. Other suburbs and communities employ different methods for assigning addresses.

The most important piece of directional information is this: the center of the Seattle grid is 1st and Yesler. Numbers and directions (either before or after the "St." or "Ave.") are based on that central intersection. North/south streets in the Downtown area are parallel to Elliott Bay, running northwest to southeast, as far north as Denny Way and as far south as Yesler Way. Outside of this area, most Seattle streets run exactly north-south or east-west. Street and house numbers increase as you move away from Downtown, with the highest numbers at the north and south end of the city limits. These north-south streets are "avenues" with the directional location at the end of the street name; for instance, 24th Ave. NW or 32nd Ave. S. Streets which run east-west are "streets" with the location at the beginning of the street name; for instance, NE 49th St. or SW Spokane St.

Most north-south running streets in the city are numbered, except for a few major streets and those between the two 1st Avenues north of Downtown. South of the Lake Washington Ship Canal (a man-made canal which bisects the city north of Downtown, and connects Lake Washington and Lake Union to the Puget Sound), most east-west running streets have names, such as Union St., E Aloha St., S Lander St., etc. North of the ship canal, east-west running streets are numbered.

There are actually two 1st Avenues north of Downtown. If you look at a map, you'll see why. At the south end of Downtown, 1st Ave. becomes 1st Ave. S, and streets increase in number to either side of it. At the north end of Downtown, the end of 1st Ave. (which has been running northwest-southeast) is several blocks west of where the south-end version of the street is. So the city planners simply added an additional 1st Ave. north of the Lake Washington Ship Canal that lines up on a map with 1st Ave. S. Street and house numbers still increase as you move east or west of these streets. Those houses between the two 1st Avenues have house numbers in the thousands instead of the hundreds to differentiate them from their nearby neighbors.

The location tags attached to the street names indicate where in the city that portion of a street is located; for instance, 15th Ave *NE* or *SW* Othello St. This fact can help you enormously when trying to find an address in the city. Downtown, streets have no location tags at all (think of it as the central point, and everything else as being north, south, east, or west of Downtown). North of Denny Way as far as the Lake Washington Ship Canal, streets are labeled as W (*west* of 1st Ave. N in Magnolia and parts of Queen Anne), N (those directly *north* of Downtown on Queen Anne and around Lake Union, between 1st Ave. N and Eastlake Ave. E) or E (those *east* of Lake Union, in Eastlake and Montlake). North of the Lake Washington Ship Canal, streets are labeled as NW (*north* of the ship canal and *west* of 1st Ave. NW, in Ballard and Broadview), N (directly *north* of Downtown between 1st Ave. NW and 1st Ave. NE, in Phinney Ridge, Green Lake, Wallingford, and Northgate), or NE (*north* of the ship canal and *east* of 1st Ave. NE, in Lake City, the University District, and Sand Point). South of Yesler Way, all streets are labeled as either S (everything *south* of Downtown — and east of 1st Ave. S — in Rainier Valley, Mount Baker, and Beacon Hill) or SW (streets *southwest* of Downtown — and west of 1st Ave. S — in West Seattle). Between the Lake Washington Ship Canal and Yesler Way and east of the edge of Lake Union, all east-west running streets are labeled as E (those *east* of Downtown, in Madrona, Leschi, the Central District, Capitol Hill, and Madison Park), but here north-south streets have no location tags.

Several streets in Seattle don't follow all of the above mentioned rules. Coincidentally, those streets tend to be the city's main thorough-fares, some of which are listed here:

Martin Luther King Jr. Way: "MLK" begins at Madison St. at the north end of the Central District, and runs south through the CD, Madrona, Leschi, Beacon Hill, Mount Baker, and Rainier Valley.

Boren Ave./Rainier Ave. S: Boren Ave. is a main street which runs northwest-southeast over First Hill. South of Jackson St., Boren Ave. becomes Rainier Ave. S, and continues southeast through the south end of the Central District and into the Rainier Valley.

Madison St.: one of the city's most convenient streets, Madison St. runs east from Downtown, through First Hill, Capitol Hill, and along the north end of the Central District, to Madison Park on Lake Washington.

Useful highways within Seattle are listed below, be careful of these "thoroughfares" at rush hour:

I-5: Interstate 5 runs north-south through the city and is the most commonly used thoroughfare in Seattle.

I-90: Interstate 90 begins at the Kingdome in Downtown Seattle and runs east out of town. The I-90 bridge is the only roadway to Mercer Island, and has more lanes in either direction than the Hwy. 520 bridge to the north.

Hwy. 520: a state highway connecting I-5 (at the north end of Capitol Hill) with the Eastside communities of Bellevue, Kirkland, and Redmond, the Hwy. 520 bridge is always packed with commuters during rush hour.

Hwy. 99: running parallel to but west of I-5 through Seattle, Hwy. 99 begins as Aurora Ave. in the north end, where it is a major thoroughfare lined with strip malls, inexpensive hotels, and other businesses. Crossing the Lake Washington Ship Canal into the city, Hwy. 99 runs through the Battery Street Tunnel and becomes the Alaskan Way Viaduct, a large stacked highway along the Waterfront. South of the Waterfront, Hwy. 99 becomes E Marginal Way S and eventually Pacific Hwy.

Hwy. 522: commonly known as Lake City Way NE, Hwy 522 begins at NE 75th St., runs northeast through the Lake City neighborhood to Lake Washington., and eventually turns into Bothell Way NE at the north end of the lake.

West Seattle Freeway: the West Seattle Freeway connects both I-5 (at Beacon Hill) and Hwy. 99 with the West Seattle peninsula.

F inding a place to live in Seattle, once an easy task, has become much more difficult as the area's population has increased relentlessly. Situated as it is between two bodies of water, with only narrow bridges and ferries for access to the popular Eastside, Seattle faces the challenge of housing a rapidly growing population around substantial geographical constraints. Couple these factors with local anti-development sentiment and a booming economy and it's easy to understand the sky-rocketing prices of area real estate. Leveling off in the early 1990s, housing prices began to rise again in the mid 1990s, accounting for Seattle's recent listing by the National Association of Realtors and the Washington Center for Real Estate Research as being among the country's-most-expensive places to buy residential real estate. Once a city made up of primarily single-family homes, the creation of duplexes and tri-plexes out of older homes is now common. Condominiums and apartment buildings account for a large portion of current building projects, as do townhouses and multi-family houses. Rental prices have also risen sharply in recent years, as demand has consistently outstripped supply in this city of mostly renting newcomers. Those interested in Seattle's immediate suburbs should expect even higher prices, especially in the Bellevue and Redmond areas.

APARTMENT HUNTING

The savvy newcomer should consider using several different methods fo find an apartment in Seattle. Searching the local classifieds is still the best way to start an apartment search, although you'll need to start calling about listings early on Saturday morning when the Sunday newspaper (the "bulldog" edition) first comes out. Another good practice is to drive through the neighborhoods you're interested in, looking for posted rental notices. Many local landlords don't run advertisements in the paper; instead they simply post a sign early in the month and wait for

prospective tenants to drive by. If you're interested in living in a neighborhood near a local university or college, late spring is the best time to
look for vacancies. These neighborhoods include Fremont, Wallingford,
or North Queen Anne, which are near Seattle Pacific University; the
University District, Green Lake, and Ravenna, which are near the
University of Washington; or Capitol Hill and the CD, which border the
Seattle University campus.

If you have the time and patience to hunt for an apartment on your
own, use the **Neighborhood** chapter of this guide to give you an idea of
the types of housing in each area. Each neighborhood profile includes a
list of neighborhood organizations, which are a good resource for finding
out about available apartments, area safety and neighborhood events.

Community newspapers are another excellent avenue for finding
apartment listings; many of them run local classifieds that will give you
first crack at vacancies that may not appear in the larger city-wide papers.

CLASSIFIED ADVERTISEMENTS

- *Seattle Post-Intelligencer/The Seattle Times* — get the joint Sunday
  edition, it has the most comprehensive rental and real estate listings. Rentals are listed under "Apartments and Houses" in the classi-
  fied advertisements. Houses for sale are listed under "Homes" in the
  "Home/Real Estate" section.
- *Seattle Weekly* — a free weekly newspaper with some rental advertisements, the *Weekly* is distributed on Thursdays and is available in
  cafés, bars, and convenience stores.
- *The Stranger* — a free weekly newspaper that can be found in
  restaurants and bars throughout Seattle, *The Stranger* is also distributed on Thursdays, and contains rental and real estate classifieds.
- **Neighborhood newspapers** — usually available free of charge at
  neighborhood businesses and cafes, these newspapers often contain rental opportunities that aren't advertised elsewhere.

OTHER PLACES TO LOOK

In addition to reading through local newspapers, check out bulletin
boards on college campuses or in laundromats and convenience stores
in the neighborhoods that interest you. All of the newspapers listed
above have "Roommate Wanted" or "Room Available" sections, worth

a look if you're on a limited budget. Shared houses are common in some areas of Seattle, particularly in the University District and the southeast side of Capitol Hill. These can be a good option if you plan to move again in several months, as many do not require a long-term lease. Here are some other suggestions:

- **Free Rental Guides** — several companies publish free rental guides. Most list newer apartment complexes or apartments that are maintained by large property management companies. You can pick up a stack of rental guides at most local grocery or convenience stores.
- **Online** — the *Seattle P-I* and *The Seattle Times* both have web sites that link to the Sunday classifieds. Two of the best known rental guides also have web sites that list available rentals:
- *Seattle Post-Intelligencer/The Seattle Times* — www.seatimes.com will link you to both papers' web sites and the classifieds.
- *For Rent Magazine* — www.aptsforrent.com
- **Greater Puget Sound Apartment Guide** — www.aptguides.com

APARTMENT SEARCH FIRMS

One way to find an apartment, particularly if your time is limited, is to use an apartment search firm. These can be especially helpful if you want to set up your rental before arriving in town; most agents will fax or mail you information and do a lot of the legwork for you. When speaking to an apartment search firm agent, find out whether the fees will be paid by you or the property owner, and be very specific about your needs and budget. The following are a few of the search firms in Seattle:

Apartment Finders, 800-473-3733
Apartment Hunters, 206-764-9244
Apartment Locators, 206-545-0125

APARTMENT SHARING SERVICES

There are two companies in Seattle that help find roommates for those who would like to share an apartment.

- **Seattle Roommate Referral**, 905 E Pike St., 206-322-2233
- **Space Finders Inc.**, 300 Vine St. Suite 16-B, 206-728-8500

CHECKING IT OUT

You're on your way to the day's first rental appointment, you haven't had breakfast, the old college friends you're staying with are getting restless, your back is aching from a bad night's sleep on their sofa-bed, and twenty other people are waiting outside the prospective apartment when you drive up — you panic, take a quick glance around, like what you see, and grab an application. Three months later you're wondering how you landed in such a dump.

To avoid this scenario, tour each apartment with a clear idea of what you want. Beyond personal likes and dislikes, there are some specific things to check for as you look:

- Is the apartment on the first floor? If so, does it have burglar bars? First floor apartments are easy targets for burglary.
- Are the appliances clean and in good working order? Test all of the stove's burners. Does the kitchen sink have one or two basins? Is there sufficient counter space? Is the freezer compartment of the refrigerator a frost-free variety?
- Check the windows to make sure they open, close and lock. Do the windows, especially the bedroom windows, open onto a busy street or alley? Alleys are especially notorious for late night car horns and loud early morning trash removal.
- Are there enough closets? Are the closets big enough to accommodate your belongings?
- Is there private storage space in a secure area?
- Is there adequate water pressure for the shower, the sink and the toilet? Turn them on and check.
- Flush all toilets and check for leaks or unusual noises.
- Check the number of electrical outlets. In older buildings it is common to have one or two outlets per room. Are there enough outlets for all your plug-in appliances?
- Are there laundry facilities in the building? Is there a laundromat within walking distance?
- How close is the building to public transportation and grocery stores?
- If you are looking at a basement apartment, check to see if there are any water stains along the walls. They're a sure sign of flooding.
- Does it smell funny? They may have just sprayed the apartment for bugs. You should think twice before taking it. If it's a multi-unit building there may be bugs in the other apartments just waiting to

move back in with you.
- Is there a smoke and/or carbon monoxide detector in the apartment?

LEASES, SECURITY DEPOSITS AND TENANT'S RIGHTS

Most landlords in Seattle require your first month's rent, a security or "damage" deposit, and a signed lease agreement prior to the tenant moving in. Many also require the last month's rent to be paid prior to renting or within the first three months. Make sure that you read your lease agreement before signing, and before paying anything. Check to see how and when the rent can be increased and by how much; don't assume that it can't be increased during the initial term of your lease. Find out how the landlord determines the percentage of the security deposit that will be returned to you; some landlords routinely keep all or part of the deposit for regular cleaning expenses when you move out. Most of these details can be negotiated before you sign the lease.

If you have any problems with your landlord while you're renting or if you feel that you were discriminated against while you were hunting for an apartment or house, the resources listed below may help:

- **City of Seattle Department of Housing and Human Services;** Housing and Community Services Division, 206-684-0721; Seattle Housing Authority, 206-615-3340; DCLU Code Violations Hotline, 206-684-7899
- **City of Seattle Human Rights Department;** Discrimination Complaints, 206-684-4500
- **Seattle Tenants Union,** 206-723-0500
- **Washington State Attorney General's Office,** 206-464-7744

RENTER'S INSURANCE

You've moved into your new apartment, and the last boxes have been cleared away. Take a look around and ask yourself, "How much would it cost to start over if everything I see was destroyed by fire?" Probably more than you think. Imagine having to replace your clothing, television, stereo, furniture, computer, and other accumulations of a lifetime. The bill would be staggering.

Typically, with renter's insurance you are protected against fire, hail, lightning, explosion, aircraft, smoke, vandalism, theft, building collapse, frozen plumbing, defective appliances, and sudden electrical damage. Renter's insurance also may cover personal liability as well as damage done (by you) to the property of others.

By now you should be convinced that renter's insurance is a good idea, especially because your belongings would not be not insured under your landlord's policy. The good news about renter's insurance is that it is not as expensive as you might believe. For $15,000 to $20,000 in coverage you probably will pay between $200 to $300 per year.

When shopping for renter's insurance, be sure to ask whether the insurance company pays as soon as the claim is filed and whether it pays cash-value or replacement value. If you have a cash-value policy, you will only be paid what your five-year-old television is worth, not what it costs to replace it. Some big-ticket items, such as home computers or jewelry, are insured only to a certain amount. Find out what these limits are. You can purchase renter's insurance through almost any area insurance agency.

Whether you get renter's insurance or not, it's a good idea to keep an inventory of all items of value and record their serial numbers

HOUSE, CONDO OR CO-OP HUNTING

If you are in the market to buy a house, and especially if you are a first time home-buyer, consider taking a real-estate class, often available at area colleges. If you don't have the time or inclination for a class, but are willing to read up yourself, look for a book on home buying how-to's. One such publication specifically about the Seattle area is *Seattle Homes: Real Estate Around the Sound* by Jim Stacey. Another invaluable resource is the Washington Center for Real Estate, call them at 800-835-9683, or visit their web site, www.cbeunix.wsu.edu/~wcrcr for a list of their services

Seattle residents love their houses. Beyond the Downtown, First Hill, and Capitol Hill neighborhoods, most streets are lined with single-family homes on roomy lots. And home values have been on the rise for most of the past decade as the local economy has boomed and interest rates have stayed low. A surge in the number of well paid technology jobs, particularly at companies on the Eastside such as Microsoft, has driven the price of homes near the Hwy. 520 bridge ever higher.

The good news is that it looks as though home values will continue to increase for the next few years. So an investment in a house, townhouse, or condominium is likely to pay off. In general, homes are slightly less expensive in those neighborhoods without direct freeway access. Affordable new homes can be found in some nearby suburbs, such as Renton, Bothell, and Edmonds (see the Surrounding Communities section of the **Neighborhoods** chapter for more information).

How should you go about finding a home to buy in Seattle? As any good real estate agent will tell you, there are three things to consider when purchasing a house: location, location, location. The **Neighborhoods** chapter of this book will give you a good overview of the neighborhoods in Seattle, as well as brief descriptions of some of the city's suburbs. From there, it's always a good idea to visit the neighborhoods you're considering. Get a feel for the area in general; visit the schools and parks; stop by during rush hour to evaluate traffic flow and freeway noise. Attend a few open houses or find a realtor in your neighborhood of choice to show you homes currently on the market. Be aware, in today's thriving real estate market many houses are selling the first day they're listed, and often for *more* than the asking price. Don't let that panic you, there are a lot of homes for sale, and if you're patient and persistent you will find one that is right for you.

When contemplating a new home purchase, you'll want to first evaluate your personal finances. How much can you afford to pay up front, and how much will you then be able to pay per month? Generally you will be able to qualify for a loan of about three or four times your yearly income, depending on your credit record and other debts. The loan won't cover your down payment and closing costs, however. In most cases closing costs, which are in addition to the down payment, run 3-7 percent of the purchase price. These can include loan origination fees, attorney's fees, title search, title insurance, inspections, and tax and insurance premiums held in escrow. As a buyer you will probably not be expected to pay the broker's fees, which are commonly paid by the seller. Expect your down payment to be 10-20 percent of the price of the home. Additional fees, such as mortgage insurance or higher loan origination fees, are often required if the down payment is less than 20 percent.

Given the current real estate market in Seattle, it's a good idea to get pre-approved for a loan before looking for houses in earnest. Most sellers will not seriously consider an offer from a buyer who is not pre-approved. The pre-approval process should not commit you to a particular lender or interest rate. It is simply a document that indicates to the seller that when you formally apply for a loan, you will most likely qualify to purchase the home. Most banks or mortgage brokers will process a pre-approval application without a fee. In addition to making your offer more attractive to the seller, the pre-approval process gives you, the buyer, an accurate idea of what size loan you will be able to receive. Just remember, that regardless of the loan amount for which you qualify, the most important thing is how much you feel comfortable paying.

Assuming that you are relatively unfamiliar with the city, you'll probably want to find a real estate agent or broker to help you with your search. Friends or co-workers may be able to recommend a good realtor. Another option is to consider the real estate agents who host the open houses you visit. The agent should be someone you trust, who listens to you, knows the city and the neighborhoods you like, and understands the market. A good realtor will not expect you to pay more than you can afford, although you may find that what you can pay for and what you want are very different things. Even with today's brisk market, you should expect that your agent will be constantly on the lookout for the style and size of home you are interested in. Most home buyers in Seattle do not require the services of a real estate lawyer in addition to their agent (often the lawyer involved is an employee of the escrow company). Nevertheless, it is a good idea to have the name of a real estate attorney available just in case. Ask friends or co-workers for recommendations, or perhaps your agent may be able to suggest a reputable attorney.

When purchasing a **house**, you are buying not only the building but also a piece of land. With your new home comes the joy of your own lawn or garden, the possibility of remodeling or renovating the house, and the pride of ownership. Before buying a house, you should hire an independent building inspector or engineer to examine the foundation and overall structure, heating and plumbing systems, and the roof. Your lender will also inspect the house, but only to determine if its value will safely secure the loan. It is always a good idea to know the defects of the house yourself; if possible, you should word your purchase offer so that you can rescind based on the inspection results. At the very least, your real estate agent should be willing to negotiate with the seller on any major flaws turned up during the inspection.

Condominiums are generally less expensive than comparably-sized houses, and can be a good option for those who can't easily afford a house in their chosen neighborhood. When you purchase a condo, what you're buying is an apartment and a piece of the land that the building is on. You own the apartment outright, so you can usually make improvements to it, rent it out, and re-sell it as you see fit. However, some restrictions apply to condo ownership. Generally, a condo association oversees the rules of the complex, making decisions about building repairs, external improvements, and landscaping. Some condo associations impose rules on subletting. Ask to see the association rules and regulations and the current operating budget, then review the paperwork with your real estate agent and, if possible, a lawyer. Consider any major improvements or repairs that will be required in the next few years, and see if the budget will be able to cover most of the cost. If your building has jointly owned amenities, such as a hot tub, roof-top deck, or pool, the association coordinates maintenance on those facilities as well. All of these services come at a cost; expect to pay between $100 and $300 in monthly association dues, as well as a one-time fee for capital improvements or emergency repairs, such as a new roof. While these dues may add up over time to little more than the maintenance on your own house, you'll need to factor them in when evaluating your monthly house payments.

A **co-op** (cooperative apartment) is another option for home ownership in Seattle. When you buy a co-op, you are actually buying shares in the ownership of a building. Co-ops tend to be much less expensive than comparable condominiums, but with some important trade-offs. Co-ops are tightly controlled by the shareholders in the building, in other words by all of the co-op owners. This can make it difficult to buy a cooperative apartment, since the co-op board will interview you, consider both your financial status and neighborly qualities, and may require several letters of reference. You may not have the option of remodeling your apartment, renting it out, or even selling it when you need to. Since the co-op board must approve any potential buyer, it makes it more challenging to sell when and to whom you want. In addition, many lenders simply do not approve mortgages for co-ops, while many co-ops do not accept anything but a full cash payment at the time of purchase. If you have the patience and financial wherewithal to buy a co-op unit, however, you will most likely get a great deal. Co-ops are most common in the Capitol Hill, Eastlake, and First Hill neighborhoods.

Those thinking about buying a condominium or co-op should seriously consider that unlike being a homeowner where you are, still, pretty much king of your castle, owning a condo or co-op means you will have to get along with a diverse group of people (your fellow owners). While these people could turn out to be great friends and neighbors, the opposite is also true and you will have no choice but to interact with them.

Finally, a few words of advice about getting a **loan**. While it's usually most convenient to get your pre-approval from a local bank, shop around when it comes to actually signing for your loan. While many banks are offering competitive interest rates, mortgage brokers can often match or beat your best offer. Make sure you ask about loan origination fees (points) when requesting interest rate quotes. Usually the lowest interest rate includes a hefty one-time fee, one that may not be mentioned until you're ready to sign the papers. The Bank Rate Monitor web site, www.bankrate.com, provides mortgage and interest rate data on over 2,000 lending institutions.

REAL ESTATE RESOURCES

Whether you're looking for a house, condominium, or co-op, you'll most likely start by touring the open houses in the areas you like. *The Seattle Times/Seattle Post-Intelligencer* Sunday edition has a Home/Real Estate section that lists many of the open houses in Seattle and surrounding communities. The paper is available on Saturday mornings, so you can get a drive-by preview. Other good resources for both open houses and other listings are the web sites of real estate agencies and home-buying journals, available at local grocery and convenience stores. A few real estate agencies, web sites, and publications are listed below. Others may be found in the Yellow Pages.

- **Abele Owner's Network**, www.owners.com
- **Bank Rate Monitor**, www.bankrate.com
- **Coldwell Banker Bain Associates**, 800-821-1431, www.cbbain.com
- **Coldwell Banker Real Estate**, 800-800-9749, www.coldwell-banker.com
- **Fannie Mae**, www.fanniemae.com
- **Home Realty, Inc.**, 206-363-8806, www.seattle-home.com/homereal/
- **John L. Scott Real Estate**, 800-872-7268, www.johnlscott.com
- **Lake Real Estate**, 206-527-1777, www.lakere.com
- **MacPherson's Better Homes and Gardens Real Estate**, 206-546-4124, www.macpherson's.com
- **Prudential Northwest Realty**, 206-932-4500, www.prudential-nw.com
- **Real Estate Seattle**, 206-722-3200, www.RealEstateSeattle.com
- **Re/Max Realty North**, 800-777-1174, www.seattlehomes4u.com
- **Seattle Real Estate On-line**, www.seattle-real-estate.com
- **Windermere Real Estate**, 206-789-7700, www.windermere.com

Once you've found a place to call home, try to arrange your home phone service, electricity, and heat, a few days before moving in. Most of the utilities listed in this chapter can be hooked up with a phone call, although, in some cases you may be required to mail or fax documents. Other services in this chapter such as auto registration or photo identification cards will require a visit to an office or bureau in person; unlike your utilities however, you can probably live without these for a few days or even weeks. Also included here is a list of broadcast media, so you can entertain yourself while waiting on on the phone or filling out forms.

UTILITIES

TELEPHONE

Because you'll need a home phone number for most applications, you'll want to get your residential telephone service established before anything else. Local telephone service in Seattle is provided by **U.S. West Communications**. Call 800-244-1111 (TTY 800-223-3131) 7 a.m.-7 p.m., weekdays to set up your new telephone account. You'll need to be prepared with the following information: home address; preferred long distance company; information on your previous phone account, including your former address and telephone number; employment and credit information. Depending on your credit status and previous telephone service history, a deposit may be required when you set up service. For more information about your local service you can check out U.S. West's web site; www.uswest.com.

The area code in Seattle, and just north and south of the city limits, is 206. Recently other area codes have been added to many of Seattle's suburbs. To call locations north and east of the city you may need to dial

425. To the south, the area code is 253. Other areas in Western Washington use the 360 area code (both north and south of Seattle) and east of the Cascades the area code is 509. Local numbers with a different area code should be dialed as 10 digits (area code + number); long distance calls require 11 digits (1 + area code + number).

LONG DISTANCE SERVICE PROVIDERS

Major long distance service providers are listed below:

- **AT&T**, 800-222-0300
- **MCI/Worldcom**, 800-950-5555
- **USSprint**, 800-877-7746

CELLULAR PHONE AND PAGING SERVICES

Since the recent national deregulation of local cellular services, there are many choices for cellular service in Seattle. The two largest companies in the city, AT&T Wireless Services and AirTouch, are faced with new competition and are subsequently offering lower rates. Another option is to buy service through a reseller, a company that resells cellular air time at slightly less than the usual rate, often without a pesky annual contract. Shop around when looking to purchase a cellular phone or cellular service, as rates and telephone prices can vary widely, and always ask about current promotions or discounts before committing yourself. Also, if you will be working for a large company or government agency, ask your employer whether there is a company cellular service plan. Often these offer much lower rates than you could get on your own. The following are some of the local cellular companies:

- **AT&T Wireless Services**, 206-624-5109 or 888-290-4613, www.attws.com
- **AirTouch Cellular**, 800-247-8682, www.west.airtouch.com/
- **GTE Wireless**, 888-GTE-4PCS
- **Sprint PCS**, 800-480-4PCS, www.sprintpcs.com

The following companies can set you up with paging services; check the Yellow Pages for other paging companies. If you don't already own a pager, you may also want to explore retail electronics stores, which sometime offer good deals on a combination pager and service purchase.

- **AT&T Wireless Services**, 425-803-1530, www.attws.com
- **AirTouch Paging**, 206-451-2370, www.paging.airtouch.com
- **PageNet**, 425-747-9646 or 800-864-PAGE
- **SkyTel**, 206-328-1961, www.skytel.com
- **Sprint Paging**, 800-4-PAGERS, www.sprint.com

ELECTRICITY

Seattle City Light supplies electricity for all residences within the city limits. Some outlying suburbs may have other electricity providers; call the suburb's municipal office for more information. The initial hook-up fee for electricity is $6.00. Seattle City Light can be contacted 8 a.m.-5 p.m., Monday through Friday, at the following numbers:

- **North of Denny Way**, 206-615-0600 (TTY 206-684-3225)
- **South of Denny Way**, 206-654-2720 (TTY 206-684-3225)

NATURAL GAS OR OIL HEAT

In Seattle, heating options consist of electric, natural gas or oil. Most likely you will go with whatever is already in use at your new house, apartment, or condominium. Unless the cost is included in your rent or condominium dues, you will be responsible for setting up a new account and for filling the existing tank (if using oil). If you decide to install a new furnace, water heater, or stove, you will need to be home when you have the line hooked up. If you chose the same fuel as what the previous resident used, you simply need to call for service, the gas or oil company will handle the rest. Natural gas is supplied for Seattle residents by **Puget Sound Energy**, 206-382-7858 (TTY 206-625-9607) 7 a.m.-5 p.m., weekdays.

Heating oil may be purchased from any of several local companies; a few are listed below. Check the Yellow Pages for additional companies.

- **Ballard Oil Co.**, 206-783-0241
- **Bowman Heating Oil**, 206-772-4447
- **Cascade Oil Company**, 206-323-6050
- **Olson Fuel Company**, 206-782-5522
- **Pacific Heating Oil Company**, 206-632-1966
- **Rainier Petroleum Inc.**, 206-623-3480

WATER

Generally, water service isn't something that you'll need to set up if you're renting. If you've purchased a home, you will need to change the current service to your name. Call the **City of Seattle Water Services** office at 206-684-5800 for more information.

CONSUMER COMPLAINTS

It's always a good idea to try to resolve billing or other disputes with the utility company directly. If that fails, however, you can file a formal complaint with the appropriate consumer complaint office. For city departments, call the **City of Seattle Complaints Line** at 206-684-8811 (voice and TTY). For state departments or independent companies, call the **Consumer Protection Complaints** line at 206-464-6684 or the **Washington State Attorney General** at 206-464-7744 (TTY 800-276-9883).

GARBAGE AND RECYCLING

Trash and recycling services are provided by the **Seattle Public Utilities Solid Waste Services Office**. Call 206-684-7600 for customer service or recorded information on rates and services. Garbage rates are standard for all residences within the city, and are based on the estimated volume of garbage that will be collected at your residence. For most apartments and condominiums, this cost is included in your monthly rent or dues. For single-family residences, a can must be purchased (either through the city or from a hardware store) and you must set up service with the city. The most common usage level is one 32 gallon can at a monthly cost of $16.10, but other options are available. There is a one-time charge of $15 to set up service or to increase your level of service. There are also charges for additional garbage collected beyond your usual level of service. Yard waste may be included as part of your garbage, although the city designates a few weeks during the year when additional yard waste can be collected at no extra charge.

The city also offers weekly recycling pick-ups at both houses and apartments in the city, but the collection day is generally different from your garbage collection day. Recycling containers for newspapers, mixed papers, aluminum, tin, and glass are provided. Again, call 206-684-7600 for customer service or recorded information on rates and services. If you live in an apartment or condominium, these services should already be provided for all tenants. If you are renting or have purchased a house, the recycling containers should already be with the house.

DRIVER'S LICENSE, STATE IDENTIFICATION

You must apply for a Washington State driver's license within 30 days of moving into the state. If you already have a valid driver's license from another state or U.S. territory, you can get a Washington State driver's license by passing the written exam only. If you fail three consecutive written exams, have an expired out of state license, or have certain medical conditions, you may be required to pass a driving exam as well. The cost of a four year license is $14.00, and there may be a $7.00 surcharge for replacing an expired license or if a driving test is required. The cost of a Washington State photo identification is $6. All licenses, temporary permits, and photo identification cards must be obtained by going to the licensing bureau office in person. Recent customer service improvements have greatly increased the efficiency of these offices, but you're still better off going on a weekday rather than a Saturday to avoid delays. Bring your current (valid or expired) license, other proof of identification, and proof of state residence, such as a utility bill or rental agreement. If you've recently been married and need your name changed on your driver's license, make sure you bring your marriage certificate as well. The Licensing Services' hours of operation are Mon., Tues., Wed., Fri.: 8:30 a.m. - 4:30 p.m., Thurs.: 9:30 a.m. - 4:30 p.m. Call ahead to schedule a driving test.

- **Downtown Seattle** (renewals only), 1200 3rd Ave., 206-464-6845
- **East Seattle**, 464 12th Ave., 206-720-3024
- **Greenwood**, 320 N 85th St., 206-545-6755
- **North Seattle**, 907 N 135th St., 206-368-7261
- **West Seattle**, 8830 25th Ave. SW, 206-933-3419

Low income seniors and disabled persons may be interested in applying for a City of Seattle Identification card, entitling them to discounts in the Seattle area. Call the **Mayor's Office for Senior Citizens**, 206-684-0500 for more information.

AUTO REGISTRATION

Getting your vehicle registered in Washington State can be an expensive task, but the penalties for driving with expired plates are far costlier. You must license your automobile or motorcycle within 30 days of becoming a Washington resident, even if your tabs from your previous state of residence are still valid. The fines for driving an unregistered vehicle are a minimum of $330.

The cost of your registration depends on the model and year of your vehicle. The basic fee for a passenger vehicle license is $27.85. In addition, you will pay various county and state fees totaling approximately $30. On top of that you may pay a $7.50 surcharge if you get your registration from a sub-agent (often worth the additional charge for the added efficiency), and a $12.00 emissions test charge (for vehicles manufactured after 1967). The largest chunk of your total registration fee, however, will be the variable excise tax, which is based on the type of vehicle, the manufacturer's suggested retail price, and a depreciation schedule established by law. This charge can easily run into the several hundred dollar range. To calculate the excise tax for your vehicle on the internet, visit the **State of Washington Department of Licensing Excise Tax Calculator** at www.vs.dol.wa.gov/excisetax/. The **State of Washington Department of Licensing** web page at www.wa.gov/dol/ offers many other tips on vehicle, vessel, and driver's licensing.

VEHICLE/VESSEL LICENSING INFORMATION

- **Department of Licensing,** 500 4th Ave., 206-296-4000 (TTY 206-296-2709)

EMISSIONS TEST INFORMATION

- **State of Washington Department of Ecology,** 800-453-4951

VEHICLE/VESSEL LICENSE SUB-AGENTS

- **Ballard Auto Licensing Agency,** Ballard Square, 2232 NW Market St., 206-781-0199
- **Bill Pierre License Agency,** 12531 30th Ave. NE, 206-361-5505
- **Georgetown License,** 5963 Corson Ave. S Suite 162, 206-767-7782
- **Puget Sound License Agency,** 3820 Rainier Ave. S, 206-723-9370

- **University License Agency,** 5615 Roosevelt Way NE, 206-522-4090
- **Wendel's License and Services,** 13201 Aurora Ave. N, 206-362-6161
- **West Seattle Licenses, Inc.,** 5048 California Ave. SW, 206-938-3111

AUTOMOBILE INSURANCE

The State of Washington requires drivers to have automobile insurance for all owned or leased vehicles, providing liability coverage for damage to the other driver's vehicle, as well as bodily damage to the driver and passengers of the other car. The fines for not carrying automobile insurance are steep, close to $400. You are required to show proof of insurance if stopped for a moving violation or if involved in an automobile accident. Coverage is available from area and national insurance companies. Contact your home-owners insurance agent first, and ask about a possible discount for carrying multiple policies with the same company. Check the Yellow Pages under "Insurance" for listings of area companies.

PARKING PERMITS

Parking in Seattle can be challenging at times, but if you're moving from another large city you'll probably be pleasantly surprised. Parking for a few hours in the business district can be extremely expensive, but there are affordable lots in some parts of Downtown. Street parking is also available throughout the Downtown area, at a cost of $1.00 per hour, but be sure to read the signs carefully. Some streets restrict parking during the busiest traffic hours; other parking meters have special time restrictions or fees. Parking fines are not insignificant — $22.00 for a street parking infraction — so you'll want to pay attention. The good news on street parking Downtown is that you only need to pay between 8:00 a.m. and 6:00 p.m. Monday through Saturday.

If you're going to be commuting to Downtown Seattle regularly, your least expensive and least stressful option would be to take the bus. If that's not the method you choose, another good idea is to set up or join a carpool and take advantage of reduced parking fees. Call the **City of Seattle Carpool Parking Permits Line** at 206-684-0818 to arrange for a carpool parking permit. The cost for Downtown parking is $150 per quarter (three months) for a two-person carpool or $75 per quarter for a three-person carpool.

If you don't have someone lined up to carpool with, Metro Transit offers Ridematch, a regional ride-sharing program that matches commuters with carpools. Another option available through Metro is a van-pool. Vanpools require 5-14 passengers and monthly fares range from $31-$85 per person. The advantages, however, are that Metro provides the van, insurance, and gasoline. In addition, the carpool parking mentioned above is free for vanpools. For more information on both the **Ridematch** and **Vanpool** programs, call 206-625-4500 or 1-800-427-8249, or visit Metro's web site, www.transit.metrokc.gov/.

Finally, if you want to drive to work by yourself every day, arrange to rent a space in a parking lot or garage. Street parking is too expensive and inconvenient for all-day parking. Your employer may offer discounts at nearby lots or offer incentives to carpool or ride mass transit.

Residential neighborhood parking has become more of an issue within the last ten years. Although there is still free street parking in each neighborhood, certain time restrictions usually apply. Some of these, such as parking for only a few hours or not being allowed to park at all on busy streets, are intended to keep the flow of traffic and business customers moving through the area. Other restrictions, which limit parking on residential streets during certain hours of the day, target habitual long-term parking by people who do not live in the area. For instance, neighborhoods with popular theaters and restaurants may have evening parking restrictions; areas with office buildings or hospitals nearby may have daytime parking restrictions. If your neighborhood has restricted parking, you'll want to get a residential parking permit. These permits can cost up to $27 for a year; charges and expiration dates are particular to each residential parking zone. Call the **City of Seattle Transportation Department** at 206-684-7623 for more information. The helpful folks there will take your address and mail you the required forms. You must provide copies of your vehicle registration and proof of address when you turn in the paperwork.

TOWED OR STOLEN CARS

There are five impound lots in Seattle that are operated by the city. If you believe your vehicle has been impounded by order of the police department, call 206-684-5444 (have your license number ready) and you will be directed to the appropriate lot. If your car was towed while on private property, you'll need to call the owner or manager of that property or the posted towing company number. To report a stolen vehicle, call the **Seattle Police Department** non-emergency line at 206-625-5011.

VOTER REGISTRATION

To register to vote in Seattle, you must be at least 18 years old, a citizen of the United States, and a legal resident of Washington State. You may register to vote at any time at several public locations, such as government offices, schools, and public libraries. You can also register through the mail or through the "Motor Voter" program. "Motor Voter" registration is completed when you apply for or renew your driver's license. It takes only an extra minute or two — well worth the convenience. You do not need to declare your political affiliation or party membership when you register. Absentee ballots are available up to 45 days before an election. The rules for receiving absentee ballots are not particularly rigid in Washington state, and many voters use absentee ballots even when they expect to be home on election day. For more information or to register by mail, call the **Voter Registration Hotline** at 800-448-4881 (TTY 800-422-8683).

LIBRARY CARDS

King County has two library systems, the Seattle Public Library and the King County Library System. Both offer an extensive selection of books and other materials, and can reserve books at other libraries in the system for your use. While Seattle residents are eligible as King County residents to belong to both library systems, all King County libraries are located outside of the city limits. Seattle Public Library cards are available at any neighborhood library (check the **Neighborhoods** chapter for listings of Seattle libraries near you). You will need to show proof of identification and proof of Seattle residency, such as a recent utility bill or driver's license. King County Library cards are also available at any King County Library and require the same information. If you already have a Seattle Library card you should bring that along as well. The following are numbers to call for more information:

- **Seattle Public Library**, Central Library, 1000 4th Ave., 206-386-4636
- **King County Library System**, Main Office, 300 8th Ave., 800-462-9600

PASSPORTS

Passports are processed at the Seattle Passport Agency, located Downtown. You may also pick up applications for passports at some neighborhood service centers in Seattle. Be sure to bring two standard identification photos, a picture I.D., and proof of U.S. citizenship, such as a previous U.S. passport, certified birth certificate, naturalization certificate, or certificate of citizenship. The cost is $60 for a new passport and $40 to renew a passport less than 12 years old. The standard turnaround time for a new passport is 25 days, but an expedited three day passport can be requested for an additional $35 fee. For more information, call the Seattle Passport Agency office directly. A recorded message lists all requirements and satellite locations. To use the internet for your passport application process go to the web site for the **Bureau of Consular Affairs**: www.travel.state.gov/.

- **Seattle Passport Agency**, U.S. Department of State, 915 2nd Ave. Suite 992, 206-220-7788 (TTY 206-220-7773)

TELEVISION

CABLE TV SERVICE

Seattle is served by TCI Cablevision for cable television. Strangely, where you live in the city determines the range of channels you'll receive with your basic cable package. Ask for more details when you set up service, or you may not get the channels you're expecting. Also, you may want to consider one of the popular satellite services that are available. Most electronics and TV stores can set you up with satellite service. If you prefer cable, the following information will help you contact the TCI new accounts office:

- **TCI Cablevision of Washington, Inc.**, 8914 Roosevelt Way NE, 206-743-5300

LOCAL TELEVISION STATIONS

For standard broadcast television, Seattle has the three main networks and a few independents and newcomers. If you've hooked up cable or satellite service, your stations may differ from those listed here.

- Channel 4, KOMO-TV, ABC
- Channel 5, KING-TV, NBC
- Channel 7, KIRO-TV, CBS
- Channel 9, KCTS-TV, PBS

- Channel 11, KSTW-TV, UPN
- Channel 13, KCPQ-TV, FOX
- Channel 22, KTZZ-TV, WB

RADIO STATIONS

Seattle residents love their music! Here's a guide to the available radio stations in Seattle.

Adult Contemporary
KGY, 1240 AM
KISS, 106.1 FM
KLSY, 92.5 FM
KMTT, 103.7 FM
KXRO, 1320 AM

Alternative Rock
KCMU, 90.3 FM
KISS, 106.1 FM
KMTT, 103.7 FM
KNDD, 107.7 FM

Christian
KCIS, 630 AM
KCMS, 105.3 FM
KGNW, 820 AM
KKOL, 1300 AM
KLFE, 1590 AM
KAZJ, 1680 AM

Classic Rock
KZOK, 102.5 FM

Classical
KING, 98.1 FM
Country
KMPS, 94.1 FM
KYCW, 96.5 FM
KKBY, 104.9 FM

Easy Listening
KEZX, 1150 AM
KIXI, 880 FM
KRWM, 106.9 FM

Jazz
KEZX, 98.9 FM
KWJZ - 98.9 FM

News, NPR
KIRO, 710 AM
KNWX, 770 AM
KOMO, 1000 AM
KPLU, 88.5 FM
KUOW, 94.9 FM

Oldies
KBSG, 97.3 FM
KJR, 95.7 FM

Rock
KISW, 99.9 FM

Sports
KJR, 950 AM

Talk Radio
KIRO, 100.7 FM
KONP, 1450 AM
KRKO, 1380 AM
KVI, 570 AM

Top 40
KPLZ, 101.5 FM
KUBE, 93.3 FM

World Music and Folk
KBCS, 91.3 FM
KCMU, 90.3 FM

FINDING A PHYSICIAN

Often a recommendation from a trusted friend or co-worker is the best place to start when looking for a doctor. Another option is to call a physician referral line or local hospital. Two local referral lines are listed below.

- **Children's Hospital & Medical Center Resource Line,** 206-526-2500
- **Northwest Hospital MED-INFO Physician Referral Line,** 206-633-4636

PET LAWS AND SERVICES

Pets in Seattle must be licensed, even those that generally are kept inside. The cost of a one year dog license is $33.00 ($15.00 if the dog is spayed or neutered). A one-year cat license is $20.00 ($10.00 if the cat is spayed or neutered). To qualify your pet for a license, you must provide proof that your pet has received a current rabies vaccination. The reduced license fee for a spayed or neutered pet requires a copy of a veterinarian's spay or neuter certificate. Low income senior citizens and disabled persons with a City of Seattle I.D. card qualify for a 50 percent discount on all fees. (See the Driver's License, State Identification section of this chapter for more information.)

All four legged pets (except cats) must be on a leash or held by the owner when in public places in Seattle, including sidewalks. In addition, Seattle has strict "scoop laws" that require the person in charge of the animal, to clean up after the pet.

Some parks have "off-leash" areas where pets are allowed to roam freely. One popular off-leash site is in Marymoor Park, in Redmond. In the Seattle city limits, only the following locations are designated off-leash areas, although others are currently under consideration.

- **Upper Golden Gardens Park,** NW 85th St. and Golden Gardens Dr. NW
- **Genesee Park,** S Genesee St. and 44th Ave. S
- **Westcrest Park,** 9th Ave. SW and SW Henderson St.

If you're interested in adopting an animal, you can visit the **Seattle Animal Control Center** at 2061 15th Ave. W, in the Interbay area, 206-386-4254. Fees range from $20 to $90 depending on the size and breed of the animal. You will be required to provide current photo identification, and your landlord's name and phone number if you live in a rental property. For more information about Seattle Animal Control and pets available for adoption, visit the SAC web site at www.ci.seattle.wa.us/rca/animal/.

For information on finding a pet-sitter or someone to walk your dog regularly, check out the listings under Pet Care Services in the **Helpful Services** chapter. Other numbers that may prove useful for those who have lost a pet or have found a stray are listed below.

- **The Humane Society for Seattle/King County,** 13212 SE Eastgate Way, Bellevue, 425-641-0080
- **King County Animal Control Shelter,** 821 164th Ave. NE, Bellevue, 206-296-3940; 21615 64th Ave. S, Kent, 206-296-7387
- **King County Animal Control Enforcement,** 206-296-7387
- **Northwest Animal Rights Network,** 1704 E Galer St., 206-323-7301
- **Progressive Animal Welfare Society (PAWS),** 15305 44th Ave. W, Lynnwood, 425-787-2500
- **Seattle Animal Control Shelter,** 2061 15th Ave. W, 206-386-4254
- **Seattle Animal Control, Animal Care Office,** 206-386-4289
- **Seattle Animal Control Service (Lost Pets),** 206-386-4254
- **Seattle Animal Control Enforcement,** 206-386-4292

SAFETY

While most Seattle neighborhoods are safe, and in fact crime rates are on the decrease, safety precautions should be taken, especially in unfamiliar areas. The following safety tips may be helpful: walk quickly and with a purpose, especially at night; don't dawdle or slow your pace, even when approached, and keep clear of alleyways, deserted areas, and dead ends. If riding in a bus, stay close to the front, near the driver. Most of all, *trust your instincts*. If you feel uneasy about a person or situation, there is probably a good reason for it.

Many neighborhoods in Seattle have block watch organizations that are registered through the **City of Seattle Crime Prevention Unit**. Call 206-684-7555 for a group in your area or for assistance in setting up your own block watch program.

For those who do a lot of travelling, check out the useful safety handbook; *Smart Business Travel: How to Stay Safe when You're on the Road*, by Stacey Ravel Abarbanel.

BANKING

O pening a bank account may be one of the first things to take care of after coming to town and finding a home. Although opening an account is a fairly simple process, it's a good idea to keep your old checking account open until you've completed the task of setting one up here. This can be particularly important if you're going to try to rent a home or apartment before opening a local account; many landlords won't accept a tenant who doesn't have a bank account.

There are many banks in the Seattle area and it's always a good idea to consider your options carefully before choosing. Factors like proximity to your home or office, hours, services offered, interest rates and fees may all influence your decision. The largest Seattle banks offer the convenience of branches throughout the Puget Sound area. There are also many smaller community banks offering competitive rates and services. Your employer or alma mater may offer membership in a credit union, which may give you an advantage on interest rates, loan fees, and low fee checking.

CHECKING ACCOUNTS

You'll probably want to call around to several banks to find out about special promotions; many banks offer special deals or extra perks for opening a checking account. Most banks will offer "free" checking for a price: maintaining a hefty balance in the account. Make sure that you understand exactly what potential fees could be charged to your account; in some cases, the lowest cost checking accounts charge you for completing a transaction with a human teller instead of using an ATM.

When opening a checking account, be sure to ask if a debit card is available to use with your account. Debit cards, often displaying a VISA or MasterCard symbol, take the place of a written check, deducting the amount of your purchase directly from your checking account, usually at no charge. They can also be used as an ATM card for cash withdrawals and deposits. However, unlike a credit card, a debit card cannot be used to reserve a car or hotel room.

To open a checking account, you'll need to visit a local branch office and bring the minimum deposit required (this amount varies from bank to bank, so call ahead). You will also need photo identification and possibly proof of address (a letter or utility bill mailed to your new address, or your rental contract). The following are a few area banks, most with several branch offices in the city.

- **Continental Savings Bank**, 800-654-1075
- **EvergreenBank**, 206-628-4250
- **First Mutual Bank**, 206-706-0894
- **KeyBank**, 800-KEY-2-YOU
- **Northstar Bank**, 206-632-0200
- **Pacific Northwest Bank**, 206-624-0600
- **Seafirst Bank**, 206-461-0800
- **Sterling Savings**, 206-789-5755
- **US Bank**, 800-872-2657
- **United Savings & Loan Bank**, 206-624-7581
- **Viking Community Bank**, 206-784-2200
- **Washington Federal Savings Bank**, 206-624-7930
- **Washington First International Bank**, 206-292-8880
- **Washington Mutual Bank**, 800-756-8000
- **Wells Fargo Bank**, 800-TO-WELLS

OTHER SERVICES

You may also want to start a savings account in addition to your checking account; most banks will open both for you at the same time. With some banks, you will save on fees by having two open accounts at the same location. Other services offered by banks include credit cards, loans, mortgages, lines of credit, and mutual fund accounts; ask about any of these that interest you.

CREDIT UNIONS

A low-cost alternative to a bank checking account is a similar type of account at a credit union. Normally, you must belong to a union or an employee organization to have access to these consumer-friendly non-profits. Two large local credit unions are the Washington State Employee

Credit Union and the Group Health Credit Union.

CONSUMER PROTECTION

If you have a problem with your bank, first try to resolve the issue through customer service or with a bank officer. If the matter concerns a discrepancy on your statement, time is usually of the essence. Find out how long you have to resolve the situation, and file a written complaint with the bank as soon as possible. If attempts to resolve the issue directly with the bank are unsuccessful, or if you are still not satisfied with the bank's explanation of certain transactions or charges, there is a state agency that handles consumer complaints against banks and other financial institutions. Contact the **State of Washington Department of Community Trade and Economic Development**, Consumer Protection Complaints Hotline, 206-464-6684.

CREDIT CARDS

As soon as you've established a new address in Seattle, you'll start receiving credit card offers in the mail. If you want to apply for a credit card even earlier:

- **American Express**, 800-THE-CARD
- **Department store credit cards**; Check at the customer service counter or at the checkout counter. Many stores offer a discount on your first purchase, with some restrictions. Department store cards are sometimes easier to qualify for than traditional credit cards, and can be used to establish a credit history if you have none.
- **Diner's Club**, 800-2DINERS
- **Discover Card**, 800-347-2683
- **VISA** and **MasterCard**; most banks offer one of these two major credit cards, and you can sign up for the card when opening your bank account. However, you may be able to find a more competitive interest rate by shopping around.

TAXES

Washington state residents pay federal income tax, but no state income tax. Instead, there is a fairly high sales tax (8.2%) that is charged on all purchases other than food. The state also has additional service taxes that are charged in some instances. After you've lived here for awhile, you'll get used to paying more than the listed price for most items. Property taxes are assessed on real estate.

When filing federal tax forms, the following numbers may be useful:

- **Federal Tax Forms**, call 800-829-3676 or stop by any public library or post office during tax filing season.
- **Federal Teletax Information System**, 800-829-4477
- **Internal Revenue Service**, 915 2nd Ave., 206-442-1040
- **Washington State Department of Revenue**, 800-647-7706

N ow that you've found a place to call home, and you've taken care of the utilities, you might benefit from some of the area's helpful services. Some of these services, such as furniture rentals, will help fill up an empty house or apartment. Others, including diaper and house cleaning services, can make your life far simpler. Below are the basics.

RENTAL SERVICES

Perhaps you've sold all but your most prized possessions to make your move easier, or maybe you're moving from a much smaller house to a sprawling new home in Seattle. Whatever the reason, you may want to use a rental service to fill in the gaps until you've had the chance to buy the perfect replacements. Those listed here are some of the area's largest rental service companies; others can be found in the Yellow Pages. All of those listed are in Seattle, unless otherwise noted. A word of advice, however: read any rental or lease agreement (matter how long or boring) before you sign it and ask questions if you don't understand anything. This will go a long way towards preventing any costly misunderstandings.

FURNITURE

Bring a list of what you need and, if possible, a floor plan or room measurements of your new home.

- **Cort Furniture Rental**, 2125 Western Ave., 206- 441-5857
- **Globe Furniture Rentals**, 406 Evans-Black Dr., 206-246-6400
- **It's Gotta Go Rental & Sales**, 2200 Western Ave., 206-441-1822
- **National Furniture Rental & Sales Inc.**, 2462 1st Ave. S, 206-682-8680
- **Quality Rentals**, 10421 16th Ave. SW, 206-248-3755

- **Rent-A-Center,** 13032 Aurora Ave. N, 206-367-3000; 9620 14th Ave. SW, 206-762-2708; 6026 Martin Luther King Jr. Way. S, 206-721-5488; 2301 S Jackson St., 206-325-3231

TELEVISION, VCR, STEREO

Most furniture rental places also offer TVs, VCRs, and stereos, but you may want to rent from an electronics specialist.

- **Northwest Radio & TV,** 7000 Greenwood Ave. N, 206-782-7447
- **T Dee Appliance, Inc.,** 13339 Lake City Way. NE, 206-361-7368

PERSONAL COMPUTERS

The following businesses offer rentals, leases, delivery, and technical support.

- **GE Capital Computer Rental Services,** 206-624-6978
- **Vernon Computer Rentals and Leasing,** 206-467-5107

DOMESTIC SERVICES

For those who need a little extra help around the house, the following services might be of interest. Check the Yellow Pages for more listings.

• DIAPER SERVICES

- **Baby Diaper Service,** 206-634-2229
- **Sunflower Diaper Service,** 206-782-4199

DRY CLEANING DELIVERY

- **Downtown Cleaners,** 920 3rd Ave., 206-622-1413
- **Fashion Care Cleaners,** 1822 Terry Ave., 206-382-9265
- **Hogan's Corner Drycleaners,** 5501 25th Ave. NE, 206-526-9754

HOUSE CLEANING

You may decide to use a house cleaning service before you move into your new home or for routine chores on an on-going basis. A few house cleaning businesses are listed below. As with all lists in this guide, inclusion here does not indicate an endorsement. If you are not satisfied with the level of service you receive from a company during the initial cleaning, you may request that they clean again at no charge.

- **Best Homemakers**, Seattle Area, 206-682-2556
- **Broomstick Cleaning**, Seattle Area, 206-285-1950
- **Dana's Housekeeper Referral Service**, Seattle Area, 206-368-7999; West Seattle Area, 206-433-0070
- **Maid Brigade**, Seattle Area, 206-362-8439
- **Maid in the Northwest**, Seattle Area, 206-622-7783; North Seattle Area, 206-365-5087
- **Merry Maids**, Seattle Area, 206-527-2984; West Seattle Area, 206-937-7083
- **Mighty Maids**, West Seattle Area, 206-938-9662
- **Northwest House Cleaning**, Seattle Area, 7801 Lake City Way NE, 206-525-2360
- **Rent-A-Yenta House Cleaning Service, Inc.**, Seattle Area, 206-325-8902
- **Sea-Maids Housecleaning Services**, Seattle Area, 206-526-5950
- **Student Cleaning**, Seattle Area, 206-527-4290
- **Superior Cleaning and Restoration**, Seattle Area, 206-633-5515

LAWN CARE & LANDSCAPING

For some, taking care of a lawn and garden is part of the dream-come-true with home ownership; for others it is a tiresome chore that they would gladly do without. For those who would rather spend their time doing something other than maintaining the lawn or for those with bigger ambitions — redesigning the landscaping on your property, for example — consider hiring a professional lawn/garden person to help you out.

- **All Season Maintenance**, 206-329-1329
- **Al's Yard Maintenance**, 206-723-0880
- **Austin Services**, 206-343-5546
- **Beautiful Gardens**, 206-328-9121
- **Bob's Lawn & Garden Service**, 206-363-8708
- **Clifford Quality Landscapes**, 206-527-1284
- **Corcoran Landscape Services**, 206-283-5296
- **DJ's Landscaping**, 206-367-0573

- **Emerald Green Lawns,** 206-363-5124
- **Evergreen Lawn & Yard Service,** 206-248-3811
- **Jacobsen Gardening & Landscaping,** 206-525-8448
- **Ken's Yard Service,** 206-932-6223
- **Lyons Landscape,** 206-784-3733
- **Nick's Careful Yard Maintenance,** 206-361-9388
- **Seattle Lawn & Garden,** Ballard Area, 206-783-7191; Queen Anne Area, 206-285-4343; West Seattle Area, 206-935-1717

PET CARE/SITTING SERVICES

Though most pets like, even need, company, if you're a pet owner but have to be away from home for long periods of time, consider hiring a surrogate in your absence.

- **Bona Fide Pet Sitting Service,** 206-547-3882
- **Comfort of Home,** 206-364-1493
- **Holiday Pet Care,** 206-726-4128
- **Pet Sitters of Puget Sound Referral Line,** 206-622-7387
- **Vonni's Critter Sitting,** 206-933-0408
- **Windance Pet Sitting,** 888-946-3738

POSTAL AND SHIPPING SERVICES

While you're between addresses and in need of a place to receive mail, you can rent a box at a local post office or choose a private receiving service. Many of the private services allow call-in mail checks and mail forwarding, but they are often more expensive than the Post Office.

MAIL RECEIVING SERVICES

- **The Mail Box,** 300 Lenora St., 206-728-1228; 300 Queen Anne Ave. N, 206-285-0919; 3213 W Wheeler St., 206-285-4843; 6201 15th Ave. NW, 206-789-7564
- **Mail Boxes Etc.,** 10002 Aurora Ave. N, 206-527-5065; 4505 University Way. NE, 206-545-4455; 4742 42nd Ave. SW, 206-933-8038; 800 5th Ave. Suite 101, 206-382-9177; 916 NE 65th St., 206-522-9732; 9594 1st Ave. NE, 206-523-7353; 1315 Madison St., 206-682-0998

- **Package Delivery Services**
- **Airborne Express**, 800-247-2676
- **DHL Worldwide Express**, 800-225-5345
- **Federal Express**, 800-463-3339
- **Roadway Package Systems**, 800-762-3725
- **United Parcel Service (UPS)**, 800-742-5877
- **U.S. Postal Service Express Mail**, 800-222-1811

MOVING

For your move to Seattle, you will most likely want to use a mover based in your current location or a national moving company. Both of these can be found in the Yellow Pages for your area. If you've had a problem with your move, the consumer phone number to call is different depending on whether your move was within Washington State or across state lines. Moves within Washington are regulated by a state agency, while a federal body regulates interstate moves. Both agencies are listed below.

- **State of Washington Utilities and Transportation Commission,** Consumer Services Division, 800-562-6150 (for in-state moves)
- **U.S. Department of Transportation**, Office of Motor Carriers, 360-753-9875 (for interstate moves)

STORAGE FACILITIES

If you are going to have an interim period before you move into a new house or apartment, or if you have more things to move than you'll have space for in your new place, you may want to put some of your belongings in storage. There are dozens of local storage companies, some of which will pick up and deliver storage trunks to your door. A few are listed below; others may be found in the Yellow Pages.

- **12th & Madison Self Storage**, 1111 E Madison St., 206-322-8408
- **A-1 Self Storage**, 2648 15th Ave. W, 206-282-0200
- **Aaron's Mini-Storage Center**, 2030 Dexter Ave. N, 206-286-9155
- **Door-to-Door Storage**, Ballard, 206-782-3990; Capitol Hill, 206-325-3886; Mount Baker, 206-723-3630; Queen Anne, 206-282-2050; University District, 206-545-7978; West Seattle, 206-932-7110
- **Downtown Self Storage**, 1915 3rd Ave., 206-441-2999

- **Magnolia Bridge Self Storage**, 1900 15th Ave. W, 206-286-1900
- **Nickerson Street Self Storage**, 1300 W Nickerson St., 206-285-5800
- **Public Storage**, 3600 Stone Way N, 206-545-9160; 1515 13th Ave., 206-329-6271; 11512 Aurora Ave. N, 206-362-5994; 10404 Martin Luther King Jr. Way S, 206-725-4777; 10020 Martin Luther King Jr. Way S, 206-723-4673
- **Roosevelt Self Storage**, 6910 Roosevelt Way NE, 206-526-0900
- **Seattle Self Storage**, 1100 Poplar Pl. S, 206-323-3000
- **Shurgard Storage**, 16 locations in the greater Seattle area, 800-SHURGARD

SERVICES FOR PEOPLE WITH DISABILITIES

There are a number of organizations in the Seattle area that serve as resources for disabled persons. The **Washington Coalition of Citizens with Disabilities (WCCD)** offers legal services, specifically for civil rights violations; an employment program, which provides assistance in finding a job; a travel training program, to help disabled persons use the Metro bus system; a technical assistance program, providing job training; and a self-advocacy program, to teach disabled persons how to speak up for their rights. The **Washington State Governor's Committee on Disability Issues and Employment (GCDE)** supports the integration of all persons with disabilities into the community and provides publications on workplace accessibility and other topics. The **Washington Assistive Technology Alliance (WATA)** is an organization which increases access to and awareness of technologies which provide assistance and accessibility for people with disabilities. The University of Washington's **Assistive Technology Resource Center (ATRC)** provides information, referral services, training, and consultation regarding assistive technology devices, services, and funding. **The Easter Seal Society of Washington** provides housing assistance programs, vocational rehabilitation, including interview skills training, job search techniques, and on the job support. They also publish a pamphlet listing accessible sites in the Seattle area.

Metro Transit issues Regional Reduced Fare Permits to individuals with disabilities. The permit costs $3 and is valid for Metro transportation, Washington State ferries, Community Transit, Pierce Transit and most other bus agencies in the region. With the permit, each bus ride is $.25; buses are equipped with wheelchair lifts and special seating. For

those individuals who require assistance in riding the bus, a special
Personal Care Attendant permit allows the disabled person's escort to
ride for free. Depending on the nature of the disability, a letter of certification from a physician, psychiatrist, psychologist, or audiologist may be
required. Call Metro Transit at 206-553-3060 (TDD 206-684-2029) for
more information and to receive a copy of the certification form.

Here's how to get in touch with the above centers, as well as several other national and local organizations.

- **Assistive Technology Resource Center (ATRC),** University of
  Washington, 800-841-8345 (Voice/TTY)
- **Community Service Center for the Deaf and Hard of Hearing,**
  1609 19th Ave., 206-322-4996 (Voice/TTY)
- **Community Services for the Blind and Partially Sighted,** 9709 3rd
  Ave. NE, Suite 100, 206-525-5556 (Voice/TTY), 800-458-4888
- **Deaf-Blind Service Center,** 2366 Eastlake Ave E Suite 206, 206-
  323-9178 (Voice/TTY)
- **Hearing, Speech and Deafness Center,** 1620 18th Ave., 206-323-
  5770 (Voice/TTY)
- **Learning Disabilities Association of Washington,** 7819 159th Pl.
  NE, Redmond, 425-882-0792
- **National Council on Disability (NCD),** 1331 F Street NW Suite
  1050, Washington, DC, 20004
- **Northwest Disability and Business Technical Assistance Center,**
  800-949-4232 (Voice/TTY)
- **Self Help for Hard of Hearing People (SHHH),** 26820 Arden
  Court, Kent, 206-854-0171 (Voice/TTY)
- **Washington Assistive Technology Alliance (WATA),** University of
  Washington, 206-685-4181, 206-616-1395 (TTY), www.wata.org
- **Washington Coalition of Citizens with Disabilities,** 4649
  Sunnyside Ave. N Suite 100,
  206-461-4550, 206-461-3766 (TTY), www.premier1.net/~wccd
- **Washington Protection and Advocacy System,** 1401 E. Jefferson
  Street Suite 506, 800-562-2702, 800-905-0209 (TTY)
- **The Washington State Governor's Committee on Disability
  Issues and Employment (GCDE),** Olympia Office, PO Box 9046,
  MS: 6000, Olympia, WA 98507-9046, 360-438-3168
- **Washington State Office of Deaf and Hard of Hearing Services,**
  PO Box 45300, Olympia, WA 98504-5300, 360-753-0703, 360-
  753-0699 (TTY)

- **Washington Telecommunications Relay Services**, 800-833-6384, 800-833-6388 (TTY), 800-833-6385 (Telebraille)

CONSUMER PROTECTION NUMBERS

If you have a complaint about a business transaction in Seattle, the following public and private agencies can serve as a resource for reporting or resolving the problem for you.

- **City of Seattle Consumer Affairs,** Consumer Complaints, 206-684-8484
- **State of Washington Consumer Concerns,** Consumer Protection Complaints and Inquiries, 206-464-6684 or 800-551-4636
- **State of Washington Consumer Concerns,** Lemon Law, 206-587-4240 or 800-541-8898 (Lemon Law complaints apply specifically to the purchase of a new or used vehicle in Washington State. Generally a vehicle is considered a "lemon" if it cannot be repaired within a reasonable amount of time, and if the vehicle is less than 30 months old. More specifics of the law are available at the phone numbers listed above.)
- **State of Washington Attorney General's Office,** 206-464-7744
- **Federal Consumer Product Safety Commission,** Western Regional Center, 600 Harrison St. Rm. 245, San Francisco, CA 94107, 415-744-2966 or 800-638-2772

CHILD CARE

As a newcomer with young children, one of the most challenging tasks you'll face is finding a day care center or babysitter you trust. Often, the best advice is to ask for referrals from friends or trusted co-workers. Before beginning your search, order a copy of a useful informational pamphlet, *Choosing Quality Child Care in King County: A Guide for Parents*. The guide costs only $5 and provides in-depth advice for those searching for child care in King County. To order, call 206-461-3708 or send an e-mail request to ccr@childcare.org.

Note: mention in this book of a particular child care organization or business is merely informational; it is *not* an endorsement or recommendation of the organization or business. We recommend that you carefully consider and scrutinize any person or organization before entrusting your youngster (s) to them.

DAY CARE

There are several companies which provide referrals to local day care facilities, including the **Child Care Resources**, which maintains a database of licensed child care providers in the King County area. For a small fee ($25 for on-line access only and $50 for on-line and telephone information), Child Care Resources offers six months of access to their database. Many local employers offer a benefits package that includes a similar service; check with your place of work for more details. In addition to using one of these services, you will want to visit the prospective day care facility (preferably unannounced) and interview staff members at the site. If possible, request names of other parents who use the facility who would be willing to talk to you. Ask them for their candid opinion about the level of service provided.

In Washington State, a license is required for anyone who is paid to care for children in their own home on a regular basis (unless the children are related to the person). Prior to receiving a license from the State of Washington Department of Social and Health Services (DSHS), a prospective day care provider must have a business license, undergo a criminal history background check, attend a first aid/CPR class which includes infant/child CPR and pediatric first aid, attend an HIV/AIDS awareness class, and pass a DSHS licensing inspection at the place of business. In addition, only licensed day care providers qualify to obtain liability insurance. However, because liability insurance is not required by the state, you'll need to ask the day care providers you interview if their business is covered.

The Service Employees International Local #925, the local union for child care workers, may be able to offer some help in your search for good child care. The SEIU district office is located at 2900 Eastlake Ave. E. Call 206-328-3010 or 206-328-7295 for more information.

- **Child Care Resources**, 1265 S Main St. Suite 210, 206-461-3708; Referral Line 206-461-3207; Internet Access, www.childcare.org/
- **Child Care Referrals**, 206-467-1552
- **Daycare Finders Inc.**, 206-932-3677
- **Evergreen Children's Association**, 206-781-8062
- **Hilltop Children's Center**, 2400 8th Ave. W, 206-283-3100
- **KidsSpace**, 3847 13th Ave. W, 206-282-3622
- **Pike Market Child Care and PreSchool**, 1501 Pike Place, #313, 206-625-0842

NANNIES

A number of agencies match families with nannies. While these services tend to be pricey, some include background checks or psychological testing during the applicant screening process. Nannies are not licensed by the state and screening processes vary among agencies, so you may want to ask for screening specifics at the various agencies.

That said, a nanny can be a wonderful addition to your family. Whether you're employed outside of the home or simply need some assistance while working at home, a considerate and hard-working nanny may be the best option for your child care needs.

- **A Nanny for U**, 425-745-9882
- **ABC Nannies**, 206-870-2989
- **All About Nannies, Inc.**, 425-482-1783
- **Annie's Nannies**, 206-784-8462
- **Around the Clock Nanny Services**, 206-367-2222
- **CareWorks**, 206-325-7510
- **Dreamboat Nannies**, 206-282-9225
- **Judi Julin R.N., Nannybroker, Inc.**, 206-624-1213
- **Keepsake Nannies**, 206-433-1936
- **McDonald Employment/Nanny Services**, 206-284-5244
- **Seattle Nanny Network, Inc.**, 206-374-8688, www.seattlenanny.com
- **Theresa Snow Homecare, Inc.**, 206-623-7091

EMERGENCY BABYSITTING

Whether you just haven't found a reliable babysitter in your neighborhood, or the one you found just called and cancelled, the following companies offer emergency baby sitting services. Be prepared pay more for immediate response.

- **Annie's Nannies**, 206-784-8462
- **Around the Clock Nanny Services**, 206-367-2222

AU PAIRS

If you'd like the convenience of a nanny at considerably lower cost, or if you're simply interested in participating in a cultural exchange, consider the services of an au pair. Young women (and a few men), usually from Europe, provide a year of child care and light housekeeping in exchange for airfare, room and board, and a small stipend. Au pairs work up to 45 hours a week, and often go to school or sightsee during their time off.

It is unquestionably a good program for those families and au pairs who understand the trade-offs of the system. Nevertheless, you may want to confirm that you and the au pair have mutual expectations for your year together. The au pair will be in a foreign country, interested in travelling and meeting people her age. While most agencies are specific when outlining responsibilities, make sure the au pair understands what is expected during her year of employment; your au pair may not have fully considered how restricted her free time will be. Additionally, some parents may have unrealistic expectations of an au pair, assuming that she will be a combination nanny, babysitter, and full time housekeeper, or expecting that she will make few friends and spend all of her time with the family. That said, if you and your au pair come to an agreement early in the relationship, and follow the guidelines detailed by the agency, you will most likely be very pleased with the au pair experience.

The U.S. Information Agency (USIA) oversees and approves organizations that arrange au pair services. The following agencies meet USIA's standards.

- **American Heritage Association/Au Pair International**, 800-654-2051
- **American Institute for Foreign Study/Au Pair in American**, 800-727-2437
- **Euraupair Intercultural Child Care Program**, 800-333-3804
- **Ayusa International/Au Pair Care**, 800-428-7247
- **Educational Foundation for Foreign Students/Au Pair EF**, 800-333-6056
- **InterExchange/Au Pair USA**, 800-287-2477
- **Exploring Cultural & Educational Learning/Au Pair Registry**, 800-547-8889

SCHOOL INFORMATION

PUBLIC AND PRIVATE SCHOOLS (K-12)

For the past several years, now deceased Superintendent John Stanford, with his controversial brand of military-style planning and organization tried to change the Seattle Public School system. As a result, test scores went up at most schools, graduation requirements became more challenging and standardized exit tests became required for students to pass up from grades five, eight, and eleven. The district also implemented new safety measures in schools by, for example, providing identification badges for high school students and expanding focused anti-violence campaigns.

The Seattle Public Schools enrollment process is fairly complicated, but most parents consider it a vast improvement over the former school assignment program. The old system did not allow voluntary school selection and instead involved busing large numbers of students throughout the city to improve the racial balance at each school. While busing successfully integrated the schools, it also took its toll on the overall well-being of the public school community. With bus rides taking as much as 90 minutes each way, many students found it difficult to get to and from school, let alone participating in after-school sports and activities. With such inconveniences, those who could afford to removed their children from the public system, choosing private schools instead.

In 1993, the school district offered the community a voluntary school selection process, which is limited only by space and the racial integration standards set by the state. The goal is to give all students their first choice school, although it remains to be seen if all first-choice school assignments are possible. Nevertheless, the district has consistently come close. Slight changes are made to the program each year, but generally the enrollment guidelines are as follows:

Elementary students are assigned to a "cluster" (one of nine geographic areas defined by the district) and to a "reference area school" (the student's default school choice) within the cluster. While both are determined by the child's home or child care address, the school nearest the home is not necessarily the reference area school. In middle and high school, the student is assigned two "base schools" which are determined by the elementary school attended. A spot for the child is guaranteed at the reference area school and at either of the base schools as long as it is the student's first choice on the enrollment application. Once accepted to a particular school, the student can remain there through graduation, as long as they continue to list it as their first choice school. If the student is granted admission to a school other than their base or reference area school, transportation may not be provided by the school district. School assignments are based first on choice, then on available space, and finally on tie-breakers. Students who do not receive their first choice school are assigned to another school in the cluster area, and then are wait-listed for the chosen school until the academic year begins. If space becomes available during that time, the student is then assigned to the originally requested school.

To enroll your child in the Seattle Public School District, you must call or visit one of the Student Assignment Services Centers to receive registration materials. The Centers can also provide you with your child's reference area or cluster assignment. To complete the registration process, you must bring proof of address, such as a rent receipt, driver's license, or pre-printed check; your child's immunization records; and proof of the student's birth date.

If you are able to register your child for school during the regular enrollment period (February for elementary, March for middle and high school), you have a much better chance of receiving your first choice school assignment. All applications received before the period deadline are processed together, with each carrying equal weight. After the normal enrollment period ends, applications are processed on a "first-come, first-served" basis. Some schools fill up quickly based on special programs or popularity; others simply have smaller buildings and cannot accommodate as many students. Alternative schools and classes, such as honors, special education, multi-cultural, or bilingual programs, often have additional requirements that restrict enrollment.

When necessary, "tie-breakers" are used during the school assignment process, and are applied in the following order:

Siblings — a student whose sibling attends the requested school will receive first preference.

Reference area (for most schools) or cluster area (for alternative schools) — if a student resides in the geographic area (as defined by the school district) that includes the school, the student will take precedence over other children outside of that area.

Integration — a student whose presence will positively affect the racial balance of the school will be chosen first.

Distance — the shortest physical distance between the school and the student's home may determine school assignment.

Lottery — finally, if none of the above criteria can be used, assignment is based on a lottery. Each student is assigned a three-digit lottery number during the enrollment process, and the student with the lowest number in a tie-breaker situation wins.

Finally, an important element of the registration program is the appeals process. If your child does not receive their first-choice school, you may appeal to the school district and, if necessary, request a hearing before the Appeals Board. It is always worth taking this step if you are truly dissatisfied with your child's school assignment.

While the Student Assignment Services Centers can provide information on any of the Seattle Public Schools, another excellent resource for statistics and information on special schools and programs is the **SchoolScout** web site. SchoolScout provides detailed profiles of each public school, including number of students, special classes and programs, and faculty qualifications. The site profiles several local private schools as well. In addition, you may want to contact School Match in Westerville, Ohio, to request its report on Seattle schools. The three-page report will include information on student-teacher ratios, test scores, and even property values in your chosen neighborhood. Call **School Match** at 800-992-5323 to order the report, which costs $19. All of the resources mentioned previously, as well as some other Seattle Public School resources are listed here.

- **SchoolScout web site**, www.komotv.com/schoolscout
- **Seattle Public Schools web site**, including links to SchoolScout public school profiles, www..sea-css.ssd.k12.wa.us/index.html
- **Student Assignment Information** (Recorded Message), 206-298-7410
- **Student Assignment Services Center (North)**, John Marshall Building, 520 NE Ravenna Blvd. Room 106, 206-729-3370
- **Student Assignment Services Center (South)**, Sharples Building, 3928 S Graham St., 206-760-4690
- **Special Education Information**, 206-298-7935
- **Special Education Family Services**, 206-298-7850
- **Student Enrollment Services Office**, 206-298-7218

If you are considering **private schooling** for your child, there are many such options in the greater Seattle area, most of which provide bus service as well. A few of the private schools in or near Seattle are listed here, many others are listed in the Yellow Pages. Entrance requirements vary widely, be sure to call or visit the school for more information.

- **Blanchet High** (9-12), 8200 Wallingford Ave. N, 206-527-7711
- **Bush School** (K-12), 405 36th Ave. E, 206-326-7736
- **Concordia Lutheran** (P-8), 7040 36th Ave. NE, 206-525-7407
- **Holy Family** (K-8), 9615 20th Ave. SW, 206-767-6640
- **Hope Lutheran/LCMS** (K-8), 4446 42nd Ave. SW, 206-935-8500
- **Islamic School of Seattle**, 720 25th Ave., 206-329-5735
- **King's Schools** (P-12), 19303 Fremont Ave. N, 206-546-7218
- **Lakeside** (5-12), 14050 1st Ave. NE, 206-368-3600
- **Meridian School** (K-5), 4649 Sunnyside Ave. N, 206-632-7154
- **Northwest School** (6-12), 1415 Summit Ave., 206-682-7309
- **St. Edward** (K-8), 4212 S Mead St., 206-725-1774
- **St. Joseph's** (K-8), 700 18th Ave. E, 206-325-0497
- **Seattle Jewish Primary** (K-4), 7330 35th Ave. NE, 206-522-5212
- **Seattle Lutheran High** (9-12), 4141 41st Ave. SW, 206-937-7722
- **Seattle Preparatory** (9-12), 2400 11th Ave. E, 206-324-0400

- **Seattle Urban Academy** (9-12), 3800 S Othello Ave., 206-723-0333
- **University Preparatory Academy** (6-12), 8000 25th Ave. NE, 206-525-2714
- **West Seattle Montessori**, (K-8), 4536 38th Ave. SW, 206-935-0427

COLLEGES AND UNIVERSITIES

In some ways, Seattle is one big college town. It is both the site of the state's largest public university, the University of Washington, and home to many other well-known private and community colleges. The colleges and universities listed below represent only a small number of the schools located in the Seattle area, others may be found by consulting the Yellow Pages. In addition to traditional colleges, there are many special interest, vocational, and technical schools in the area.

- **University of Washington,** (main entrance on 17th Ave. NE and NE 45th St.), 206-543-2100, www.washington.edu; founded in 1861, the University of Washington is a public research university attended by about 35,000 students. Known internationally for its bio-medical research, the UW also has outstanding masters programs in business and law and is a well-respected undergraduate institution. The university hosts guest speakers, dance troupes, and musicians throughout the year. In the fall, the Husky Football team attracts alumni and sports fans from across the state.
- **North Seattle Community College**, 9600 College Way N, 206-527-3600, www.nsccux.sccd.ctc.edu/; located in a surprisingly pleasant concrete building near Northgate, NSCC is a versatile community college which offers day and evening classes for undergraduates and professionals. The school's continuing education program offers a variety of up-to-the-minute computer courses for all levels of users.
- **Seattle Central Community College**, 1701 Broadway, 206-587-3800, www.edison.sccd.ctc.edu; a school of 10,000 students, SCCC is located in the Capitol Hill neighborhood, offering both undergraduate and professional education classes. It also operates two satellite branches, the Maritime Training Academy and the Wood Construction Programs. In addition, SCCC runs the Seattle Vocational Institute, providing short-term job training programs.

- **South Seattle Community College,** 6000 16th Ave. SW, 206-764-5300, www.sccd.ctc.edu/south; located in West Seattle, South Seattle Community College offers both vocational and academic classes.
- **Seattle Pacific University,** main entrance on 3rd Ave. W and W Nickerson St., 206-281-2000, www.spu.edu/; located in the north end of Queen Anne, SPU is a private Christian university offering degrees in liberal arts, fine arts, business, and education, among others. The university's picturesque campus makes it a pleasant school to attend.
- **Seattle University,** 900 Broadway, 206-296-6000, www.seattleu.edu/; an independent Jesuit university located on First Hill, SU offers courses in a wide variety of subjects, including graduate programs in law, nursing, and software engineering, as well as undergraduate degrees in philosophy, theology, and the sciences.

During and after your move to Seattle you will undoubtedly need to purchase a few items for the home. To assist you in this endeavor, we offer a brief guide to area retailers. Shopping is popular in Seattle, perhaps because it is can be done even in the rain. With Seattle's continuing economic boom, many area malls have been extensively remodeled, and now include a host of upscale stores. Bellevue Square and University Village in particular have become destinations for fashionable and affluent shoppers. Every mall and shopping district in Seattle includes several espresso stands and take-out dining options, while the more fashionable locations offer an array of trendy eateries and swank cocktail lounges.

Those shopping locations listed in this chapter are either in Seattle or nearby suburbs such as Lynnwood, Tukwila or the Eastside. All addresses are in Seattle unless otherwise noted.

MALLS

Most Seattle area malls offer a combination of stores; from the reasonably priced, practical stores to the more luxurious boutiques. As Seattle's economy has prospered in recent years, the less expensive mall shops have been replaced by specialty boutiques or popular national chains. Dollar and discount stores are now often located outside of the malls themselves, either across the street or a few blocks away. Below are just a few:

- **Alderwood Mall**, I-5 and Alderwood Mall Blvd., Lynnwood, WA, 425-771-1121
- **Bellevue Square**, NE 8th and Bellevue Way, Bellevue, WA, 425-454-4340

- **Factoria Mall**, 128th Ave. SE and SE 38th St., Bellevue, WA, 425-747-7344
- **Northgate Mall**, I-5 and Northgate Way, Seattle, WA, 206-362-8768
- **Pacific Place**, 600 Pine St., Seattle, WA, 206-405-2655
- **Redmond Town Center**, 7730 Leary Way NE, Redmond, WA, 206-867-0808
- **Southcenter Shopping Center**, I-5 and I-405, Tukwila, WA, 206-246-7400
- **University Village Shopping Center**, 25th Ave. NE and Montlake Ave. NE, Seattle, WA, 206-523-0622
- **Westlake Center**, 400 Pine St., Seattle, WA, 206-467-1600

SHOPPING DISTRICTS

While nearly every neighborhood in Seattle has its own small retail core, the following Seattle districts are well-known for their shopping opportunities.

If you are in a spending mood, some of the best shopping **Downtown** can be found in and around the soaring new Pacific Place mall at the intersection of 6th Ave and Pine St. Just west, you'll find the equally impressive new Nordstrom flagship store in the former Frederick & Nelson building. Since 1993 this area of Downtown has been undergoing a concerted and expensive retail makeover as many upscale locally owned retailers as well as big names in international fashion and entertainment have located in this part of the city.

Originally a simple farmers' market, the exceedingly popular **Pike Place Market** is located Downtown at 1st Ave and Pike St. In addition to the traditional fish, meats, fruits and vegetables, stalls are also filled with local arts, crafts, flowers, teas, and clothing. Surrounding the marketplace, unique clothing shops, gardening and home decorating stores, antique malls, and importers share space with tiny restaurants and fragrant bakeries.

Located at the north end of Fremont Bridge, the **Fremont** shopping district is known for kitschy boutiques, vintage clothing stores, funky bakeries, and the local Red Hook Brewery. Fremont is a great location to visit for a strong cup of coffee and enjoyable window shopping. Every Sunday during the summer the **Fremont Fair** attracts local artisans and their wares.

Capitol Hill's busy **Broadway** shopping district runs along

Broadway, from E Roy St. to Madison St. Usually teeming with people until late at night, the district has almost as many restaurants, cafes, and bakeries as retail stores. Shops cater to a young and bohemian crowd, with several new and used music stores, bookstores such as the popular Bailey-Coy Books, costume jewelry and bead shops, tattoo and body-piercing parlors, movie theaters, and funky clothing stores.

DEPARTMENT STORES

Nordstrom originated in Seattle, and still dominates the local market for high-end clothing and shoes. However, Seattle offers many alternatives for both home and personal shopping. A few of the largest stores are listed below.

- **The Bon Marche**, located Downtown at 3rd Ave. and Pine St., as well as multiple mall locations, 206-506-6000.
- **Lamonts**, multiple mall locations, 206-367-7690
- **Marshall's**, multiple locations, 206-575-0141
- **Mervyn's**, multiple locations, 206-439-1919
- **Nordstrom**, located Downtown at 500 Pine St., as well as multiple mall locations, 206-628-2111.
- **J.C. Penney**, multiple mall locations, 206-361-2500
- **Sears Roebuck and Co.**, 15711 Aurora Ave. N, 206-364-9000

SPORTING GOODS AND OUTDOOR WEAR STORES

Whether you're heading out of town for a rugged hike or spending an hour at the park with a frisbee, these stores have what you're looking for. Seattle residents take their sports and recreational activities seriously, so there are many places to find just the right equipment.

- **2nd Base** (used), 1101 E Pine St., 206-325-2273
- **Action Athletics**, 5416 Shilshole Ave. NW, 206-781-8301
- **Athletic Supply**, 24 Westlake Ave. N, 206-623-8972
- **Avanti Sports**, 3503 NE 45th St., 206-527-8866
- **Avid Angler Fly Shoppe**, 11714 15th Ave. NE, 206-362-4030
- **Bicycle Center**, 4529 Sandpoint Way NE, 206-523-8300
- **Big 5 Sporting Goods**, 1740 NW Market St., 206-783-0163; 2500 SW Barton St., 206-932-2212; 4315 University Way NE, 206-547-2445

- **Chubby & Tubby,** two locations; 7906 Aurora Ave. N, 206-524-1810; 3333 Rainier Ave. S, 206-723-8800
- **Discount Divers Supply,** 2710 Westlake Ave. N, 206-298-6998
- **Exercise Equipment Center,** 318 Westlake Ave. N, 206-621-8333
- **Fast Lady Sports,** University Village, 206-522-2113
- **Feathered Friends,** 119 Yale Ave. N, 206-292-2210
- **Fiorini Sports,** 4720 University Village Place NE, 206-523-9610
- **Footzone,** 919 E Pine St., 206-329-1466
- **Northwest Outdoor Center on Lake Union,** 2100 Westlake Ave. N, 206-281-9694
- **Niketown,** 1500 6th Ave., 206-447-6453
- **NordicTrack Fitness,** 561 Northgate Mall, 206-361-6700
- **Olympic Sports,** 10700 5th Ave. NE, 206-363-3007
- **Outdoor Emporium,** 420 Pontius Ave. N, 206-624-6550
- **Outdoor & More,** 510 Westlake Ave. N, 206-340-0677
- **Patagonia,** 2100 1st Ave., 206-622-9700
- **Patrick's Fly Shop,** 2237 Eastlake Ave. E, 206-325-8988
- **Performance Bicycle Shop,** 811 NE 45th St., 206-633-3877
- **Play It Again Sports** (used), 901 E Pike St., 206-329-8605
- **Polare,** 2215 Alaskan Way, Pier 66, 206-441-4049
- **Pro Guide & Mountain Supply,** 8954 Aurora Ave. N, 206-528-7515
- **Puetz Golf Centers,** 11762 Aurora Ave. N, 206-362-2272
- **REI** (Recreational Equipment Inc.), 222 Yale Ave. N, 206-223-1944
- **Seattle Athletic & Exercise,** 842 NE Northgate Way, 206-364-5890
- **Second Bounce** (new and used), 513 N 36th St., 206-545-8810
- **Sound Sports,** 80 Madison St., 206-624-6717
- **Sporthaus Schmetzer Inc.,** 12524 Lake City Way NE, 206-365-2161
- **The Sports Junction,** 4519 2 California Ave. SW, 206-938-2555
- **Sports Specialties,** 2319 2nd Ave., 206-441-8412
- **Super Jock 'n Jill,** 7210 E Green Lake Drive N, 206-522-7711
- **Swallows' Nest,** 2308 6th Ave., 206-441-4100
- **Terrasystems Modern Outfitters,** 1335 5th Ave., 206-292-6916
- **Three GI's,** 9037 14th Ave. NW, 206-782-5860
- **Urban Surf,** 2100 N Northlake Way, 206-545-9463
- **Velo Stores,** 1535 11th Ave., 206-325-3292
- **Warshal's Sporting Goods,** 1000 1st Ave., 206-624-7300
- **Wiley's Water Ski Shop,** 1417 S Trenton St., 206-762-1300
- **Winter's Surplus,** 6169 4th Ave. S, 206-763-2722

WAREHOUSE STORES

Warehouse stores now offer good deals on almost everything from clothing and groceries to furniture and appliances. The only caveat is that you often have to buy in bulk so unless you have room for 100 rolls of toilet paper . . . . Both of those listed have membership requirements; call for more details.

- **Costco Wholesale**, 4401 4th Ave. S and other area locations, 206-622-3136
- **Sam's Club**, 13550 Aurora Ave. N, 206-362-6700

FACTORY DISCOUNT STORES AND OUTLET MALLS

In many cases, you can find great bargains in these places, in other cases you may not. Pay attention to price and merchandise quality.

Most of these malls are quite a drive from Seattle, so check the locations on a map or call ahead for directions before you leave the city.

- **Factory Stores of America**, 461 South Fork Ave. SW, North Bend, WA, 425-888-4505
- **Gig Harbor Factory Stores**, 2709 Jahn Ave. NW, Gig Harbor, WA, 360-858-7255
- **SuperMall of the Great Northwest**, 1101 SuperMall Way, Auburn, WA, 253-833-9500

ELECTRONICS

For your stereo, television, cellular phone, and home theater purchases, you'll find a wide variety of electronics stores in Seattle. While J.C. Penney and The Bon Marche no longer have home electronics departments, large department and warehouse stores such as Sears and Costco are worth a visit when shopping around for home audio or video options. One Seattle location well-known for its concentration of electronics stores is just north of the University District on Roosevelt Way NE, between NE Ravenna Blvd. and NE 65th St. Stores in that area and throughout Seattle are listed below.

- **The Audio Connection**, 5621 University Way NE, 206-524-7251
- **Bang & Olufsen**, 412 University St., 206-467-4494

- **Classic Audio,** 7313 Greenwood Ave. N, 206-706-1561
- **Definitive Audio,** 6017 Roosevelt Way NE, 206-524-6633
- **Famous Audio Company,** 517 S Main St., 206-521-9794
- **The Good Guys,** 601 106th Ave. NE, Bellevue, 425-688-0029; 31858 Pacific Hwy. S, Federal Way, 206-839-9740; 19800 44th Ave. W, Lynnwood, 425-640-5514; 300 Andover Park W, Tukwila, 206-575-8000
- **Hawthorne Stereo,** 6303 Roosevelt Way NE, 206-522-9609
- **King Audio,** 4914 Martin Luther King Jr. Way S, 206-723-1204
- **Madison Audio,** 909 Western Ave., 206-292-9262
- **Magnolia Hi-Fi,** 6308 Roosevelt Way NE, 206-525-1961
- **Northwest Radio and TV,** 7000 Greenwood Ave. N, 206-782-7447
- **Radio Shack,** multiple locations, 206-364-8670
- **Rainier Audio,** 2000 23rd Ave. S, 206-329-9229
- **SpeakerLab,** 6220 Roosevelt Way NE, 206-523-2269
- **Stereo Warehouse,** 14915 Aurora Ave. N, 206-365-5622
- **Video Only,** 707 Westlake Ave. N, 206-623-3388

COMPUTERS

There are many options these days for purchasing a computer. Many manufacturers have web sites or 800 numbers that allow you to order a computer from home. Large and small computer dealers abound in any large city, including Seattle. Besides new computers, used PCs are also available. The Yellow Pages have dozens of listings for the Seattle area, only a handful are included here.

NEW COMPUTER VENDORS

- **Adcom Systems,** 8917 Lake City Way NE, 206-524-6828
- **Best Computers,** 3600 Stone Way N, 206-545-4216
- **Boise Technology,** 435 Westlake Ave. N, 206-224-6000
- **CompUSA,** 100 108th St. NE, Bellevue, 425-452-9511; 17400 Southcenter Parkway, Tukwila, 206-575-2922; 6007-A 244th St., SW, Montlake Terrace, 425-744-0165; 12526-A Totem Lake Blvd., Kirkland, 425-820-1600.
- **CompuStar Computers,** 2373 Eastlake Ave. E, 206-329-3840
- **Computer Stop,** 14125 NE 20th St., Bellevue, WA, 425-644-5400
- **The Computer Store,** 815 NE 45th St., 206-522-0220
- **Comprosoft,** 6209 15th Ave. NW, 206-784-8140

- **Office Depot,** 13501 Aurora Ave. N, 206-364-2404; 4900 25th Ave. NE, 206-527-3220; 1751 Airport Way S, 206-587-2582
- **PC Warehouse,** 305 NE 45th St., 206-632-1901
- **University Bookstore Computer and Electronics Center,** 4300 University Way NE, 206-545-4382
- **USConnect,** 601 Union St., 206-224-7690
- **Westwind Computing,** 510 NE 65th St., 206-522-3530

USED COMPUTER VENDORS

- **Computer Renaissance,** 2827 2nd Ave., 206-448-9566
- **Re-PC,** 1565 6th Ave. S, 206-623-9151

HOME FURNISHINGS

A home furnishings store may be one of the first places you'll visit as you try to fill your new home or pad. For a huge selection of reasonably priced contemporary furnishings, check out the IKEA store. Also, many department stores offer a good selection of traditional home furnishings. Call ahead for details.

FURNITURE

- **The Bon Marche,** Downtown at 3rd Ave. and Pine St., as well as multiple mall locations, 206-506-6000
- **Ethan Allen Home Interiors,** 2209 NE Bellevue Redmond Rd., Redmond, 425-641-3133; 4029 200th St. SW, Lynnwood, 425-775-1901; 17333 Southcenter Parkway, Tukwila, 206-575-4366
- **Dania Furniture Collections,** 6416 Roosevelt Way NE, 206-524-9611
- **IKEA Home Furnishings,** 600 SW 43rd, Renton, WA, 800-570-4532
- **Levitz Furniture,** 17601 Southcenter Pkwy., Tukwila, WA, 206-575-0510
- **Miller-Pollard Interiors,** 4741 University Village Plaza NE, 206-527-8478; 4218 E Madison St., 206-325-3600
- **Oak Barn Furniture,** 4918 196th St. SW, Lynnwood, 425-776-0566; 17600 W Valley Hwy., Tukwila, 425-251-9345; 15301 NE 24th St., Bellevue, 425-643-5800
- **Olsen Furniture,** 5354 Ballard Ave. NW, 206-782-6020
- **Ryan's Fine Furniture,** 11306 Lake City Way NE, 206-364-4030
- **Z Gallerie,** 1331 5th Ave., 206-749-9906

BEDS AND BEDDING

- **All About Down,** 352 N 78th St., 206-784-3444
- **Alternative Futon Company,** 400 Minor Ave. N, 206-623-5264
- **Bedrooms & More,** 300 NE 45th St., 206-633-4494
- **Case Littell Furniture,** 8214 Greenwood Ave. N, 206-782-3131
- **Comfort by Akiko,** 705-A E Pike St., 206-328-3173
- **Down Factory,** 3427 4th Ave. S, 206-467-7072
- **Feathered Friends,** 1415 10th Ave., 206-328-0887
- **Futon of North America,** 970 Denny Way, 206-625-9663; 3409 Stone Way N, 206-634-0630; 1716 E Olive Way, 206-328-0338; 4700 University Way NE, 206-522-5202
- **Mattress World,** 8300 Aurora Ave. N, 206-522-7433
- **McKinnon Furniture,** 1015 Western Ave., 206-622-6474
- **Scandia Down,** 129 Bellevue Square, Bellevue, 425-455-5535
- **Sleep Country USA,** multiple locations, 800-99SUNNY
- **Sleep Train,** 809 NE Northgate Way, 206-364-8150; 16830 Southcenter Parkway, Tukwila, 206-575-0205
- **Soaring Heart Futon & Natural Bed Company,** 101 Nickerson St. Suite 400, 206-282-1717
- **The Well Made Bed,** 2671 N University Village Mall, 206-523-8407

CARPETS AND RUGS

If you're looking for an Oriental rug, a fun place to begin your search is in the many galleries and shops in the Pioneer Square area of Downtown.

- **ABC Carpet Company,** 1110 19th Ave. E, 206-323-8567
- **Aladdin Rug Collection,** 202 1st Ave. S, 206-622-7777
- **Besaw Store of Floors,** 2600 California Ave. SW, 206-937-7516
- **Birdim Turkish Rugs & Kilims,** 7321 Greenwood Ave. N, 206-782-9205
- **Caravan Carpets,** 3500 Fremont Ave. N, 206-547-0449
- **Carpet Exchange,** 1251 1st Ave. S, 206-624-7800
- **Carpet World,** 920 NW Leary Way, 206-782-4856
- **The Color Store,** 1122 E Madison St., 206-328-3908
- **Color Tile & Carpet,** 2710 1st Ave. S, 206-622-3880
- **Consolidated Carpet,** 200 N 85th St., 206-789-7737; 11724 Lake City Way NE, 206-440-8609
- **Decker Brothers Interiors,** 4435 California Ave. SW, 206-937-7707

- **Nielsen Brothers Carpets and Flooring**, 2031 NW 56th St., 206-783-3040
- **Pande Cameron**, 815 Pine St., 206-624-6263
- **Pitcher Brothers House of Carpets**, 5034 University Way NE, 206-522-4611
- **Ravenna Interiors**, 2251 NE 65th St., 206-525-5794
- **Terry Bue Gallery**, 2100 N 45th St., 206-633-3134
- **Yam Oriental Rugs**, 78 S Washington St., 206-622-2439

HOUSEWARES (GENERAL)

- **City People's Mercantile**, 500 15th Ave. E, 206-324-9510; 3517 Fremont Ave. N, 206-632-1200; 5400 Sandpoint Way NE, 206-524-1200
- **Cost Plus Imports**, 2103 Western Ave., 206-443-1055
- **Eddie Bauer Home Store**, 1330 5th Ave., 206-622-2766; University Village, 206-527-2646
- **Pier 1 Imports**, Pier 70, 206-448-4072; 4345 University Way NE, 206-545-7397
- **Pottery Barn**, 1420 5th Ave., 206-682-9312; University Village, 206-522-6860
- **Restoration Hardware**, University Village, 206-522-2775
- **Sur La Table**, 84 Pine St., 206-448-2244
- **The Mrs. Cooks**, University Village, 206-525-5008
- **Williams Sonoma**, 400 Pine St., 206-624-1422

LAMPS AND LIGHTING

Many hardware and department stores also stock a wide selection of lamps and lighting fixtures. The Bon Marche, Eagle Hardware, and Home Depot are worth a visit when looking for contemporary lighting options.

- **Antique Lighting Company**, 1000 Lenora St. Suite 314, 206-622-8298
- **Bogart, Bremmer, & Bradley Antiques**, 8000 15th Ave. NW, 206-783-7333
- **Hansen Lamp and Shades**, 6510 Phinney Ave. N, 206-783-6859
- **Harold's Lamps and Shades**, 1912 N 45th St., 206-633-2557
- **Highlights**, 999 Western Ave., 206-382-9667
- **Lighting Supply, Inc.**, 2729 2nd Ave., 206-441-5075

- **Seattle Lighting**, 222 2nd Ave. S, 206-622-4736

HARDWARE STORES

For paint and wallpaper, and anything else you might need to make your new house "home," the following list might be useful.

- **City People's Mercantile**, 500 15th Ave. E, 206-324-9510; 3517 Fremont Ave. N, 206-632-1200; 5400 Sandpoint Way NE, 206-524-1200
- **Chubby & Tubby**, 7906 Aurora Ave. N, 206-524-1810; 3333 Rainier Ave. S, 206-723-8800
- **Crawford-Waage Ace Hardware**, 2217 3rd Ave., 206-441-4393
- **Eagle Hardware and Garden**, 12525 Aurora Ave. N, 206-366-0365; 2700 Rainier Ave. S, 206-760-0832
- **Five Corners True Value Hardware**, 305 W McGraw St., 206-282-5000
- **The Home Depot**, 2759 Utah Ave. S, 206-467-9200
- **Junction True Value Hardware**, 4747 44th Ave. SW, 206-932-0450
- **Madison Park True Value Hardware**, 1837 42nd Ave. E, 206-322-5331
- **Magnolia Ace Hardware**, 2420 32nd Ave. W, 206-282-0055
- **RR Hardware**, 6512 15th Ave. NE, 206-522-7810
- **Stephenson Ace Hardware**, 9000 Roosevelt Way NE, 206-522-3324
- **Stewart Lumber & Hardware**, 1761 Rainier Ave. S, 206-324-5000
- **Stoneway Hardware and Supply**, 4318 Stone Way N, 206-545-6910
- **Tweedy & Pop Ace Hardware**, 1916 N 45th St., 206-632-2290
- **University True Value Hardware**, 4731 University Way NE, 206-523-5353
- **Welch True Value Hardware**, 2211 S Jackson St., 206-322-1306
- **Winkelman True Value Hardware**, 14401 Greenwood Ave. N, 206-363-7211

SECOND HAND SHOPPING

A favorite Seattle past-time. What better way to spend a drizzly afternoon than digging for treasures that cost only pennies?

THRIFT STORES

- **Chicken Soup Brigade Thrift Store**, 1508 11th Ave., 206-329-4563
- **Children's Hospital Thrift Store**, 2026 3rd Ave., 206-448-7609
- **Shop and Save**, 1425 NW Market St., 206-781-0641
- **Value Village**, 8700 15th Ave. NW, 206-783-4648; 12548 Lake City Way NE, 206-365-8232; 1525 11th Ave., 206-322-7789

ANTIQUE STORES

Don't forget about antique and vintage furniture, lamps, and fixtures when shopping for your home. In many cases the quality and craftsmanship of an antique will more than match that of a contemporary piece of furniture. There are many antique and vintage stores in the Seattle area, particularly near the Pike Place Market and in the Greenwood, Ballard, and Fremont neighborhoods. Several small towns beyond the city limits, most notably Duvall, Monroe, and Snohomish, are also known for their many antique stores.

A few of Seattle's antique stores and malls are listed below. Also, check the Sunday newspapers for estate sales or auctions. Most are open to the public, some also hold previews so you can judge whether to arrive early for the sale or auction.

- **Antiques at Pike Place**, 92 Stewart St., 206-441-9643
- **Bogart, Bremmer, & Bradley Antiques**, 8000 15th Ave. NW, 206-783-7333
- **The Downtown Antique Market**, 2218 Western Ave., 206-448-6307
- **Fremont Antique Mall**, 3419 Fremont Place N, 206-548-9140
- **Greenwood Antique Mall**, 8414 Greenwood Ave. N, 206-297-1904
- **Market Street Antique Mall**, 2026 NW Market St., 206-782-1125
- **Pelayo Antiques**, 7601 Greenwood Ave. N, 206-789-1999; 8421 Greenwood Ave. N, 206-789-1333

FOOD

If you enjoy eating out, one of the first things you'll want to do when you arrive in Seattle is begin to explore your dining options. Seattle is well-known for having a large number of eateries, ranging from greasy spoons to sophisticated seafood restaurants. Every neighborhood in Seattle has at least one espresso stand, a cafe or bakery, and a local pub or micro-brewery. Ask around, check in the local newspapers for reviews or get a copy of *Zagat's Seattle Restaurant Survey* (see **A Seattle Reading List**) for recommendations. Restaurants are not profiled in this book, but the following information will help you find just the right ingredients for cooking at home.

GROCERY STORES

All of the large grocery stores in the city are open 24 hours a day, and most feature well-stocked delis and on-site bakeries. The current trend in the new and remodeled stores is to offer in-house floral sections, espresso stands, and take-out food counters with sandwiches, salads and hot entrees. Many have adjoining businesses such as bakery, bagel, or coffee shops, and small bank branches. **QFC, Safeway, Larry's Market, Thriftway,** and **Albertson's** each have several locations throughout the city. QFC stores are known for their high quality produce; Safeway for having in-store pharmacies; Larry's for their well-stocked wine selections and knowledgeable wine stewards; Thriftway and Albertson's for their smaller stores that lend a more personal touch.

Two warehouse stores in the Seattle area offer excellent deals on bulk foods as well as other household items. These are **Costco, 206-622-3136,** and **Sam's Club, 206-362-6700.** Both have membership requirements, call ahead for details.

Another grocery shopping option is the food cooperative. Seattle's largest is **PCC** (Puget Consumers Co-Op), with seven neighborhood stores in the city. PCC Natural Markets offer a wide selection of natural and organic foods. Call ahead (206-547-1222) or stop by any location for membership information.

FARMERS' MARKETS

If you're searching for the highest quality in fruits, vegetables, or berries, your best bet is to buy right from the growers. During the summer, you can often find corn, cherries, raspberries, strawberries, apples and peaches being sold from truck beds on city street corners. For a bigger selection, try one of the farmers' markets in Seattle. The largest is **Pike Place Market,** in Downtown Seattle at the west end of Pike St. Don't be fooled by the fact that Pike Place is a popular tourist attraction; it is also a year-round destination for locals in search of fresh produce — a succulent nectarine, perfect tomato or flavorful Walla Walla sweet onion. You can also find fresh fish and shellfish, homemade jams, jellies and honey, and brilliantly colored tulips, daffodils, and dahlias. Other local farmers' markets are open during the spring and summer in Seattle neighborhoods as well, including the Fremont and Capitol Hill Farmers' Markets. These markets are usually open on the weekends only, but like Pike Place they offer fresh produce from local farmers and arts and crafts from area artists.

ETHNIC MARKETS

Small grocery stores specializing in delicacies from other parts of world are scattered throughout the Seattle area. Immigrants and natives alike are attracted to these unique stores making some of them very popular. Below are a few that you can visit to find specific ethnic foods, but there are many others in addition to those listed here.

AFRICAN
- **East African Grocery and Deli**, 2205 E Union St., 206-860-8211
- **Kilimanjaro Market**, 12519 Lake City Way NE, 206-440-1440

ASIAN
- **An Dong Market**, 206 12th Ave. S, 206-328-0060
- **Asia Market**, 9615 15th Ave. SW, 206-762-8658
- **Center Oriental Grocery**, 9641 15th Ave. SW, 206-762-5620
- **Foulee Market**, 2050 S Columbian Way, 206-764-9607
- **Hop Thanh Supermarket**, 1043 S Jackson St., 206-322-7473
- **Phnom Penh Market**, 7123 Martin Luther King Jr. Way S, 206-723-4341
- **Uwajimaya**, 519 6th Ave. S, 206-624-6248
- **Vientian Asian Grocery**, 6059 Martin Luther King Jr. Way S, 206-723-3160
- **Viet Hoa Market**, 676 S Jackson St., 206-621-8499
- **Viet Wah Supermarket**, 1032 S Jackson St., 206-329-1399

GREEK-MIDDLE EASTERN
- **Aladdin Gyro-Cery**, 4139 University Way NE, 206-632-5253

INDIAN-PAKISTANI
- **Pakistani and Indian Grocery**, 12325 Roosevelt Way NE, 206-368-7323

SPANISH-MEXICAN-LATIN AMERICAN
- **El Mercado Latino**, 1514 Pike Pl., 206-623-3240
- **La Bodeguita Specialty Foods**, 2528A Beacon Ave. S, 206-329-9001

TAKEOUT MEALS

If you're tired after a long day of work and prefer to eat in without the hassle of cooking, consider picking up some food to go. Nearly all restaurants offer take-out, as well as some local grocery stores and specialty foods shops. Most of the chain grocery stores, particularly Larry's Market and QFC, have a wide selection of take-out meals. Here are some other places to consider:

- **Komen's Live Market**, 3701 NE 45th St., 206-343-LIVE
- **Pasta & Co.**, 1001 4th Ave. Plaza, 206-624-3008; 2109 Queen Anne Ave. N, 206-283-1182; 815 Pike St., 206-322-4577; University Village, 206-523-8594

DRINKING WATER

Most Seattle residents drink plain tap water, though some use a simple home filtering system, such as a Brita water pitcher. For those less trusting souls, there are several companies that will deliver drinking water to your home or business. Here are just a few:

- **Cascade Water**, 206-935-4088
- **Cullyspring Water Co.**, 206-722-6500
- **Mountain Mist Water Co.**, 800-232-7332
- **Pure Water Corporation**, 206-763-7873

Seattle isn't just a mecca for alternative rock and its fans, but also for art, classical music, opera, comedy, and theater lovers. It's really no mystery why residents flock to film openings, live theater, traveling Broadway shows, even literary readings — months of inclement winter weather guarantees large audiences for most performances, and in the summer, entertainers simply move to the enticing outdoors. Concerts are held in local parks, on the Waterfront, and at "The Gorge," a huge amphitheater in the Columbia River gorge which attracts big names in contemporary and classic rock, blues, and jazz. Several summer festivals also feature fabulous musical and theatrical performances; see **A Seattle Year** for more details.

Like nearly every major city in the U.S., tickets to most shows in Seattle can be purchased through Ticketmaster at 206-628-0888 or online at www.ticketmaster.com. For especially popular events, such as rock concerts and professional sports playoffs, you may have no choice but to buy from Ticketmaster. For many events and performances, however, you can often avoid paying the extra Ticketmaster fees (which add up) by purchasing tickets directly at the event venue's box office.

CLASSICAL MUSIC, COMMUNITY CHOIRS, AND SYMPHONIES

- **Seattle Symphony,** 200 University Street, 206-215-4747
  The symphony presents weekly performances September through June in the new, $118 million Benaroya Hall. This accoustic masterpiece with seating for 2500 should enhance the group's popularity.

- **Northwest Chamber Orchestra,** 1305 4th Ave. Suite 522, 206-343-0445
  The area's only professional chamber orchestra, the group presents

performances of contemporary and classical works, September through May.

- **Seattle Men's Chorus**, 319 12th Ave., 206-323-0750
A popular local choir, representing Seattle's large gay community, the Seattle Men's Chorus is well-known for its raffish and entertaining performances. A wonderful place to catch the group is at Bumbershoot, a music and arts festival held at the Seattle Center over Labor Day weekend. They also present several regular and charity shows each year.

DANCE

- **Pacific Northwest Ballet (PNB)**, Seattle Opera House, Seattle Center, 206-441-9411
The Pacific Northwest Ballet presents six programs September through June, including several performances of short contemporary works and one or two longer traditional pieces. The annual Christmas show is a beloved version of the Nutcracker, featuring sets designed by author and illustrator Maurice Sendak.

OPERA

- **Seattle Opera**, Seattle Opera House, Seattle Center, 206-389-7600
World renowned, the Seattle Opera features five productions from August to May, as well as a bi-yearly summer presentation of The Ring cycle by Wagner. A typical season will include several traditional performances of popular operas, as well as contemporary works or a fresh take on an old standard. The opera routinely attracts international stars for lead roles, and longtime patrons recognize the local performers filling out each performance.

THEATER

Somehow Seattle seems to maintain the minimum number of season ticket subscribers necessary to support the many local theatrical companies, but you'll find that this is really a city of last-minute ticket buyers. Even the most popular shows may not sell out until the day of the performance. It's usually in your best interest to call ahead, however. In most

cases there is little difference in price between tickets to one or two performances or to the whole season — something you'll probably want to
know before the season is half over.

- **A Contemporary Theater (ACT),** 700 Union St., 206-292-7676
  Referred to as "ACT theater" or "the CT" by loyal audiences, A
  Contemporary Theater presents contemporary works by both estab-
  lished and little-known playwrights.

- **Bathhouse Theater,** 7312 West Green Lake Dr. N, 206-524-9108
  Located on Green Lake in a cozy brick building which used to serve
  as the lake's bathhouse (hence the name), the theater produces
  classic shows with a good dose of humor. Now in its 28th season,
  the theater is noted for its annual Shakespeare play, often an updat-
  ed or musical version of the classic.

- **Empty Space Theater,** 3509 Fremont Ave. N, 206-547-7500
  Situated on the top floor of a building in the center of the Fremont
  neighborhood, the Empty Space Theater has been producing contemporary shows in Seattle for over 25 years. The Empty Space is a
  favorite of Seattle theater-goers, who enjoy the boisterous comedies
  and cutting edge dramas performed (and often written) by talented
  local players.

- **Intiman Theater,** Playhouse, Seattle Center, 206-269-1900
  The Intiman Theater, once considered the poor cousin to the nearby
  Seattle Repertory Theater (also at the Seattle Center), has really come
  into its own in recent years. Presenting a variety of modern and classic works, the Intiman addresses contemporary issues with ambitious
  and dynamic interpretations of new and established plays.

- **Paramount Theater,** 911 Pine St., 206-682-1414
  The recently refurbished Paramount Theater hosts travelling productions of Broadway shows, as well as some concerts and special
  charitable functions. The plush lobby and ornate performance hall
  make this an elegant venue for any play or musical.

- **Seattle Children's Theater,** Charlotte Martin Theater, Seattle
  Center, 206-441-3322
  Seattle Children's Theater offers six productions each season, plus

school matinees and two school touring productions. The season runs from September to June.

- **Seattle Repertory Theater,** Bagley Wright Theater, Seattle Center, 206-443-2222
  Perhaps Seattle's best-known theater, "The Rep" presents an eclectic mix of classical and contemporary plays each season, from October to April. The theater often performs plays that have recently completed successful Broadway runs, but never hosts touring shows. In addition, the Rep premiers new works by contemporary playwrights.

- **The 5th Avenue Theater,** 1326 5th Ave., 206-625-1900
  Like the Paramount Theater, The 5th Avenue hosts travelling productions of major Broadway shows, as well as some concerts. The performance hall is exquisitely decorated with Oriental style carvings and opulent fabrics.

- **The Group Theater,** Center House, Seattle Center, 206-441-1299
  For over 20 years, The Group Theater has presented multi-cultural theater for the local community, including its traditional holiday presentation of "Voices of Christmas."

IMPROVISATIONAL THEATER

A combination of stand-up comedy and acting, improvisational theater uses audience suggestions to create a scene, which is then usually played for laughs. Most improv groups perform only on the weekends; make sure you call ahead as times and locations change.

- **Jet City Improv,** 3940 Brooklyn Ave. NE, 206-781-3879
- **TheatreSports,** 1428 Post Alley, 206-781-9273

COMEDY CLUBS

Although there are only a few comedy clubs in Seattle, those listed attract nationally known comics to the city.
- **Comedy Underground,** 222 S Main St., 206-628-0303

- **Giggles Comedy Nite Club**, 5220 Roosevelt Way NE, 206-526-JOKE

CONTEMPORARY MUSIC

Seattle burst on the national music scene several years ago as the home of "Grunge" rock. Bands like Pearl Jam, Soundgarden, Alice In Chains, and Nirvana may have put the city on the map for alternative music, but many other music genres thrive in Seattle. The following bars, clubs, and concert halls are best known for the category under which they are listed, but many book a variety of acts. Check out *The Rocket* or *The Stranger* — both free local newspapers that can be found in bars, cafes, and music stores — to find out which bands will be playing each venue.

BLUES AND FOLK
- **Fiddler's Inn.** 9219 35th Ave. NE, 206-525-0752
- **Larry's Greenfront**, 209 1st Ave. S, 206-624-7665
- **The Latona**, 6423 Latona Ave. NE, 206-525-2238
- **New Orleans**, 114 1st Ave. S, 206-622-2563
- **Old Timer's Café**, 620 1st Ave. S, 206-623-9800

COUNTRY
- **Sylvia's Little Red Hen**, 7115 Woodlawn Ave. NE, 206-522-1168

IRISH AND CELTIC
- **The Dubliner Pub**, 3405 Fremont Ave. N, 206-548-1508
- **Kells**, 1916 Post Alley, 206-768-728-1916
- **The Owl 'n Thistle**, 808 Post Ave., 206-621-7777

JAZZ
- **Dimitrou's Jazz Alley**, 2033 6th Ave., 206-441-3303
- **Paragon Bar and Grill**, 2125 Queen Anne Ave. N, 206-283-4548
- **The Pink Door**, 1919 Post Alley, 206-443-3241
- **Tula's Restaurant and Bar**, 2214 2nd Ave., 206-443-4221

REGGAE
- **Bohemian Café**, 111 Yesler Way, 206-447-1514

ROCK AND ALTERNATIVE
- **Ballard Firehouse**, 5429 Russell Ave. NW, 206-784-3516
- **Central Saloon**, 207 1st Ave. S, 206-622-0209

- **Crocodile Café,** 2200 2nd Ave., 206-441-5611
- **Doc Maynard's,** 610 1st Ave., 206-682-4649
- **Fenix and Fenix Underground,** 315-323 2nd Ave. S, 206-467-1111
- **The Highliner,** 1735 W Thurman St., 206-283-2233
- **OK Hotel,** 212 Alaskan Way S, 206-621-7903
- **RKCNDY,** 1812 Yale St., (no phone number)
- **Showbox,** 1426 1st Ave., 206-628-3151

NIGHTCLUBS AND DISCOS

- **Down Under,** 2407 1st Ave., 206-728-4053
- **Machine Werks,** 112 5th Ave., 206-441-0715
- **Neighbors,** 1509 Broadway, 206-324-5358
- **Re-Bar,** 1114 Howell St., 206-233-9873
- **Squish,** 722 E Pike St., 206-322-4024
- **Vogue,** 2018 1st Ave., 206-443-0673

MUSEUMS

What better activity to do on a rainy day than stroll through the quiet (and dry) halls of a fine museum? While some believe there could certainly be a few more museums in Seattle, those already here offer interesting and diverse exhibits. Many of the museums host travelling exhibits, so call ahead to find out the latest and to check about days and hours of operation — for example, several museums are closed on Monday.

- **Burke Museum,** University of Washington campus, near the intersection of NE 45th St. and 17th Ave. NE, 206-543-5590
  The Thomas Burke museum houses fascinating exhibits on Pacific Rim geology, natural history, and anthropology. Native American artifacts, including masks, beads, and totem poles, and displays of dinosaur skeletons and fossils are especially popular with children. Open seven days a week, 10-5, Thursdays until 8 p.m. General admission is $5.50, $2.50 for students, and children five and under are free.

- **Coast Guard Museum of the Northwest,** Pier 36, 1519 Alaskan Way S, 206-217-6993
  Coast Guard memorabilia, photographs, model ships, and other

nautical items are on display at this museum. Tours of Coast Guard cutters are available on the weekends. Open Monday, Wednesday, Friday, Saturday, Sunday, 1-5. No admission charged.

- **Frye Art Museum,** 704 Terry Ave., 206-622-9250
  Located on First Hill in an International Style building designed in 1952 by Paul Thiry, the Frye Art Museum houses a collection of 19th century paintings by European artists, as well as a large collection of works by 18th century German artists. Open Tuesday, Wednesday, Friday, Saturday 10-5; Thursday 10-9; and Sunday 12-5. No admission charged.

- **Henry Art Gallery,** University of Washington campus, near the intersection of 15th Ave NE and NE 41st St., 206-543-2280
  The 19th century and early 20th century American and European collection originally donated by local businessman Horace C. Henry is still the backbone of this museum's collection. Housed in a recently renovated brick Tudor designed by Carl Gould, it provides a pleasant respite from the bustle of the city. Hours of operation are Tuesday - Sunday, 11-5, Thursday until 8 p.m. General admission is $5.00, $3.50 for seniors, and no charge for students. Thursday evenings, 5-8 p.m., are free.

- **Museum of Flight,** 9404 E Marginal Way S, 206-764-5720
  Located on the original site of the Boeing Company, the museum presents a complete history of flight and aviation technology. This is a great museum for kids and adults alike, with interactive exhibits, archival film footage, colorful full-scale reproductions of some of Boeing's first airplanes, including early bi-planes and military jets, hanging from the ceiling. The Red Barn, which housed the first Boeing airplane factory, is also part of the exhibit. Open daily from 10-5, Thursdays until 9 p.m. General admission is $9.00, $7.00 for seniors, $4.00 for children ages 5-17, and free for those 4 and under. The first Thursday evening of the month (5-9 p.m.) is free for everyone.

- **Museum of History and Industry,** 2700 24th Ave. E, 206-324-1126
  Local Northwest history is presented in this museum near the University of Washington. A popular museum with children, exhibits include old-fashioned fire engines, model ships, and figureheads. History buffs will enjoy the large collection of archival photographs and the many artifacts of Seattle's fishing, lumber, and shipping

industries. Hours are Saturday and Sunday, 10-5; Tuesday through Friday, 11-5; closed Mondays. Admission charges range from $5.50 for adults down to $1.00 for 2-5 year olds.

- **Nordic Heritage Museum**, 3014 NW 67th St., 206-789-5707
  This museum chronicles the history of the Scandinavian immigrants who settled in the Ballard neighborhood and other areas of the Pacific Northwest. The museum also helps keep Nordic heritage strong in the Ballard community by providing traditional dance and language classes, by showcasing Scandinavian films, hosting lectures, and by sponsoring the popular neighborhood Scandinavian festivals. Hours of operation are Tuesday through Saturday, 10-4; Sunday, 12-4; closed Mondays. Admission charges range from $4.00 for adults down to $2.00 for students, K-12.

- **Pacific Science Center**, Seattle Center, 206-443-2001
  Not your traditional museum by any means, the Pacific Science Center has over 200 interactive exhibits on science and nature. Children in particular enjoy the hands-on activities, which approach learning in fun and creative ways. Open daily from 10-6. General admission ranges from $7.50 for adults down to no charge for those under two.

- **Seattle Art Museum (SAM)**, 100 University St., 206-654-3100
  Located near the Pike Place Market, the Seattle Art Museum houses an exceptional art collection, which includes a variety of African, Chinese, and Native American pieces as well as European and American art. SAM is Seattle's preeminent art museum, showcasing international travelling exhibits of photography, painting, and sculpture. Open Tuesday - Sunday, 10-5, Thursday until 9 p.m. Suggested admission for adults is $6.00, $4.00 for seniors and students, and those 12 and under are admitted free. The first Thursday of the month admission is free.

- **Seattle Asian Art Museum**, 1400 E Prospect St., 206-654-3100
  Housed in a 1933 Art Deco building designed by Carl Gould, and previously occupied by the Seattle Art Museum, this gallery presents art from Japan, China, Southeast Asia, Korea, and India. The museum is a focal point of Volunteer Park, located at the northeast corner of Capitol Hill. Open Tuesday - Sunday, 10-5, Thursday until 9 p.m. Suggested admission for adults is $6.00, $4.00 for seniors and stu-

dents, and those 12 and under are admitted free. The first Thursday of the month admission is free.

- **Seattle Children's Museum**, Center House, Seattle Center, 206-441-1768
  Intended for children ages 1-8, this delightful interactive museum also presents special multi-cultural programs on the lower level of the Center House. Open Monday - Friday, 10-5, Saturday and Sunday, 10-6. Admission is $5.50, ages 1-12, and $4.00 for adults.

- **Wing Luke Asian Museum**, 407 7th Ave. S, 206-623-5124
  Housed in a converted garage in the historic International District, the nationally-recognized Wing Luke Asian Museum showcases pan-Asian culture, history and art. Open Tuesday through Friday, 11-4:30, Saturday and Sunday, Noon-4.

ART GALLERIES

On the first Thursday of every month, Pioneer Square art galleries stay open late in the evening for what locals call the "gallery walks." This can be a great way to see the exhibits without fighting daytime traffic and crowds. Call ahead for hours and showings or look in the local newspapers for weekly reviews. Listed below are some of the galleries in Downtown Seattle:

- **Benham Studio/Gallery**, 1216 1st Ave., 206-622-2480
- **Linda Cannon Gallery**, 617 Western Ave., 206-233-0404
- **Center on Contemporary Art**, 65 Cedar St., 206-728-1980
- **Davidson Galleries**, 313 Occidental Ave. S, 206-624-7684
- **Foster/White Gallery**, 3112 Occidental Ave. S, 206-622-2833
- **G. Gibson Gallery**, 122 S Jackson St. Suite 200, 206-587-4033
- **Gallery Magna**, 310 Occidental Ave. S, 206-223-9563
- **Grover/Thurston Gallery**, 309 Occidental Ave. S, 206-223-0816
- **Lisa Harris Gallery**, 410 Occidental Ave. S, 206-624-3315
- **Linda Hodges Gallery**, 410 Occidental Ave. S, 206-624-3034
- **Kimzey Miller Gallery**, 1225 2nd Ave., 206-682-2339
- **Greg Kucera**, 608 2nd Ave., 206-624-0770
- **Lead Gallery & Wine Bar**, 1022 First Ave., 206-623-6240
- **Kurt Lidtke Gallery**, 318 2nd Ave. S, 206-622-5082
- **Meyerson & Nowinski**, 123 S Jackson St., 206-223-1700

- **Robbie Mildred Gallery,** 207 Harvard Ave. E, 206-325-5228
- **Milky World Gallery,** 111 Battery St., 206-374-0933
- **Jeffrey Moose Gallery,** 1333 5th Ave., 206-467-6951
- **Bryan Ohno Gallery,** 155 S Main St., 206-667-9572
- **Seafirst Gallery,** 701 5th Ave., 206-585-3200
- **Soil,** 82 University St., 206-623-5950
- **William Traver Gallery,** 110 Union St., 206-587-6501
- **Donald Young Gallery,** 1103 E Pike St., 206-860-1651

LITERARY LIFE

Seattle, with it's many rainy days and coffee worship, is a great bookstore town. It's no surprise then that area residents flock to fiction and poetry readings and myriad book-signings and events. Seattle is even home to that bookstore without any shelves, amazon.com.

The Seattle Weekly and *The Stranger* have listings of upcoming readings and author signings or you can call your local bookstore for their calendar of events.

- **B. Dalton Bookseller,** Northgate Mall, 206-364-5810
- **Bailey-Coy Books,** 414 Broadway E, 206-323-8842
- **Barnes & Noble** ,600 Pine St., 206-264-0156; 2700 NE University Village, 206-517-4107; 300 Andover Park W, 206-575-3965
- **Beks Bookstore,** 1201 3rd Ave., 206-224-7028; Rainier Square, 206-624-1328
- **Benjamin Books,** SeaTac Airport, 206-241-5920
- **Borders Books & Music,** 1501 4th Ave., 206-622-4599
- **Brentano's Bookstore,** Westlake Mall, 206-467-9626
- **City Books,** 1305 Madison St., 206-682-4334
- **DeGraff Books,** 98 Union St., 206-621-0535
- **The Elliott Bay Book Company,** 1st Ave. S and S Main St., 206-682-6600
- **Fremont Place Book Company,** 621 N 35th St., 206-547-5970
- **Liberty Book Company,** 10338 Aurora Ave., N, 206-523-1227
- **M. Coy Books,** 117 Pine St., 206-623-5354
- **Madison Park Books,** 4105 E Madison St., 206-328-7323
- **Magnolia's Bookstore,** 3206 W McGraw St., 206-283-1062
- **Queen Anne Avenue Books,** 1629 Queen Anne Ave., N, 206-283-5624

- **Seattle University Book Store**, Seattle University,1108 E. Columbia St., 206-296-5820
- **Second Story Books**, 1815 N 45th St., 206-547-4605
- **Square One Books**, 4724 42nd Ave., SW, 206-935-5764
- **Third Place Books**, 17171 Bothell Way (Lake Forest Park Towne Centre), 206-366-3333
- **Tower Books**, 20 Mercer St., 206-283-6333
- **University Bookstore,** 4326 University Way NE, 206-634-3400; 4th and University, 206-545-923
- **Waldenbooks,** Northgate Mall, 206-365-2923
- **Wit's End Bookstore,** 770 N 34th St., 206-547-2330

S eattle's landscape is the result of various geologic forces; the hills and mountains created by shifting plates far beneath the earth's surface, the lakes and waterways carved out by a great system of glaciers and several ice ages. Add to this a rainy climate broken almost daily by bright sunlight, and throw in lush indigenous evergreens and colorful rhododendrons, and it is no wonder that Seattle residents spend so much time outdoors. The city's park system, which includes many lakes, provides abundant opportunities for enjoying the area's natural beauty.

Most of Seattle's park system was designed in 1903 by J.C. Olmsted, son of Frederick Law Olmsted who planned New York's City's Central Park and many of the great urban parks across the country. Olmsted was hired by the Seattle park board to design a boulevard system that would link much of the city's park land, which had been purchased between 1897 and 1903. The result is impressive with approximately 20 miles of winding parkway, connecting many of Seattle's major greenspaces. The following is a brief description of the area's most popular parks, although in addition to those listed here, many neighborhoods also have small parks, athletic fields, and playgrounds. To get more information on any of the parks listed here, call the **Seattle Parks and Recreation Department** at 206-684-4075.

Seward Park, in the southeast corner of Seattle, is located on the 277-acre Bailey Peninsula. In addition to a beach and original bathhouse, the park has a system of nature trails perfect for solitary walks or bird-watching (bald eagles are occasionally sighted here). The 1920s bathhouse now serves as an artists' studio, offering a variety of ceramics classes for adults and children; call 206-722-6342 for class availability. From here, a narrow greenbelt follows Lake Washington Blvd. north to **Mount Baker Park**, near the site of the SeaFair hydroplane races which take place each August. The **Mount Baker Rowing and Sailing Center**

hosts beginning rowing and sailing classes, and is home to both an adult and a high school crew team. Call the center at 206-386-1913 for details. Further north along the lake shore, **Leschi Park** offers summer swimming and year-long views of the colorful boats in the marina, while nearby **Madrona Park** provides stunning views of the lake from a sandy beach. Several miles north, **Madison Park** is located on Lake Washington at the far east end of Madison St. Though not a part of the Olmsted plan, it originated in the 1890s as the site of a summer amusement park. Today it is a popular sunny day hang-out, offering the perennial summer favorites of picnicking, swimming, and sunbathing.

West along Madison Ave., the **Washington Park Arboretum** picks up the Olmsted planned parkway in Madrona. The Arboretum is a 255-acre woodland, managed by the University of Washington. Though it was a part of the Seattle park system as early as 1904, it was developed by the university as an arboretum in 1936. Originally filled with native Northwest plants and trees, today the Washington Park Arboretum is home to more than 5,500 flowers, trees, and shrubs from all over the world. It includes the beautifully sculptured **Japanese Tea Garden**, designed in 1960 by Japanese architect Juki Iida, and at the north end of the Arboretum, the **Museum of History and Industry** hosts fascinating exhibits of Seattle's industrial history and maritime heritage.

Crossing the Montlake Bridge, the Olmsted parkway cuts a path through the UW campus and continues to **Ravenna Park**, which follows a steep ravine northwest to **Cowen Park** and then **Green Lake**. Green Lake is perhaps Seattle's most popular public park. It is surrounded by almost three miles of paved walkway, attracting bicyclists, in-line skaters, runners, and strolling couples. In Seattle, where locals are undaunted by drizzle and early winter darkness, Green Lake has become a year-round mecca for early morning and late evening walkers and joggers. During the summer, fields at the east side of the lake fill with volleyball teams, the basketball courts host informal but competitive pick-up games, and in-line skaters can be found playing hockey in the drained kiddie pool. The Seattle Parks Department's **Green Lake Small Craft Center** (206-684-4074) sponsors boating classes for novice sailors at the south end of Green Lake, and beginning wind-surfers set sail from the eastern shore. Another Seattle tradition, the annual SeaFair Milk Carton Derby, launches from the shore each July, and there are many other events held on Green Lake throughout the year. At the south end of Green Lake, **Woodland Park** offers tennis courts, lawn bowling, and grassy picnic areas, as well as the **Woodland Park Zoo**, a seasonal favorite of adults and kids alike. One particularly popular program is the Bird of Prey program, where kids delight in watching trained Raptors in flight. Small children enjoy the petting zoo, and pony rides which are available during the summer. The zoo is located in the Phinney Ridge neighborhood, at Phinney Ave. N and N 50th St., call 206-684-4800 for hours. Also worth a visit is the spectacular **Rose Garden**, just outside of the zoo's south gate, call 206-684-4863 for details and special events information.

Discovery Park, on the western point of Magnolia, is the largest of the Olmsted-designed parks. With over 500 acres of wooded trails and flowery meadows, towering sea cliffs and windy beaches, everyone can find something to do at this park. Visit in the evening to watch the sun set over the Olympics, or come during the day for a pleasant hike down to the beach. Clay cliffs overhang the rocky beach, providing hours of fun for kids. Nearby quiet meadows are great places for picnics or impromptu bird-watching. You may see bald eagles, hawks, falcons, or even an osprey. From the beach you may catch sight of migrating seabirds, and views of the **West Point Lighthouse**. The **Daybreak Star Cultural Center**, in the center of the park, celebrates Native American culture with art exhibits and special programs. Call 206-285-4425 for details.

Not all of Seattle's popular parks were part of the Olmsted plan. **Golden Gardens Park**, located at the north end of Ballard, features one of Seattle's few truly sandy beaches, luring swimmers, picnickers, and volleyball players through the summer months. **Gasworks Park**, at the north end of Lake Union, is built around the dramatic skeleton of the old gasworks factory and offers stunning views of the Downtown skyline. The park attracts kite-flyers and Frisbee players, and is a starting point for the **Burke-Gilman Trail**, a paved walkway which heads east from Gasworks to Lake Washington, then along the lake shore to the Eastside. The giant sundial atop the park's central hill is always worth a visit. Gasworks Park hosts an annual Independence Day celebration; lucky visitors can watch a spectacular fireworks display over Lake Union, set to music by the Seattle Symphony. On the Lake Washington waterfront near Sand Point, **Matthews Beach Park** is a popular summer destination for sunbathers and swimmers, and is also a stop on the Burke-Gilman Trail. Only a mile or so south, **Magnuson Park** has softball fields and a boat launch to Lake Washington. Magnuson Park is also the entrance to the famous Soundgarden, a unique wind chime sculpture. Finally, **Alki Beach Park** in West Seattle is one of the city's most dynamic parks. Alki is a great place to watch sunsets over the Olympics or enjoy a spectacular view of Downtown Seattle. During the summer, in-line skaters, bicyclists, and serious beach volleyball players flock to this park. The beach resort atmosphere adds to the charm of this narrow strip of land along the northwest shore of West Seattle.

To enjoy other breathtaking views of Downtown, two parks in the Queen Anne neighborhood can't be beat. **Kerry Park**, on the southwest corner of the hill, overlooks Elliott Bay and the Downtown skyline. **Bhy Kracke Park**, which winds narrowly up the southeast corner of Queen Anne, presents fabulous views of Downtown and Lake Union.

On the northeast corner of Capitol Hill, **Volunteer Park** also provides incredible views of Downtown, as well as the Puget Sound and Olympic Mountains. For an even more dazzling view, climb to the top of the 75-foot water tower. In Volunteer Park you'll also find the **Seattle Asian Art Museum**, and a 1912 conservatory filled with orchids and other tropical plants. Just north of the park, the **Lake View Cemetery** contains the graves of several prominent Seattle citizens, including "Doc" Maynard and Bruce Lee.

If you're in the mood for something slightly more adventurous than a city outing, consider a trip to one of Washington's many state or national parks. **Mount Rainier National Park** activities include skiing, hiking, camping, and mountain-climbing. Call 360-569-2211 for more information. **Olympic National Park**, on the Olympic Peninsula, also offers hiking, camping, and mountain-climbing opportunities. For an up-close look at the mountains without the hike, visit **Hurricane Ridge** near Port Angeles. You can drive to the ridge and view the mountains from the comfort of the visitors center. Also worth a visit while is **Sol Duc Hot Springs**, in the center of the park. For more information on the Olympic National Park, call 360-452-0330. **North Cascade National Park**, the third of Washington's three national park's, offers stunning views, hundreds of hikes and an outstanding museum. To receive information on any of Washington's 125 state parks, call the **Washington State Parks and Recreation Commission** at 360-902-8500 or 800-223-0321 (TDD 360-664-3133). Also, for further outdoor recreation ideas, read the **Quick Getaways** chapter of this book.

Seattle has much to offer in the way of sports and recreation. For weekend warriors who enjoy playing games as much as they like watching them, there are plenty of indoor and outdoor activities available, whether it be a recreational pick-up game at one of Seattle's many parks, or participation in an organized league. And for avid spectators, there is professional and college action galore.

SPECTATOR SPORTS

PROFESSIONAL BASEBALL

Seattle is home to one of the rising stars of professional baseball, the Seattle Mariners. After many years of being a sub-500 team, the Mariners are now making their yearly mark in the play-offs, much to the delight of area baseball fans. There are also two minor league teams that play in the surrounding communities.

The American League's **Seattle Mariners** play approximately 80 home games. They used to play in the covered Kingdome, but now they have a baseball only facility. Opened in the spring of 1999, the new facility offers improved amenities including seating designed specifically for baseball, and a retractable roof for those notorious Seattle rain showers. Because of the Mariners' recent success, tickets are more in demand than they were several years ago. You can order tickets by calling 206-622-HITS. For a Mariners schedule and more information, check out the team's web site at www.mariners.org.

The **Tacoma Rainiers** are a Triple-A club playing in the Pacific Coast league. A farm team for the Mariners, the Rainiers play many games during the spring and summer in Cheney Stadium. There are usually several fun theme nights throughout the season with extra entertainment and prizes. For a schedule or tickets call 206-752-7707 or check the web site at www.rainiers.fonlink.com.

The **Everett Aquasox** host their home games at Everett Memorial Stadium in downtown Everett. The Aquasox are a Single-A farm team for the Seattle Mariners, and offer many exciting games during the summer. Contact their office at 425-258-3673, or visit their web sight, www.aquasox.com.

PROFESSIONAL BASKETBALL

The National Basketball Association's **Seattle SuperSonics** play their home games at the Key Arena, located at the Seattle Center. The Sonics are a perennial contender in the NBA, having made the play-offs for the last several years and the NBA finals in 1996. They also possess an NBA championship from the 1979 season, the only professional team in Seattle to achieve such national recognition. Sonics games are always popular, so call ahead for tickets at 206-283-DUNK, or visit their web site at www.nba.com/sonics/.

PROFESSIONAL FOOTBALL

The **Seattle Seahawks** are a National Football League team, playing their home games in the Kingdome. The Seahawks, once one of the hardest tickets to come by in Seattle, have fallen short of making the playoffs in the last several seasons. The team was recently purchased by billionaire Paul Allen, who also owns the Portland Trailblazers, and there is much hope among fans that the change in ownership will translate into a winning season. For tickets, call 888-NFL-HAWK. Check out the Seahawks web site at www.seahawks.

PROFESSIONAL HOCKEY

In addition to hosting the Seattle Sonics, the Key Arena is home to the **Seattle Thunderbirds**, a Western Hockey League team. The Thunderbirds always draw a large and enthusiastic crowd for competitive games and the occasional brawl. Tickets and information can be had at 206-448-7825 or www.seattle-thunderbirds.com.

PROFESSIONAL SOCCER

The **Seattle Sounders,** offer the Seattle area professional soccer. The

Sounders are part of the USISL A-league, and play their home games at the Memorial Stadium in the Seattle Center. Though soccer is traditionally less popular than other major league sports in U.S. cities, the Sounders have a loyal following of boisterous fans. Call 800-796 KICK for tickets, or visit the team's web site at www.seattlesounders.com.

COLLEGE SPORTS

Attending college games often can be even more exciting than watching professional teams. The frenzied fans and the youthful energy of the participants usually make for an exhuberant experience. The largest draw in the area for college sports are the University of Washington teams, which play on the UW campus near Lake Washington. The UW offers many first class sporting events:

BASEBALL

The Huskies have a men's baseball team and a women's softball team both of which play at Husky Ballpark. Call 206-543-2200 or go to www.gohuskies.com for more information.

BASKETBALL

The Husky Women's Basketball team is an annual contender in the NCAA championship tournament, and the Husky Men's team, which has been in a rebuilding phase during the last few years, made the NCAA championship tournament in 1998. Both play their home games at Hec-Ed Pavilion on the UW campus. Check www.gohuskies.com on the web or call 206-543-2200 for tickets and information.

FOOTBALL

The Husky Football team is usually nationally ranked and has a long list of national championships. Games are played at Husky Stadium, which is one of the best college football venues in the nation. Not only does it offer great seating for the game, but the stadium also offers fans a panoramic view of Lake Washington and snowcapped Mount Rainier. The football games are popular with students and many alumni are season ticket holders, so it's often difficult to get tickets. Call 206-543-2200 or go to www.gohuskies for more information.

PARTICIPANT SPORTS AND ACTIVITIES

Ask a Seattle resident what he or she loves most about the Puget Sound area, and the most likely response will be the outdoor recreation opportunities. From simply watching the sunset over the Olympics in a nearby neighborhood park, to climbing to the summit of Mount Rainier, there are hundreds of activities for every level of athlete throughout the four seasons. Summer brings the inviting expanse of Lake Washington for water-skiing; fall offers breathtaking autumn foliage and pleasant muddy hikes; winter provides cottony white mountains ready for skiing, snowmobiling, and snowshoeing; and spring proffers cool mornings perfect for long bike rides, kayaking, or rowing. These are only a few of the recreational activities possible in and around Seattle.

If you're looking for general information on local parks, kiddie pools, tennis courts, or community programs, a good place to begin is with the **Seattle Parks and Recreation Department** 206-684-4075, or your local community center (listed in the **Neighborhoods** chapter). In addition to playgrounds, ball fields, basketball courts, and tennis courts, neighborhood community centers offer aerobic classes, dance lessons, pottery and art classes, and other activities.

BASKETBALL

Considering the unpredictable nature of Seattle's weather, you might think that basketball would be near the bottom of the list as a favorite sport around here. That's definitely not the case. Lively pick-up games are common in Seattle's playgrounds and community centers, and there are many organized leagues at gyms and athletic clubs. If you're interested in league play or workshops, consider the health clubs listed later in this chapter or call Seattle's Parks and Recreation Department (see above). For a casual but competitive pick up game, try any of the following public courts and community centers.

- **37th Avenue South Park,** 37th Ave. S and S Holly St., 206-684-4075
- **Alki Playground,** 58th Ave. SW and SW Stevens St., 206-684-4075
- **B.F. Day Playground,** N 40th St. and Fremont Ave. N, 206-684-4075
- **Barnett Park,** E Jefferson St. and Martin Luther King Jr. Way, 206-684-4075

- **Bayview Playground,** 24th Ave. W and W Raye St., 206-684-4075
- **Beacon Hill Playground,** 14th Ave. S and S Holgate St., 206-684-4075
- **Benefit Playground,** 39th Ave. S and S Benefit St., 206-684-4075
- **Brighton Playfield,** 42nd Ave. S and S Juneau St., 206-684-4075
- **Bryant Playground,** 40th Ave. NE and NE 65th St., 206-684-4075
- **Burke-Gilman Park,** NE 52nd St. and Sandpoint Way NE, 206-684-4075
- **Cascade Playground,** N 3rd St. and Pontius Ave N, 206- 684-4075
- **Christie Park,** 9th Ave. NE and NE 43rd St., 206-684-4075
- **Colman Playground,** 23rd Ave. S and S Grand St., 206-684-4075
- **Cowen Park,** University Way NE and NE Ravenna Blvd., 206-684-4075
- **Delridge Park,** SW 45th St. and Delridge Way SW, 206-684-4075
- **Denny Park,** Dexter Ave. N and Denny Way, 206-684-4075
- **Discovery Park,** 36th Ave. W and W Government Way, 206-684-4075
- **East Queen Anne Playground,** 2nd Ave. N and N Howe St., 206-684-4075
- **Georgetown Playfield,** Corson Ave. S and S Horner St., 206-684-4075
- **Gilman Playground,** 11th Ave. NW and NW 54th St., 206-684-4075
- **Golden Gardens Park,** NW 85th St. and Seaview Ave. NW, 206-684-4075
- **Green Lake,** N 73rd St. and W Green Lake Way N, 206-684-4075
- **Hiawatha Basketball Courts,** California Ave. SW and SW Lander St., 206- 684-4075
- **Hughes Playground,** 29th Ave. SW and SW Holden St., 206-684-4075
- **Hutchinson Playground,** 59th Ave. S and S Pilgrim St., 206-684-4075
- **I-90 Lid Park,** Martin Luther King Jr. Way S and S Massachusetts St., 206-684-4075
- **Jefferson Community Center,** S 38th St. and Beacon Ave. S, 206-684-4075
- **Kerry Park,** W Highland Drive and 2nd Ave. W, 206-684-4075
- **Lakeridge Park,** Rainier Ave. S and Cornell Ave. S, 206-684-4075
- **Loyal Heights Basketball Courts,** 20th Ave. NW and NW 77th St., 206-684-4075
- **Madrona Basketball Courts,** 34th Ave. E and E Spring St., 206-684-4075
- **Maplewood Playground,** Corson Ave. S and S Angeline St., 206-684-4075

- **Meridian Playground,** Meridian Ave. N and N 50th St., 206-684-4075
- **Miller Playfield,** 19th Ave. E and E Republican St., 206-684-4075
- **Nathan Hale Playfield,** 35th Ave. NE and NE 100th St., 206-684-4075
- **Othello Playground,** S Othello St. and 45th Ave. S, 206-684-4075
- **Pinehurst Playground,** 14th Ave. NE and NE 120th St., 206-684-4075
- **Pratt Park Basketball Courts,** Yesler Way and 20th Ave. S, 206-684-4075
- **Prentis Frazier Park,** 24th Ave. E and E Harrison St., 206-684-4075
- **Rainier Basketball Court,** Rainier Ave. S and S Oregon St., 206-684-4075
- **Ravenna-Eckstein Playground,** 21st Ave. NE and NE 65th St., 206-684-4075
- **Regrade Park,** 3rd Ave. and Bell St., 206-684-4075
- **Riverview Basketball Court,** 12th Ave. SW and SW Othello St., 206-684-4075
- **Roanoke Park,** 10th Ave. E and E Roanoke St., 206-684-4075
- **Ross Playground,** NW 43rd St. and 3rd Ave. NW, 206-684-4075
- **Sandel Playground,** NW 90th St. and 1st Ave. NW, 206-684-4075
- **Van Asselt Playground,** 32nd Ave. S and S Myrtle St., 206-684-4075
- **View Ridge Playfield,** NE 45th St. and 70th Ave. NE, 206-684-4075
- **Ware Park Playground,** S Jackson St. and 29th Ave. S, 206-684-4075

BASEBALL/SOFTBALL

Every spring, as the cherry trees blossom, Seattle residents flock to local fields to play baseball or softball. Call the Seattle Parks and Recreation Department to reserve an athletic field for a casual game between friends, or put together your own team and participate in a league. Most leagues are organized privately or through local community centers (listed in the **Neighborhoods** chapter). The following resources may also be helpful.

- **Bellevue Baseball/Softball Athletic Association,** 425-746-4592
- **Emerald City Softball Association,** 206-322-7769
- **Mind & Matter Adventure Club,** 206-324-9991
- **Puget Sound Senior Baseball League,** 425-488-8881
- **Redmond Parks and Recreation Department,** 425-556-2312
- **Roosevelt-University-Greenlake Little League,** 206-524-0784, www.cris.com/~Rugll/
- **Seattle Sport and Social Club,** 206-328-7772

- **Shoreline Community Center,** 206-546-5041
- **United States Amateur Baseball Association,** 425-776-7130, www.usaba.com

If you're simply in the mood for an impromptu game with friends or some casual batting practice, the neighborhood parks listed below have ball fields. To reserve an individual field, call the **Seattle Parks and Recreation Individual Field Reservation Line** at 206-684-4077.

- **Carkeek Park,** 950 NW Carkeek Park Rd., 206-684-4075
- **Cowen Park,** 5700 NE Ravenna Blvd., 206-684-4075
- **Dearborn Park,** 2800 S Brandon St., 206-684-4075
- **Green Lake Park,** 5701 E Green Lake Way N, 206-684-4075
- **Judkins Park & Playfield,** 2200 S Charles St., 206-684-4075
- **Laurelhurst Park,** 4554 NE 41st St., 206-684-4075
- **Lawton Park,** 2700 W Emerson St., 206-684-4075
- **Lincoln Park,** 8603 Fauntleroy Way, 206-684-4075
- **Magnuson Park,** 6500 Sand Point Way NE, 206-684-4075
- **Ravenna Park,** 2000 NE 58th St,, 206-684-4075
- **Woodland Park,** 5000 Phinney Ave. N, 206-684-4075

BICYCLING

In Seattle, bicycling is popular as both a sport and a means of transportation. Despite the unpredictable weather and hilly tophograhpy, many Seattlelites bike to work and to do errands. Bicycle lanes have become more common on major thoroughfares throughout the city. Green Lake is a popular destination for recreational bicyclists, as are many locations along the Burke-Gilman trail. For a fun and scenic ride, bike the Burke-Gilman trail from Gasworks Park on Lake Union to Matthews Beach on Lake Washington. The trail is also used as a shortcut for many University of Washington students riding to school each morning.

Cascade Bicycle Club, the largest cycling club in the United States, is based in Seattle. With over 5000 members, CBC sponsors several rides each day, for riders of all skill levels, as well as several annual events. Contact CBC at 206-522-BIKE, or check out their comprehensive web site at www.cascade.org. While CBC sponsors mainly street bicycling events, those interested in track racing should contact the **Marymoor Velodrome Association** at 206-675-1424 or visit their web site, www.iscn.com/marymoor. Racing events are held regularly in Marymoor Park in Redmond.

The following are a few of the most popular annual street rides in the Seattle area:

The **Cannonball,** organized by the **Redmond Cycling Club** (425-739-8610) and held in late June, is a one-day trek from Seattle to Spokane along I-90.

Chilly Hilly, held in late February and sponsored by CBC, is a 28-mile bicycle tour around Bainbridge Island, and marks the official opening of bicycle season in the Pacific Northwest.

The **Daffodil Classic,** an annual ride sponsored by the **Tacoma Wheelmen's Bicycle Club** (253-759-2800), is held in mid-April. There are several routes, ranging from 20 to 100 miles.

The **Kitsap Color Classic,** a ride through Kitsap County on the Olympic Peninsula, is held in early October when the leaves begin to turn. This ride is sponsored by CBC.

The **RAMROD** (Ride Around Mount Rainier in One Day) is sponsored by the Redmond Cycling Club (425-739-8610) and takes place in late July. It is a 150+ mile race around Mount Rainier, and is perhaps the most challenging in the area, with 10,000 feet of climbing during the race.

The **Seattle-to-Portland (STP)** is a two-day non-competitive bike ride from Seattle to Portland, sponsored by the CBC. Riders can choose to participate for one or two days; those riding for two days stay overnight midway. The STP takes place in mid-July and is the best-known bicycling event in the area.

Just as popular as traditional bicycling, **mountain biking** is a favorite recreational activity for many Seattle residents. Seattle's hills provide great practice routes, and there are several scenic and challenging mountain bike trails just a short drive out of the city. An excellent resource for local mountain biking information is the **Backcountry Bicycle Trails Club** at 206-283-2995 or www.dirtnw.com/bbtc/index.html. If you're new to the sport, the club offers a "boot camp" for first-time trail riders. For information on nearby trails, check out a copy of the **King County Parks and Trails Atlas**, available at King County Public Libraries. A copy of the trail map only can be purchased at REI or downloaded from www.metrokc.gov/parks/atlas/atlas2/morew.htm.

BOATING

Seattle residents love boats of all shapes, sizes, and colors. Even on cloudy days, you'll probably see several boats out on the lakes or in the Puget

Sound. Colorful spinnakers dot the sound each weekend as sailing races are held near Shilshole Bay. On sunny days, float planes arriving at Lake Union dodge the many sailboats which crowd the surface of the lake, and the early morning calm of Lake Washington entices a crowd of ski boats filled with eager water-skiers.

ROWING, CANOEING, AND KAYAKING

- **Falcon Rowing Club**, 3307 3rd Ave. W, 206-281-2743
- **Lake Washington Rowing Club**, 910 N Northlake Way, 206-547-1583
- **Moss Bay Rowing and Kayak Center**, 1001 Fairview Ave. N, 206-682-2031
- **Mount Baker Rowing and Sailing Center**, 3800 Lake Washington Blvd. S, 206-386-1913
- **Northwest Outdoor Center**, 2100 Westlake Ave. N, 206-281-9694
- **Pacific Water Sports**, 16055 Pacific Hwy. S, 206-246-9385
- **Green Lake Small Craft Center**, 5900 W Green Lake Way N, 206-684-4074
- **Seattle Canoe Club**, 5900 W Green Lake Way N, 206-684-4074
- **Washington Kayak Club**, 206-433-1983

SAILING AND SPEED BOATING

- **Elliott Bay Yachting Center**, 2601 W Marina Place, 206-285-9499
- **Mount Baker Rowing and Sailing Center**, 3800 Lake Washington Blvd. S, 206-386-1913
- **Seattle Sailing Club**, 7001 Seaview Ave. NW, 206-782-5100
- **Wind Works Sailing School and Charters**, 7001 Seaview Ave. NW, 206-784-9386

YACHT CLUBS

- **Corinthian Yacht Club of Seattle**, 7755 Seaview Ave. NW, 206-789-1919
- **Queen City Yacht Club**, 2608 Boyer Ave. E, 206-323-9602
- **Rainier Yacht Club**, 9094 Seward Park S, 206-722-9576
- **Seattle Yacht Club**, 1807 E Hamlin St., 206-325-1000
- **Shilshole Bay Yacht Club**, 7001 Seaview Ave. NW, 206-789-3311
- **Tyee Yacht Club**, 3229 Fairview Ave. E, 206-324-0200

OTHER BOATING RESOURCES

- **Boating Safety Classes**, 800-336-BOAT
- **Puget Sound Water Quality Authority**, 800-54-SOUND
- **Seattle Police Harbor Patrol Unit**, 206-684-4071
- **Seattle Boat Ramp Supervisor**, 206-684-7249
- **US Coast Guard 24 hour Emergency**, 206-286-5400

BOWLING

Bowling is most popular during Seattle's wet, gray winter months. The following bowling alleys organize leagues regularly, but also welcome amateur and first-time bowlers.

- **Imperial Lanes**, 2101 22nd Ave. S, Seattle, (206) 325-2525
- **Hi-Line Lanes**, 15733 Ambaum Blvd. SW, Seattle, (206) 244-2272
- **Kenmore 50 Lanes**, 7638 NE Bothell Way, Bothell, (425) 486-2776
- **Leilani Lanes**, 10201 Greenwood Ave. N, Seattle, (206) 783-8010
- **Magic Lanes**, 10612 15th Ave. SW, Seattle, (206) 244-5060
- **Roxbury Lanes**, 2823 SW Roxbury St., Seattle, (206) 935-7400
- **Sunset Bowl**, 1420 NW Market St., Seattle, (206) 782-7310
- **West Seattle Bowl**, 4505 39th Ave. SW, Seattle, (206) 932-3731

FISHING AND SHELLFISH GATHERING

The fishing and shellfishing opportunities in Washington are nothing short of amazing. Although the area is famous for salmon and Dungeness crab, you'll also find clams, mussels, oysters, trout, and steelhead. If you're gathering shellfish with a local, you may even get a glimpse of a geoduck. Geoduck, pronounced "gooey-duck," are huge razor clams indigenous to Washington's ocean beaches. Like clams, you'll need to dig for geoduck, although they're a lot tougher to catch (they're fast!) and you probably won't want to eat one anyway.

Several types of salmon and trout migrate through the waters of Western Washington. Chinook are the largest of the Pacific salmon and spawn in the Columbia and Snake Rivers, as well as other small rivers and streams. Coho or silver salmon are a popular sport fish in the Puget Sound, and can also be found in coastal tributaries. Sockeye salmon are a flavorful salmon, found in Lake Washington, Baker Lake, Quinault Lake, Ozette Lake, and Lake Wenatchee. Pink salmon, or humpback salmon, spawn only every other year and so appear in Washington waters during odd-numbered years only. Chum salmon can be found in small coastal streams, but are not particularly tasty and so are not popular as a sport fish. Steelhead trout and cutthroat trout, named for the red markings just below the head of the fish, live in freshwater streams and Puget Sound bays. Although cutthroats are common throughout North America, those in Washington are the only ones that spend the warm summer months in saltwater.

Lakes and rivers in Washington yield an unusual catch of fish, including many non-native species. When settlers arrived here in the mid-1800s, they caught trout, char, whitefish, and a few other small fish in the freshwater lakes and streams. As more people moved to the area and the trout population began to dwindle proportionately, additional species of fish were imported. While trout (including cutthroat, steelhead, brook, and brown trout) are still the most popular fish in Washington's many rivers, the state's lakes and rivers are now stocked with a variety of fish from sunfish and catfish, to perch and pike.

Favorite locations for trout fishing near Puget Sound are the Skagit, Snoqualmie, Skykomish, and Green Rivers. Other plentiful rivers in the state include the Columbia, Cowlitz, Kalama, and Hoh Rivers. Bottomfish such as halibut, cod, and rockfish are common in Neah Bay, the Hood Canal, and around the San Juan Islands. Lake Washington and the Puget Sound have limited amounts of sturgeon, which are more prevalent in the Columbia and Snake Rivers. If you're looking for largemouth bass, try Moses Lake, Silver Lake, Long Lake, Sprague Lake, or the Columbia River. Smallmouth bass are commonly found in the Columbia, Snake, and Yakima Rivers, and in Lake Washington, Lake Sammamish, and Lake Stevens. You may catch yellow perch in Lake Washington, Lake Sammamish, or Lake Stevens, while you're more likely to find walleyes in Eastern Washington lakes such as Moses Lake, Lake Roosevelt or Soda Lake. If you're a fan of catfish, you'll find brown bullheads in Lake Washington, Moses Lake, or Liberty Lake and channel catfish in Fazon Lake and Sprague Lake. Tiger muskies (pike) are commonly found in Mayfield Lake in Lewis County, while northern pikes swim in Long Lake near Spokane.

The Washington Department of Fish and Wildlife (WDFW) regulates fishing and shellfish gathering throughout the state, acting as both a conservation and licensing entity. The agency provides many helpful publications on a variety of fish and wildlife subjects, which can be ordered by phone or downloaded from the department's web site. Fishing licenses are required for all state residents over 15 years old, and for all non-residents, regardless of age. Licenses are valid for one year, and must be displayed at all times while fishing or gathering shellfish. License fees and restrictions vary according to the fish or shellfish collected; prices range from $7.00 to $36.00 for residents. Licenses may be purchased from most sporting goods stores. Disabled persons qualify for a free license, but must call or write the WDFW to order it, rather than purchasing one through a retail store.

- **Washington State Department of Fish and Wildlife**, 600 Capitol Way N, Olympia, 360-902-2700
- **Washington State Department of Fisheries**, Saltwater Fish and Shellfish, 206-753-6600
- **Washington State Department of Wildlife**, Freshwater Fish, 206-779-1311

FRISBEE

While many Seattle parks have adequate open spaces for a game of frisbee, a few parks are especially popular with enthusiasts. Gasworks Park, at the north end of Lake Union, combines a wide expanse of green lawn with pleasant breezes off the lake surface. Discovery Park in Magnolia has a good sized grassy meadow in which to play, and Woodland Park near Green Lake offers a quiet shady expanse.

If ultimate frisbee is your game of choice, you may want to try one of several regular pick-up games in the area. Common locations are Dahl Field on Wednesday and Friday evenings, Magnuson Park on Wednesday evenings, and Marymoor Park in Redmond on Wednesday evenings and Saturday mornings. League play is organized privately or through the **Northwest Ultimate Association**. The following resources will help you in your search for a competitive ultimate frisbee game:

- **Northwest Ultimate Association**, discnw@speakeasy.org; www.speakeasy.org/discnw/
- **Seattle Ultimate Hotline**, 206-781-5840

GOLF

Three public golf courses, run by the City of Seattle Parks and Recreation Department, are listed below. In addition, the parks department offers a short course near Green Lake and a golf center, with miniature golf course and driving range, near Queen Anne. Walk-ons are often allowed, or call 206-301-0472 to arrange a tee time. While there are many other golf courses in the greater Seattle area, most are private or semi-private courses. Check the local Yellow Pages for more information.

- **Green Lake Pitch & Putt**, 5701 Green Lake Way N, 206-632-2280
- **Interbay Family Golf Center**, 2501 15th Ave. W, 206-285-2200
- **Jackson Park Golf Course**, 1000 NE 135th St., 206-363-4747
- **Jefferson Park Golf Course**, 4101 Beacon Ave. S, 206-762-4513
- **West Seattle Golf Course**, 4470 35th Ave. SW, 206-935-5187

HIKING

If you like to hike, you'll *love* living in Seattle. Not only are there several short hikes in local parks, such as Discovery Park and Seward Park, but just outside of the city there are hundreds of trails for hikers of all fitness levels. Mountaineers Books publishes a series of useful books that describe nearly every trail in Washington. Another helpful resource is the Trailfinder feature on Microsoft's seattle.sidewalk web site, www.seattle.sidewalkapps.com/trailfinder/, which allows you to pick trails that meet certain mileage, duration, and location specifications. The following resources may also be helpful when choosing a hike.

- **Mountaineers Books**, 1011 SW Klickitat Way, 206-223-6303
- **National Park Service**, www.nps.gov
- **The Mountaineers Club**, 300 3rd Ave. W, 206-6310
- **Washington Trails Association**, 1305 4th Ave. Suite 512, 206-625-1367, www.halcyon.com/wta/quick.html

HORSEBACK RIDING

Horseback rides and lessons are available in many of Seattle's surrounding rural communities.

- **Big Horse Farm**, 206-567-4908
- **Sheryl Butler, English Riding Instructor**, 425-485-6040
- **Elk Run Stable**, 425-888-4341
- **Horse Country — Ponies Too**, 425-392-0111
- **Lake Serene Pony Farm & Day Camp**, 425-743-2112
- **Lori's Sammamish Stables**, 425-868-5299
- **Skyland Ranch**, 360-793-2611

- **Tiger Mountain Outfitters**, 425-392-5090

ICE SKATING

While most bodies of water in Seattle never freeze, and certainly don't allow for safe outdoor ice skating, indoor rinks offer skate rentals, lessons, and open ice sessions. Several indoor rinks are listed below. During the holiday season, an ice rink is open to the public for **Winterfest**, which runs from November to January at Seattle Center. Call 206-684-7200 for details.

- **Highland Ice Area**, 18005 Aurora Ave. N, Shoreline, 206-546-2431
- **Lynnwood's Sno-King Ice Arena**, 19803 68th Ave. W, Lynnwood, 425-775-7511

IN-LINE SKATING

In-line skating is a popular activity on Seattle's paved paths, particularly at Green Lake, Alki Beach, and on the Burke-Gilman trail. Some skaters even turn vacant parking lots into impromptu rinks for trick skating or pick-up hockey games. Several sporting goods stores offer in-line skating rentals. The stores listed here offer easy access to a paved walkway.

GREEN LAKE
- **The Good Sport**, 7900 E Greenlake Drive N, 206-526-8087
- **Gregg's Greenlake Cycle**, 7007 Woodlawn Ave. NE, 206-523-1822

BURKE-GILMAN TRAIL
- **Urban Surf**, 2100 N Northlake Way, 206-545-9463, www.urbansurf.com

For in-line skating lessons, try the following resources:

- **Get In Line — Inline Skating School**, 206-938-8011
- **Seattle In Line Arena**, 3800 West Marginal Way SW, 206-937-2966

RACQUET SPORTS

TENNIS

Outdoor public tennis courts dot the city and are generally open on a first-come, first-served basis, although reservations may be requested through the Seattle Parks and Recreation Department. The Seattle Tennis Center in the Mount Baker neighborhood, also run by the Seattle Parks and Recreation Department, offers lessons and indoor and outdoor courts.

- **Seattle Parks and Recreation Department**, Outdoor Court Information/Reservations, 206-684-4082
- **Seattle Tennis Center**, 2000 Martin Luther King Jr. Way S, 206-684-4764

RACQUETBALL

A few racquetball courts are open to the public in the greater Seattle area.

- **Kent Commons**, 525 4th Ave. N, Kent, 253-859-4171
- **Lynnwood Recreation Center**, 18900 44th Ave. W, Lynnwood, 425-771-4030
- **Mountlake Terrace Recreation Pavilion**, 5303 228th SW Mountlake Terrace, 425-776-9173
- **White Center Park**, 1321 SW 102nd St., Seattle, 206-296-4542

RACQUET CLUBS

Private racquet clubs and health clubs offer lessons and court rentals for a variety of games, including tennis, racquetball, and squash. Call ahead for details, as activities and services vary.

- **Auburn Racquetball Club**, 311 3rd Ave. NE, 253-833-9731
- **Olympic Athletic Club**, 5301 Leary Way NW, 206-789-5010

ROCK CLIMBING

Rock climbing is a popular sport in Washington, with several local climbing clubs and walls, as well as many nearby outdoor destinations. Closest perhaps is Little Si, near North Bend along I-90. Leavenworth, a Bavarian-style village on Hwy. 2, attracts a variety of climbers. If you're new to the sport, visit the Leavenworth area and start with the boulders near Icicle Creek, many of them have bars embedded in the rock for easy top-roping. More difficult climbs near Leavenworth can be found at Castle Rock and the Peshastin Pinnacles. Near Stevens Pass, the Index Town Wall provides challenging routes for climbers of all levels, and close to the town of Vantage, basalt columns near the Columbia River offer good climbing for experienced climbers only. Nearby, an area known as The Feathers is appropriate for beginners. In the Olympics, Flapjack Lakes Trail leads to challenging rock-climbing.

If you've never tried rock-climbing before, or if you're an experienced climber who wants to stay in practice without leaving the city, the following climbing walls and clubs offer a variety of rock-climbing experiences. Most of the clubs offer rock-climbing lessons, as do those organizations listed under "Lessons and Guide Resources" below.

CLIMBING WALLS

- **REI Pinnacle** (indoor), 222 Yale Ave. N, 206-223-1944
- **University of Washington Climbing Rock** (outdoor), south of Husky Stadium on Montlake Ave. NE, 206-543-9433
- **Schurman Rock** (outdoor), Camp Long, 5200 35th Ave. SW, 206-684-7434
- **Glacier** (outdoor), Camp Long, 5200 35th Ave. SW, 206-684-7434
- **Marymoor Climbing Wall** (outdoor), Marymoor Park, Redmond, 206-296-2964

ROCK-CLIMBING CLUBS

- **Stone Gardens**, 2839 NW Market St., 206-781-9828
- **Vertical World**, 2123 W Elmore St., 206-283-4497; 15036-B NE 95th St., Redmond, 425-881-8826

LESSONS AND GUIDE RESOURCES

- **Cascade Alpine Guides**, 800-981-0381
- **Mountain Madness**, 206-937-8389
- **The Mountaineers**, 300 3rd Ave. W, 206-284-6310
- **REI**, 222 Yale Ave. N, 206-223-1944; 15400 NE 20th St., Bellevue, 425-643-3700
- **Wilderness Sports**, 14340 NE 20th St., Bellevue, 425-746-0500

RUNNING

Considering the weather in Seattle, you might think that running wouldn't be the sport of choice in the city. For some reason, though, the rain just makes area runners more determined and dedicated. The most popular running locations in Seattle are Green Lake (the inner loop is 2.8 miles, the outer loop is slightly over 3 miles), Burke-Gilman Trail, Myrtle Edwards Park, and Alki Beach in West Seattle. Listed below are several running clubs in Seattle, which sponsor weekly club runs and annual events.

- **Eastside Runners**, 425-313-7828
- **Seattle Frontrunners** (Gay/Lesbian), 206-320-9195
- **Seattle Hash House Harriers**, 206-528-2050
- **West Seattle Runners**, 206-938-2416

Many races are held annually throughout Seattle. Some of the most popular are the **St. Patrick's Day Dash** (4 miles) held in March, the **Jingle Bell Run** (5K) held in early December, and the **Race for the Cure** (5K) held in mid-October. The **Torchlight Run** (8K), held in August as part of the SeaFair celebration, is both a run and an eclectic pre-parade event, with prizes given for best costume and group theme. The **Beat the Bridge Run** (8K) is a favorite local run, so named because the object is to cross the University Bridge before the bridge goes up. Comedians and musicians entertain those runners who get stuck behind the bridge until the bridge is lowered again. The best option for getting information on upcoming races is to contact a local running club or running store. The following stores advertise races and also sponsor weekly group runs.

- **Fast Lady Sports**, University Village, 206-522-2113
- **Super Jock 'n Jill**, 7210 E Green Lake Drive N, 206-522-7711
- **Super Jock 'n Jill Runners Hotline**, 206-524-7867

SKIING AND SNOWBOARDING

The highways over the Cascade Mountains lead to several ski resorts that are only a few hours away. **Whistler**, a few hours drive north of Vancouver, B.C., is considered one of the best ski resorts in North America. Skiing and snowboarding are both popular activities at nearby resorts, which usually offer lessons for all levels of skiers. Call ahead for details and lodging reservations.

WASHINGTON STATE SKI AREAS

- **Crystal Mountain**, located near Mount Rainier, 33 miles east of Enumclaw on Hwy. 410, 360-663-2558 or 888-OnTheMt.
- **Mission Ridge**, located 12 miles east of Wenatchee on Hwy. 2, 509-663-6543 or 800-374-1693, www.missionridge.com.
- **Mount Baker**, located 56 miles east of Bellingham on Hwy. 542, 360-734-6771.
- **Stevens Pass**, located 65 miles east of Everett on Hwy. 2, 206-812-4510, www.stevenspass.com.
- **The Summit at Snoqualmie** (includes Alpental, Hyak, Ski Acres, and Snoqualmie ski areas), 60 miles east of Seattle on Hwy. 90, 206-236-1600.
- **White Pass**, near Mount Rainier, 50 miles west of Yakima on Hwy. 12, 509-672-3100, www.skiwhitepass.com.

OUT OF STATE SKI AREAS

- **Mount Bachelor**, located 22 miles southwest of Bend, OR, 541-382-2442 or 800-829-2442, www.mtbachelor.com.
- **Mount Hood Meadows**, located 80 miles east of Portland near Hood River, OR, 503-227-7669 or 800-SKIHOOD.
- **Mount Washington**, located 80 miles north of Nanaimo on Vancouver Island, B.C., 250-338-1386, www.vquest.com/alpine.
- **Silver Mountain**, located 70 miles east of Spokane in Kellogg, ID, 800-204-6428, www.silvermt.com.
- **Schweitzer**, located 86 miles northeast of Spokane near Sandpoint, ID, 208-263-9555 or 800-831-8810, www.schweitzer.com.
- **Whistler** (includes Whistler and Blackcomb ski areas), 75 miles north of Vancouver, BC, 604-664-5625 or 800-WHISTLER, www.whistler-resort.com.

SNOWMOBILING

In Washington, snowmobiling is allowed on many forest and park trails. Snowmobiles are available for rent near most ski areas and in other wilderness areas throughout the state. Rentals generally include a short lesson that covers riding techniques and safety tips. The following resources may be helpful if you're planning a day of snowmobiling.

- **Washington State Parks and Recreation Commission,** 800-233-0321 (TDD 360-664-3133), www.parks.wa.gov/
- **Washington State Parks Groomed Trail Conditions Line,** 800-233-0321
- **Washington State Snowmobile Association,** 1690 Winona Lane, Walla Walla, 800-783-9772

WASHINGTON STATE SNOWMOBILE SNO-PARK INFORMATION

- **Chelan Ranger District,** 509-682-2576
- **Cle Elum Ranger District,** 509-674-4411
- **Lake Easton State Park,** 509-656-2230
- **Lake Wenatchee Ranger District,** 509-763-3103
- **Mount Adams Ranger District,** 509-395-3353
- **Mount Baker Ranger District,** 360-856-5700
- **Mount St. Helens Ranger District,** 360-750-3900
- **Okanogan County,** 509-422-7319
- **Naches Ranger District,** 509-653-2205
- **Packwood Ranger District,** 360-494-0600
- **Pomeroy Ranger District,** 509-843-1891
- **Randle Ranger District,** 360-497-1121
- **Spokane County Parks and Recreation,** 509-456-4730
- **Stevens County,** 509-684-6905
- **White River Ranger District,** 360-825-6585
- **Wind River Ranger District,** 509-427-3200

SNOWMOBILE RENTALS

- **Cascade Snowmobile Rentals,** 509-649-2444
- **Mountain Springs Lodge,** 509-763-2713 or 800-858-2276, www.mtsprings.com
- **Stampede Pass Snowmobile Rentals,** 206-941-7425, www.tcm-net.com/~snomo
- **Winthrop Snowmobile Rentals,** 800-488-3857

SOCCER

While a few high schools have teams, most children and adults play competitive soccer in private leagues. The following are soccer resources throughout the greater Seattle area.

- **Capitol Hill Youth Soccer Club**, 2127 Boyer Ave. E, 206-324-3473
- **Co-Rec Soccer Association**, 206-329-1548
- **Eastside Youth Soccer Association**, Bellevue, 425-462-6616
- **Everett Soccer Arena**, 2201 California St., Everett, 425-745-4322
- **Greater Seattle Soccer League** (GSSL), 9750 Greenwood Ave. N, 206-782-6831, www.gssl.org
- **LVR Youth Soccer Club**, 206-525-6045
- **Lake Hills Soccer Club**, 2107 170th Ave. NE, Bellevue, 425-643-1029
- **Lake Washington Youth Soccer Association**, 8141 161st Ave. NE, Redmond, 425-883-3009, www.lwysa.org
- **Magnolia Soccer Club**, 3213 W Wheeler St., 206-283-5321
- **Mount Baker/Lakewood Youth Soccer Club**, 206-725-2286
- **Northwest Soccer & Sports Center** (indoor soccer), 2610 Bay Street E, Tacoma, 253-627-BALL, www.nwssc.com
- **Queen Anne Soccer Club**, 206-281-9579
- **Seattle Youth Soccer Association**, 206-365-6146
- **Silver Lake Soccer Club**, Bothell, 425-481-2665
- **Soccer Ventures**, 3721 SW Barton St., 206-938-3048
- **Washington State Soccer Association**, 7802 NE Bothell Way, Bothell, 425-485-7855, www.wssa.org
- **Washington State Youth Soccer Association**, 14900 Interurban Ave. S, Suite 120, 206-246-5161
- **Woodinville Indoor Soccer Center**, 12728 NE 178th, Woodinville, 425-481-5099

SWIMMING

When hot weather hits Seattle, folks head in droves to the few swimming beaches in the city. Lifeguards are generally on duty at Seattle beaches 11:00 a.m. to 8:00 p.m. from June 20 through Labor Day (except in inclement weather). It should be noted, however, that swimming in the Puget Sound, even in summer, is an acquired (though acquired by many) taste. Following are city parks with swimming areas:

- **Green Lake Park** (two swimming areas), 7201 E Green Lake Way N and 7312 W Green Lake Drive N, 206-684-4075

- **Madison Park,** 1900 43rd Ave. E, 206-684-4075
- **Madrona Park,** 800 Lake Washington Blvd. , 206-684-4075
- **Magnuson Park,** 6500 Sand Point Way NE, 206-684-4075
- **Matthews Beach Park,** 9300 51st Ave. NE, 206-684-4075
- **Mount Baker Park,** 2301 Lake Washington Blvd. S, 206-684-4075
- **Pritchard Island Beach Park,** 8400 55th Ave. S, 206-684-4075
- **Seward Park,** 5900 Lake Washington Blvd. S, 206-684-4075

Wading pools are open for the little ones in a few parks, play-grounds, and community centers in Seattle. Park wading pools are open daily (provided the temperature is over 70 degrees), from 11:00 a.m. to 8:00 p.m. Community center and playground wading pools are open weekdays only and hours vary. Call the city's **Wading Pool Hotline** at 206-684-7796 to find out which wading pools are open for swimmers. Here are a few of the city's most popular wading pools:

- **Green Lake Park,** 7312 W Green Lake Drive N, 206-684-4075
- **Lincoln Park,** 8603 Fauntleroy Way, 206-684-4075
- **Magnuson Park,** 6500 Sand Point Way NE, 206-684-4075
- **Volunteer Park,** 1400 E Galer St., 206-684-4075

For those interested in year-round swimming, Seattle city pools offer a variety of open swim sessions, lessons, and lap-swimming options. Many host swim club practices for Masters and all ages programs.

- **Ballard Pool,** 1471 NW 67th St., 206-684-4094
- **Colman Pool** (outdoor), 8603 Fauntleroy Way SW, 206-684-7494
- **Evans Pool,** 7201 E Green Lake Drive N, 206-684-4961
- **Madison Pool,** 13401 Meridian Ave. N, 206-684-4979
- **Meadowbrook Pool,** 10515 35th Ave. NE, 206-684-4989
- **Medgar Evers Pool,** 500 23rd Ave., 206-684-4766
- **Mounger Pool** (outdoor), 2535 32nd Ave. W, 206-684-4708
- **Queen Anne Pool,** 1920 1st Ave. W, 206-386-4282
- **Rainier Beach Pool,** 8825 Rainier Ave. S, 206-386-1944
- **Southwest Pool,** 2801 SW Thistle St., 206-684-7440

Several swim clubs hold regular practices at pools around Seattle, many offering a variety of practices for all levels of experience. Call ahead for details as prices and entrance requirements vary widely. An excellent resource for competitive swimming information in Washington is **Pacific Northwest Swimming** (PNS), 402 S 333rd St., Suite 103, Federal Way, 888-300-SWIM or 206-661-7748. The organization maintains a comprehensive web site at www.pns.org. Several local swim clubs are listed below. Because many practice at multiple locations, business office addresses are given for some clubs.

- **Cascade Swim Club**, P.O. Box 77043, Seattle 98177, Head Coach: Steve Witcher, 206-367-9069, Club Contact: Jody Woodruff, 206-546-1036
- **Excel Swim Club**, 1819 NW Blue Ridge Dr., Seattle 98177, Head Coach: Tom Linde, 206-781-0880
- **Husky Swim Club**, P. O. Box 66248, Seattle 98166, Head Coach: Erin Dunn 206-575-0808
- **Medgar Evars Tiger Sharks**, 4051 Letitia Ave., Seattle 98118 Head Coach: John Walker 206-722-3779
- **Queen Anne Swim Club**, P.O. Box 19856, Seattle 98109, Head Coach: Stephanie Boden, 425-338-9537
- **Shadow Seals**, 5552 35th Ave. N.E., Seattle 98105, Head Coach: Kiko VanZandt, 206-526-2182
- **Shilshole Aquatic Club**, P.O. Box 17442, Seattle 98107, Head Coach: Doug Rusk, 206-781-0827, Club Contact: Bon Bernard, 206-782-1165
- **Sundodger Swim Club**, 4756 University Village Pl. NE, #431, Seattle 98105, Head Coach: Jana Ellis, 206-543-6644
- **Swim Seattle**, P.O. Box 51115, Seattle 98115, Head Coach: Andy Pym, 206-365-4907
- **West Seattle YMCA Dolphins Swim Team**, 4515 36th Ave. SW, Seattle 98126, Head Coach: Jenny Richter, 206-935-6400 ext. 138

WATER-SKIING

During the warm summer months you'll see hundreds of people water-skiing on Lake Washington. In Seattle, many skiers launch their boats early in the morning from Magnuson Park in Sand Point and head out to the middle of the lake. Other lakes in Washington that are popular for water-skiing are Lake Sammamish in Bellevue and Lake Chelan, north of Wenatchee. For equipment and supplies, try the following resources:

- **Active Water Sports Waterski Pro Shop**, 800-832-7547
- **Extremely Board**, 1145 NW Gilman Blvd., Issaquah, 425-391-4572

- **HO Sports**, 17622 NE 67th Court, Redmond, 425-885-3505
- **Looney Tunes Sports**, 10643 NE 68th St., 425-827-4451
- **O'Brien International**, 14615 NE 91st St., Redmond, 425-881-5900
- **Pro Tour Watersports**, 13131 NE 124th St. Suite A, Kirkland, 425-814-1395
- **Ski Masters Water Sports Warehouse**, 425-481-2754
- **Straight-Line Water Sports**, 425-881-3377
- **Sturtevant's Sports**, 622 Bellevue Way NE, Bellevue, 425-454-6465 or 888-454-7669, www.sturtevants.com
- **Three-Sixty Wakeboards**, 12015 NE 8th St., Bellevue, 425-637-0360
- **Wiley's Water Ski Shop**, 1417 S Trenton St., 206-762-1300

WIND-SURFING

While Green Lake, Lake Union, the Puget Sound, and Lake Washington are all popular destinations for wind-surfing enthusiasts, the Columbia River Gorge is the ultimate thrill for experienced wind-surfers. Located on the southern border of Washington near Hood River, Oregon, the gorge is challenging and exciting for veteran surfers, but can be rough and even dangerous for beginners. The following resources provide information and lessons for both experienced wind-surfers and beginners.

- **Columbia Gorge Windsurfing Association**, 202 Oak Street Suite 150, Hood River, OR, 541-386-9225
- **Crazyboardhead**, 206-655-8867, www.home.earthlink.net/~crzybdhd/wind/index.html
- **Northwest Boardsailing Association**, 10906 30th Drive SE, Everett, 206-441-6667
- **United States Windsurfing Association**, 202 Oak St. Suite 300, Hood River, OR, 541-386-8708
- **Urban Surf**, 2100 N Northlake Way, 206-545-9463, www.urbansurf.com

HEALTH CLUBS

Whether you're trying to stay in shape during the off-season, getting in shape for the summer or simply prefer aerobics or weight-lifting to outdoor sports, Seattle is full of health clubs and gyms. Most offer aerobics and step aerobics classes, as well as personal training programs. Some clubs also offer yoga, swimming workouts, nutrition and preventive health classes as well as the latest trendy workout regimen. Call or visit the club that you're interested in to get the details on their programs.

- **1201 Nautilus**, 1201 3rd Ave., 4th Floor, 206-583-8848
- **Allstar Fitness**, multiple locations, 206-282-5901
- **Anderson's Nautilus at Greenlake**, 7203 Woodlawn Ave. NE, 206-524-7000
- **Aqua Dive Swim & Fitness Club**, 12706 33rd Ave. NE, 206-364-2535
- **Ballard Health & Fitness Center**, 2208 NW Market St., 206-706-4882
- **Bally Total Fitness**, multiple locations, 800-695-8111
- **Body Power Gym**, 539 NE Northgate Way, 206-367-4262
- **Cross Train Concepts Conditioning Studio**, 1446 NW 53rd St., 206-782-2199
- **Every Body Health and Fitness**, 2609 S Jackson St., 206-324-6062
- **Fitness for Women**, 4815 California Ave. SW, 206-937-7733
- **Gateway Athletic Club**, 700 5th Ave., 206-343-4692
- **Gold's Gym**, 9701 Aurora Ave. N, 206-524-5543
- **Hart's Athletic Club**, multiple locations, 800-262-0880
- **Ideal Exercise**, 13754 Aurora Ave. N, 206-364-9944
- **Living Well Lady Fitness Center**, 2656 NE University Village Mall, 206-522-9318
- **Magnolia Athletic Club**, 3320 W McGraw St., 206-283-1490
- **Metropolitan Health Club**, 1519 3rd Ave., 206-682-3966
- **Olympic Athletic Club**, 5301 Leary Ave. NW, 206-789-5010
- **One on One**, 5007 3rd Ave. S, 206-764-1661
- **Pro-Robics**, multiple locations, 206-283-2303
- **Seattle Athletic Club**, 2020 Western Ave., 206-443-1111
- **Seattle Fitness Club**, 83 S King St., 206-467-1800
- **Seattle Women's Health & Fitness**, 509 Olive Way, 206-292-0900
- **Sound Mind & Body**, multiple locations, 206-547-2086
- **The Vault**, 804 Second Ave., 206-224-9000
- **Washington Athletic Club**, 1325 6th Ave., 206-622-7900
- **Westlake Club**, 1275 Westlake Ave. N, 206-283-9320
- **World Gym Fitness Centers**, multiple locations, 800-563-WRLD
- **XGYM**, 2505 2nd Ave. S, 206-728-XGYM
- **YWCA Health & Fitness Center**, multiple locations, 206-461-4868

As with all metropolitan areas in the U.S., Seattle offers a wide variety of religious organizations and communities, as attested to by the sheer number of churches, synagogues, and temples. For a more complete listing of the many places to worship in Seattle and surrounding areas, check the Yellow Pages.

AFRICAN METHODIST EPISCOPAL

- **First African Methodist Episcopal Church**, 1522 14th St., 206-323-9642
- **Primm Tabernacle African Methodist Episcopal**, 4455 S Brandon St., 206-723-2142
- **Walker Chapel African Methodist Episcopal Church**, 800 28th St. S, 206-325-8468

AFRICAN METHODIST EPISCOPAL ZION

- **Catherine Memorial African Methodist Episcopal Zion Church**, 5943 Martin Luther King Jr. Way S, 206-723-7973
- **Ebenezer African Methodist Episcopal Zion Church**, 1716 23rd Ave., 206-322-6620

ANGLICAN

- **St. Paul Anglican Church**, N 40th St. and Meridian Ave. N, 206-526-9020

APOSTOLIC

- **The Apostolic Faith**, 7420 9th Ave. E, 206-522-1350
- **Bethel Christian Church of the Apostolic Faith**, 200 24th Ave. S, 206-324-2141

- **Grace Apostolic Temple,** 6718 Martin Luther King Jr. Way. S, 206-723-5433
- **Jesus the Rock Full Gospel Church,** 555 16th Ave., 206-325-4358

ASSEMBLIES OF GOD

- **Ballard Assembly of God,** 2051 NW 61st St., 206-784-2064
- **Calvary Temple,** 6810 8th Ave. NE, 206-525-7473
- **Latin American Assemb. of God Temple El Redentor,** 5500 17th Ave. S, 206-768-1868
- **North Seattle Christian Fellowship,** 12345 8th Ave. NE, 206-367-6500
- **Queen Anne Christian Center,** 1716 2nd Ave. N, 206-283-6944
- **Seattle Outreach Ministries of the Assemb. of God,** 4402 S Graham St., 206-722-3319
- **The Gathering,** 129 Belmont Ave. E, 206-322-7702
- **Westwood Christian Assembly,** 9252 16th Ave. SW, 206-763-0585

BAPTIST

- **Ballard Baptist Church,** 2004 NW 63rd St., 206-784-1554
- **Chinese Baptist Church,** 5801 Beacon Ave. S, 206-725-6363
- **Damascus Baptist Church,** 5237 Rainier Ave. S, 206-725-9310
- **Fellowship Baptist Church,** 817 S 3rd St., 206-227-0781
- **Fremont Baptist Church,** 717 N 36th St., 206-632-7994
- **Haller Lake Baptist Church,** 14054 Wallingford Ave. N, 206-364-1811
- **Queen Anne Baptist Church,** 2011 1st Ave. N, 206-282-7744
- **Rosehill Missionary Baptist Church,** 7550 Martin Luther King Jr. Way S, 206-721-0426
- **Wedgwood Community Church,** 8201 30th Ave. NE, 206-522-5778

BUDDHIST

- **Dharmadhatu Buddhist Meditation Center,** 919 E Pike St., 206-860-4060
- **Rissho Kosei-Kai,** 5511 Martin Luther King Jr. Way S, 206-725-4268
- **Seattle Buddhist Temple,** 1427 S Main St., 206-329-080

CHRISTIAN SCIENCE

- **First Church of Christ-Scientist,** 16th Ave. E and E Denny Way, 206-324-3020
- **Third Church of Christ-Scientist,** 17th Ave. NE and NE 50th St., 206-522-5755
- **Fourth Church of Christ-Scientist,** 1119 8th Ave., 206-623-3632
- **Sixth Church of Christ-Scientist,** 2656 42nd Ave. SW, 206-932-6004
- **Seventh Church of Christ-Scientist,** 2555 8th Ave. W, 206-282-9255
- **Thirteenth Church of Christ-Scientist,** 3500 NE 125th St, 206-362-7646

CHURCH OF CHRIST

- **Church of Christ — Iglesia Ni Cristo,** 6020 Rainier Ave. S, 206-723-0346
- **Church of Christ — North Seattle,** 13315 20th Ave. NE, 206-367-9232
- **Church of Christ — West Seattle,** 4220 SW 100th St., 206-938-0212
- **Madison Park Church of Christ,** 1115 19th Ave., 206-324-6775

CHURCH OF GOD IN CHRIST

- **Berean Church of God in Christ,** 3417 Rainier Ave. S, 206-725-0745
- **Faith Temple Community Church of God in Christ,** 2623 E Union St., 206-322-4091
- **Madison Temple Church of God in Christ,** 2239 E Madison St., 206-323-4900
- **Survival Church of God in Christ,** 8459 50th Ave. S, 206-725-9366

CHURCH OF JESUS CHRIST OF LATTER DAY SAINTS

- **Church of Jesus Christ of Latter Day Saints — Seattle Stake,** 4001 44th Ave. SW, 206-935-0215

COVENANT

- **First Covenant Church,** 400 E Pike St., 206-322-7411
- **Interbay Covenant Church,** 3233 15th Ave. W, 206-283-9660

EASTERN ORTHODOX

- **Russian Orthodox Cathedral of St. Nicholas,** 1714 13th Ave, 206-322-9387
- **St. Demetrios Greek Orthodox Church,** 2100 Boyer Ave. E, 206-325-4347
- **St. Nectarios American Orthodox Church,** 10300 Ashworth Ave. N, 206-522-4471

EPISCOPAL

- **Church of the Epiphany,** 1805 38th Ave., 206-324-2573
- **Church of the Holy Apostles,** 2440 SW Roxbury St., 206-767-5150
- **St. Andrew's Episcopal Church,** 111 NE 80th St., 206-523-7476
- **St. John the Baptist Episcopal Church,** 4210 SW Hanford St., 206-937-4545
- **St. Mark's Episcopal Cathedral,** 1245 10th Ave. E, 206-323-0300

EVANGELICAL

- **Evangelical Chinese Church,** 651 NW 81st St., 206-789-6380
- **Maple Leaf Evangelical Church,** 1059 NE 96th St., 206-525-3707
- **Medhane-Alem Evangelical Church (Ethiopian),** 1729 Harvard Ave., 206-720-0181
- **Sonrise Evangelical Free Church,** 610 SW Roxbury St., 206-762-2488

FRIENDS (QUAKERS)

- **Friends Memorial Church,** 7740 24th Ave. NE, 206-525-8800
- **University Friends Meeting,** 4001 9th Ave. NE, 206-547-6449

HINDU

- **Vedanta Society of Western Washington (Ramakrishna Mission of India),** 2716 Broadway E, 206-323-1228

INDEPENDENT/INTERDENOMINATIONAL

- **Church of Mary Magdalene,** 811 5th Ave., 206-621-8474

- **Emmanuel Bible Church**, 503 N 50th St., 206-632-5539

ISLAM

- **Islamic (Idriss) Mosque**, 1420 NE Northgate Way, 206-363-3013
- **Jamaatul Ikhlas**, 1350 E Fir St., 206-322-6246

JEHOVAH'S WITNESSES

- **Central Congregation**, 333 19th Ave. E, 206-325-4192
- **Ballard and North Park Congregation**, 9240 6th Ave. NW, 206-783-9940
- **Rainier Congregation**, 5933 39th Ave. S, 206-722-1250
- **SW Cambridge and White Ctr. Congregation**, 2121 SW Cambridge St., 206-762-5486

JEWISH

REFORM
- **Temple Beth Am**, 2632 NE 80th St., 206-525-0915
- **Temple de Hirsch Sinai**, 1511 E Pike St., 206-323-8486

CONSERVATIVE
- **Congregation Beth Shalom**, 5031 University Way, NE, 206-524-0075

ORTHODOX
- **Bikur Cholim-Machzikay Hadath**, 5145 S Morgan St., 206-721-0970
- **Chabad-Lubavitch Chabad House**, 4541 19th Ave. NE, 206-524-1411
- **Congregation Ezra Bessaroth**, 5217 S Brandon St., 206-722-5500
- **Emanuel Congregation (Modern Orthodox)**, 3412 NE 65th St., 206-525-1055

LUTHERAN

- **Beacon Lutheran Church**, 1720 S Forest St., 206-322-0251
- **Bethel Chinese Lutheran Church**, 6553 40th Ave. NE, 206-524-7631

- **Central Lutheran Church of the Holy Trinity,** 1710 11th Ave., 206-322-7500
- **Crown Lutheran Church,** 1501 NW 90th St., 206-784-1930
- **Gethsemane Lutheran Church-ELCA,** 911 Stewart St., 206-682-3620
- **Grace Lutheran Church-WELS,** 11501 Phinney Ave. N, 206-363-8551
- **Hope Lutheran Church-Missouri Synod,** 4456 42nd Ave. SW, 206-937-9330
- **Luther Memorial Church-ELCA,** 13047 Greenwood Ave. N, 206-364-2510
- **Queen Anne Lutheran Church-ELCA,** 2400 8th Ave. W, 206-284-1960
- **University Lutheran Church,** 1604 NE 50th St., 206-525-7074
- **Zion Evangelical Lutheran Church-Missouri Synod,** 7109 Aurora Ave. N, 782-6734

METHODIST

- **Ballard Free Methodist Church,** 1460 NW 73rd St., 206-784-6111
- **Beacon United Methodist Church,** 7301 Beacon St., 206-722-5042
- **Curry Temple (Christian Methodist Episcopal),** 172 23rd Ave., 206-325-9344
- **Green Lake United Methodist Church,** 6415 1st Ave. NE, 206-526-2900
- **Haller Lake United Methodist Church,** 13055 1st Ave. NE, 206-362-5383
- **Rainier Avenue Free Methodist Church,** 5900 Rainier Ave. S, 206-722-5616
- **Seaview United Methodist Church,** 4620 SW Graham St., 206-932-7609

NAZARENE

- **Ballard Church of the Nazarene,** 6541 Jones Ave. NW, 206-784-1418
- **Beacon Hill Church of the Nazarene,** 4352 15th Ave. S, 206-762-2136
- **First Church of the Nazarene,** 4401 2nd Ave. NE, 206-632-4560

- North Seattle Church of the Nazarene, 13130 5th Ave. NE, 206-367-5955
- West Seattle Church of the Nazarene, 4201 SW Juneau St., 206-932-4581

PENTECOSTAL

- Bethany Temple Church, 1122 26th Ave. S, 206-328-1816
- Englesia De Dios Pentecostal Church, 2400 E Spruce St., 206-328-9717
- Full Gospel Pentecostal Federated Church, 5071 Delridge Way SW, 206-935-1511
- Holy Ground Pentecostal Temple, 4515 Rainier Ave. S, 206-723-5260

PRESBYTERIAN

- Beacon Hill Presbyterian Church, 1625 S Columbian Way, 206-762-0870
- Bethany Presbyterian Church, 1818 Queen Anne Ave. N, 206-284-2222
- Bethel Presbyterian Church, 11002 Greenwood Ave. N, 206-362-3600
- Green Lake Presbyterian Church, 6318 Linden Ave. N, 206-789-7320
- Japanese Presbyterian Church, 1801 24th Ave. S, 206-323-5990
- Korean Antioch Presbyterian Church, 6020 Beacon Ave. S, 206-725-5645
- West Side Presbyterian Church, 3601 California Ave. SW, 206-935-4477

ROMAN CATHOLIC

- Holy Family Church, 9615 20th SW, 206-767-6640
- Our Lady of Fatima Church, 3218 W Barrett St., 206-283-1456
- Our Lady of Guadalupe Church, 7000 35th Ave. SW, 206-935-0358
- St. James Cathedral, 804 9th Ave., 206-622-3559
- St. John Chrysostom Byzantine Catholic Church, 1305 S Lander St., 206-329-9219

- **St. Joseph Church,** 732 18th Ave. E, 206-324-2522
- **St. Margaret's Church,** 3221 14th Ave. W, 206-282-1804
- **St. Peter Catholic Church,** 2807 15th Ave. S, 206-324-2290

SEVENTH DAY ADVENTIST

- **Ballard Seventh Day Adventist Church,** 2054 NW 61st St., 206-783-1661
- **Green Lake Seventh Day Adventist Church,** 6350 E Green Lake Way N, 206-522-1330
- **Seward Park Seventh Day Adventist Church,** 5200 S Orcas St., 206-725-5253
- **West Seattle Seventh Day Adventist Church,** 7901 35th Ave. SW, 206-932-4211

UNITARIAN

- **University Unitarian Church,** 6556 35th Ave. NE, 206-525-8400
- **Admiral Congregational United Church of Christ,** 4320 SW Hill St., 206-932-2928
- **Beacon Avenue United Church of Christ,** 6230 Beacon Ave. S, 206-725-7535
- **Broadview Community United Church of Christ,** 325 N 125th St., 206-363-8060
- **Prospect United Church of Christ,** 1919 E Prospect St., 206-322-6030

UNITY

- **Seattle Unity Church,** 200 8th Ave. N, 206-622-8475
- **Vineyard Christian Fellowship of Seattle,** 4142 Brooklyn Ave. NE, 206-547-4354

WESLEYAN

- **Crown Hill Wesleyan Church,** 9204 11th Ave. NW, 206-783-6400

When you're new in town, volunteering provides the perfect opportunity to get acquainted with the community at large and to make new friends in the process. In addition to meeting people with similar interests, you'll be helping organizations that are often short on cash and resources. Seattle has many charitable and philanthropic organizations, offering services, food, and clothing, or donations to education or medical research. If you're not sure where you'd like to begin, the following volunteer placement services can point you in the right direction:

- **United Way of King County**, 107 Cherry St., 206-461-3655
- **Volunteers of America**, 6559 35th Ave. NE, 206-523-3565

Volunteer opportunities also can be found in the Yellow Pages and in newspaper advertisements. The following is a sample of possibilities, listed by category:

AIDS

- **AIDS Memorial Vigil-Seattle Chapter**, 1122 E Pike St. Suite 699, 206-233-1145
- **Bailey-Boushay House**, 2720 E Madison St., 206-322-5300
- **Chicken Soup Brigade**, 1002 E Seneca St., 206-328-8979
- **Multifaith AIDS Projects (MAPS)**, 1729 Harvard Ave., 206-324-1520
- **Northwest AIDS Foundation**, 127 Broadway E Suite 200, 206-329-6923
- **People of Color Against AIDS Network**, 5100 Rainier Ave. S, 206-721-0852

ALCOHOL AND DRUG DEPENDENCY

- **Addiction Recovery Systems for Sexual Minorities**, 726 Broadway Suite 102, 206-328-7595

- **Cascade Calvary Center,** 13751 Lake City Way NE, 206-364-4422
- **Catholic Community Services,** 100 23rd Ave. S, 206-325-5162
- **Central Seattle Recovery Center,** 1401 E Jefferson St. Suite 300, 206-322-2970
- **Guardian Recovery Program,** 2608 3rd Ave., 206-522-5856
- **Salvation Army Adult Rehabilitation Center,** 1000 4th Ave. S, 206-587-0503

CHILDREN

- **Big Brothers of King County,** 2719 E Madison St., 206-461-3630
- **Big Sisters of King County,** 1100 Virginia St. Suite 210, 206-461-3636
- **Boy's and Girl's Clubs of King County,** 206-461-3890
- **Childhaven,** 316 Broadway, 206-624-6477
- **Children's Home Society of Washington,** 3300 NE 65th St., 206-524-6020
- **Girl's Inc. of Puget Sound,** 708 Martin Luther King Jr. Way, 206-720-2912

CULTURAL IDENTITY

- **Afri-Relief and Development,** 4716 Rainier Ave. S, 206-760-9098
- **Chinese Information and Service Center,** 409 Maynard Ave. S Suite 203, 206-624-5633
- **El Centro de la Raza,** 2524 16th Ave. S, 206-329-9442
- **Filipino Youth Activities Inc.,** 810 18th Ave., 206-461-4870
- **Japanese American Citizens League,** 671 S Jackson St., 206-623-5088
- **Jewish Family Service,** 1601 16th Ave., 206-461-3240
- **Jewish Federation of Greater Seattle,** 2031 3rd Ave., 206-443-5400
- **Korean Community Counseling Center,** 302 N 78th St., 206-784-5691
- **Seattle Indian Center,** 510 24th Ave. S, 206-329-0676
- **Seattle Samoan Center Inc.,** 4714 Rainier Ave. S Suite 101, 206-322-0252
- **Society of African Americans USA,** 1218 E Cherry St., 206-860-0531

- **United Indians of All Tribes Foundation**, Daybreak Star Art Center, Discovery Park, 206-285-4425
- **Urban League of Metropolitan Seattle**, 105 14th Ave., 206-461-3792

DISABILITY ASSISTANCE

- **Creative Activities for Physically Disabled**, 201 N 85th St., 206-789-6525
- **Deaf-Blind Service Center**, 2366 Eastlake Ave. E, 206-323-9178
- **Easter Seal Society of Washington**, 521 2nd Ave. W, 206-281-5700

ENVIRONMENT

- **Cascadia Quest**, 810 18th Ave. Suite 206, 206-322-9296
- **Earth Ministry**, 1305 NE 47th St., 206-632-2426
- **Earth Share of Washington**, 1402 3rd Ave., 206-622-9840
- **Friends of the Earth**, 4512 University Way NE, 206-633-1661
- **Greenpeace**, 4649 Sunnyside Ave. N, 206-632-4326
- **Seattle Audubon Society**, 8050 35th Ave. NE, 206-523-8243
- **Sierra Club**, Cascade Chapter, 8511 15th Ave., NE, 206-523-2147

FOOD BANKS

- **Beacon Avenue Food Bank**, 6230 Beacon Ave. S, 206-722-5105
- **Downtown Food Bank**, 1531 Western Ave. Suite P, 206-626-6462
- **Northwest Harvest**, 711 Cherry St., 206-625-0755

GAY AND LESBIAN

- **Lambert House Gay Youth Center**, 1818 15th Ave. NE, 206-322-2735
- **Lesbian Resource Center**, 1808 Bellevue Ave., 206-322-3953
- **The Pride Foundation**, 1801 12th Ave., 206-323-3318
- **Stonewall Recovery Services**, 430 Broadway Ave. E, 206-461-4546

HEALTH AND HOSPITALS

Most hospitals welcome volunteers — just give the nearest one a call. For specific health issues, contact one of the following organizations:

- **Alzheimer's Association**, 1422 NW 85th St., 206-783-6600
- **American Cancer Society**, 2120 1st Ave. N, 206-283-1152
- **American Heart Association**, 4414 Woodland Park Ave. N, 206-632-6881
- **American Lung Association**, 2625 3rd Ave., 206-441-5100
- **March of Dimes Birth Defects Foundation**, 1904 3rd Ave. Suite 230, 206-624-1373
- **Multiple Sclerosis Society**, 192 Nickerson St. Suite 100, 206-284-4236

HOMELESS SERVICES

- **Family Services**, 615 2nd Ave. Suite 150, 206-461-3883
- **HELPS Mission**, 315 NW 84th St. Suite 305, 206-784-1969
- **Jubilee Women's Center**, 620 18th Ave. E, 206-324-1244
- **Millionair Club**, 2515 Western Ave., 206-728-5600
- **Sacred Heart Shelter**, 232 Warren Ave. N, 206-285-7489
- **Strand Helpers**, 5747 Martin Luther King Jr. Way S, 206-723-6082
- **Union Gospel Mission**, 318 2nd Ave., 206-622-5177

HUMAN SERVICES

- **American Red Cross**, 1900 25th Ave. S, 206-323-2345
- **Emergency Feeding Program**, 4620 S Findlay St., 206-723-0647
- **Goodwill**, Rainier Ave. S and S Dearborn St., 206-329-1000
- **Habitat for Humanity**, 306 Westlake Ave. N, 206-292-5240
- **Salvation Army**, 1101 Pike St., 206-447-9944

LEGAL AID

- **American Civil Liberties Union**, 705 2nd Ave., 206-624-2180
- **Volunteer Legal Services**, 206-623-2551

LITERACY

- **Literacy Action Center**, 8016 Greenwood Ave. N, 206-782-2050
- **Literacy Council of Seattle**, 811 5th Ave., 206-233-9720
- **Washington Literacy**, 2209 Eastlake Ave. E, 206-461-3623

MEN'S SERVICES

- **Dads Against Discrimination**, 206-623-DADS

POLITICS - ELECTORAL

- **Democratic Central Committee of King County**, 1411 4th Ave., 206-622-9157
- **Freedom Socialist Party — National Office**, 409 Maynard Ave. S, 206-682-0990
- **International Socialist Organization**, PO Box 9056 Queen Anne Station, 206-292-8809
- **Labor Party — Seattle Chapter**, PO Box 61087, 206-382-5712
- **League of Women Voters of Washington**, 1411 4th Ave., 206-622-8961
- **Libertarian Party of Washington State**, PO Box 20732 Broadway Station, 206-329-5669
- **Populist Party of Washington State**, 1916 Pike Place Suite 695, 206-781-0367
- **Republican Party — King County**, 1305 Republican St., 206-467-1996

POLITICS - SOCIAL

- **American Veterans Association**, 206-781-5873
- **Blacks in Government**, Region X, 810 3rd Ave., 206-624-4870
- **Hands Off Washington**, 1122 E Pike St. #532, 206-323-5191.
- **Peace Action of Washington**, 5828 Roosevelt Way NE, 206-527-8050

REFUGEE ASSISTANCE

- **Lutheran Refugee Program**, 4130 University Way NE, 206-547-5306

SENIOR SERVICES

- **Greenwood Senior Center**, 525 N 85th St., 206-461-7841

- **Northwest Senior Activity Center**, 32nd NW and NW Market St., 206-461-7811
- **Pike Market Senior Center**, 1931 1st Ave., 206-728-2773
- **Ravenna-Bryant Senior Center**, 2121 NE 68th St., 206-527-0718
- **Senior Center of West Seattle**, 4217 SW Oregon St., 206-932-4044
- **Senior Services of Seattle/King County**, 1601 2nd Ave. Suite 800, 206-448-5757
- **Southeast Seattle Senior Center**, 4655 S Holly St., 206-722-0317

WOMEN'S SERVICES

- **Center for the Prevention of Sexual and Domestic Violence**, 936 N 34th St., 206-634-1903
- **Catherine Booth House — Salvation Army Shelter for Abused Women**, 206-281-4600
- **Junior League of Seattle**, 4119 E Madison St., 206-324-3638
- **New Beginnings for Battered Women and Their Children**, 206-783-4520
- **Refugee Women's Alliance**, 3004 S Alaska St., 206-721-0243

YOUTH

- **Central Area Youth Association**, 119 23rd Ave., 206-322-6640
- **Central Youth and Family Services**, 1901 Martin Luther King Jr. Way S, 206-322-7676
- **Southwest Youth and Family Services**, 4555 Delridge Way SW, 206-937-7680
- **University District Youth Center**, 4516 15th Ave. NE, 206-526-2992
- **Youth Advocates**, 2317 E John St, 206-322-7838

BY CAR

Most Seattle residents drive everywhere — to work, church, the grocery store, Downtown, etc. Perhaps it's the hills or the inclement weather, but many people here spend as much time in the car each day as they do eating their meals. Despite efforts by the city and King County to reduce the number of single-occupancy vehicles on the road, I-5 and both bridges to the Eastside are always crowded during rush hour. Buses, carpools, and ride-sharing programs present alternatives to the solitary commute. The city offers incentives to businesses that encourage their employees to share the commute (or walk or bicycle) to work, something you may want to investigate at your office. Enhancements to the existing transit systems are in the works. In 1996, Seattle voters approved a $3.9 billion plan to build a comprehensive mass-transit system of commuter trains and express buses.

Here are a few tips for making your commute a little easier:

H.O.V. (High Occupancy Vehicle) lanes or "diamond lanes" are located on Interstates 5, 405, and 90. These lanes are reserved for carpools (minimum two or three passengers, depending on the lane), buses, and motorcycles. If you need to travel over one of the Lake Washington bridges (I-90 or Hwy. 520) during rush hour, these lanes are the way to go. You'll be able to fly past the rest of the traffic and cut to the front of the line at the bridge deck. For information on carpool parking permits, which can be used for discounted or free parking in Downtown Seattle, call the city's **Carpool Parking/Permits** line at 206-684-0818. For information on ride-sharing options, call Metro's **Ridematch** line at 206-625-4500 or 800-427-8249, or visit Metro's web site, www.transit.metrokc.gov/.

Metered ramps are on-ramps equipped with traffic lights to control the flow of traffic. Most in-city ramps to I-5 are now metered, although the lights only operate during high-volume hours. Metered ramps usually have an HOV on-ramp lane, which allows carpool vehicles on without stopping.

Traffic reports are available on all major radio stations during rush hour. These can be invaluable once you've identified some alternate routes to your usual destinations. Start listening to the radio as soon as you get up in the morning or about a half hour before leaving work, and make adjustments accordingly.

You can call the **Washington State Department of Transportation** (WSDOT) traffic line at 206-DOT-HIWY (206-368-4499) to get information on current traffic conditions, including traffic flow statistics and accident and construction reports. If you have access to the internet, you can also check local freeways on the WSDOT web site at www.wsdot.wa.gov/regions/northwest/NWFLOW/. This URL offers traffic flow maps, live camera shots of area freeways, and other helpful commuter graphics.

As you get to know Seattle, you'll certainly find your own alternatives to the major freeways, highways, and thoroughfares. Until then, here are some of the main arteries:

The main north-south roadway is I-5, connecting Seattle with Oregon to the south and British Columbia to the north. Running smack through the middle of the city, this freeway is both a blessing and a curse for those living near it. If you're already near it and if it's moving at all, it is usually the quickest way to other neighborhoods in the city. However, if you're more than ten minutes from the freeway, it's often quicker to take local streets across town.

Another north-south thoroughfare in the city is Aurora Ave. (Hwy. 99), which parallels I-5 as far as the Seattle Center, then cuts under the city and follows the waterfront. The section of Hwy. 99 along the waterfront is a stacked freeway known as "the viaduct." North of the Green Lake area, Aurora can be fairly slow because of the main traffic lights. South of the lake and through the Downtown area, Aurora is a reliable alternative to I-5, especially for those coming from the Greenwood, Phinney Ridge, Fremont, or Wallingford neighborhoods. If you travel to the airport often from any of these neighborhoods, find a good map and trace out the shortcut to the airport which includes Hwy. 99, Hwy. 509, then Hwy. 518. This can easily save you 30 minutes during rush hour.

The main east-west freeway in Seattle is I-90, which connects Seattle with Eastern Washington. The I-90 bridge is usually the best of the two Lake Washington bridges, because it has several lanes going in each direction as well as a reversible H.O.V. lane. Because I-90 begins at the Kingdome, give yourself extra time on Seahawks game days.

The other east-west highway, Hwy. 520, runs from I-5 just north of Capitol Hill to the Eastside. The 520 Bridge is one of the worst stretches of road during rush hour. Even if there isn't an accident on the bridge, the amazing views of the lake and Mount Rainier as well as bright sunlight slow traffic on the bridge decks. The "high rises" (the high portions of the bridge) at the west end of the bridge also cause traffic backups because drivers have to slow for the curves and accelerate for the incline. If you can't use I-90 as your regular route over the lake, set up a carpool and take advantage of the HOV lanes or try to use an on-ramp as close to the bridge itself as possible.

Another route from Seattle to the Eastside is I-405, which generally runs north-south on the east side of Lake Washington. I-405 goes through Renton, Bellevue, Kirkland and Bothell, connecting with I-5 south of Seattle near Southcenter Mall, and north of Seattle in Lynnwood. Depending on your destination and the time of day, an I-5 to I-405 route might be the quickest way around the lake.

The West Seattle Freeway starts at I-5 near Beacon Hill and travels west to the West Seattle peninsula, crossing Hwy. 99 on the way. This is the main thoroughfare in and out of the north end of West Seattle.

BY BUS

Currently buses are the primary form of mass transit in Seattle. Mass transit boosters hope that the passage of commuter rail ballot initiatives means a better regional mass transit system is on its way. Only time will tell.

Metro Transit provides buses that are generally clean and on-time, although they make frequent time-consuming stops as they traverse the city. Express buses are much faster but go to fewer destinations. Crosstown buses are limited and transfers are often necessary when travelling between neighborhoods. The good news is that the bus fares are reasonable (adult fares are $1.00/off-peak, $1.25/peak, youth fares are $.75, and seniors and persons with disabilities are $.25) and most of Downtown is part of a ride-free zone, meaning that passengers can use the bus for free in the Downtown area as long as they disembark before crossing Denny Way or Yesler Way (most bus drivers announce the end of the ride-free zone). The ride-free area in Downtown is the result of the unusual way that fares are collected on Metro buses. Rather than always paying when you get on the bus, fares are collected either at beginning of the ride (if you're travelling toward Downtown) or at the end of the ride (if you're travelling away from Downtown). A sign at the front of the bus will let you know when to pay your fare.

Bus passes and ticket books are available and can save a lot of money for regular passengers. Some employers, institutions, and community organizations provide free or discounted passes for employees and members, as part of the Employer Commute Services sponsored by King County Metro. Bus passes are available at over 100 locations in the city, including some drug stores and cash machines, or you can call **Metro** at **206-624-PASS** to purchase by phone.

Bus schedules are posted at all bus stops (but only for the buses that use that route), or you can call **Metro's Automated Schedule Information Line** at **206-BUS-TIME**. **Metro's 24-hour Rider Information Line** at **206-553-3000** connects you to a Metro employee who can assist you with schedule and route information, as long as you can provide your starting point and destination information. Metro Transit also has an informative and comprehensive web site at www.transit.metrokc.gov/.

In addition to buses, Metro also runs two unique public transportation systems. A relic of the Seattle World's Fair, the Monorail runs between Westlake Center in the Downtown shopping district and the Seattle Center, and the Waterfront Trolley uses an old railroad track to travel from the International District to the north end of the Waterfront, making several stops along the way.

Finally, the following are contact numbers for other public transportation systems outside of Seattle. Community Transit covers most of Seattle's neighboring communities, Everett Transit covers the greater Everett area north of Seattle, and Pierce Transit provides bus service in Tacoma.

- **Community Transit**, 425-778-2185 or 800-562-1375
- **Everett Transit**, 425-257-8803
- **Pierce Transit**, 800-562-8109

BY FERRY

Because there are no bridges connecting Seattle with the Olympic Peninsula, many area residents commute to and from work daily by ferry. The Washington State Ferries system is the largest in the United States and includes ten routes that serve the Puget Sound area. The routes used for commuting to the city are the Seattle-Bremerton, Seattle-Bainbridge Island, and Seattle-Vashon Island, which dock at a terminal on the Seattle waterfront; the Fauntleroy-Vashon-Southworth, serving West Seattle, Vashon Island and the Olympic Peninsula; and the Edmonds-Kingston, which departs from a terminal in Edmonds, 20 minutes north of Seattle. Other routes serve the San Juan Islands, British Columbia, Whidbey Island, and Tacoma.

Those routes used for commuting to Seattle can be very busy in the morning and evening hours. If you're walking on, you probably won't have any problem getting on the ferry, even if you arrive just a few minutes before departure. If you're driving on, you'll need to arrive early or be prepared to take a later ferry. This is also true when taking a car on any ferries on weekends or holidays. The wait time for those wanting to ferry their vehicles at some of the San Juan Islands routes can be several hours on summer holiday weekends.

Fares vary according to season and route. Passenger only round-trip fares are about $3.50 (usually collected at the eastern terminal of the ferry route only). Vehicle and driver one-way fares are $6.00 on most routes, and are always collected in both directions. Additional fees may be charged for oversized vehicles. Discounts are available for frequent passengers, children, disabled persons, and senior citizens.

Schedules also vary by season and route. Ferry information pamphlets are available at all ferry terminals, as well as at some transit information booths in the city. For more information, call the **Washington State Ferries'** information line at 206-464-6400 or 800-84-FERRY or visit the comprehensive web site at www.wsdot.wa.gov/ferries.

TAXIS

Unless you are Downtown, on Capitol Hill, or at the airport, you'll probably need to call ahead to arrange for a taxi. A few of Seattle's many taxicab companies are listed here; others can be found in the Yellow Pages.

- **Broadway Cabs**, 206-622-4800
- **Checker Cab**, 206-762-5533
- **Emerald City Taxi**, 206-624-6666
- **Farwest Taxi**, 206-622-1717
- **Graytop Cab**, 206-282-8723
- **Orange Cab**, 206-522-8800

- **Yellow Cab**, 206-622-6500

SEATTLE-TACOMA INTERNATIONAL AIRPORT

The Seattle-Tacoma International Airport, known locally as Sea-Tac, is located south of Seattle at 17801 Pacific Hwy. S. For parking rates and information, airport weather conditions, and general information, call 206-431-4444. When travelling to the airport by car, use the following directions from Seattle:

- Take I-5 south to the Southcenter/Sea-Tac Airport exit and follow the signs to get on Hwy. 518. From Hwy. 518 take the Sea-Tac Airport exit and stay to the left as you exit. This will put you on the main road into the airport, which is clearly marked with signs to baggage claim, airline counters, and parking.

Alternate directions from Downtown, Ballard, Phinney Ridge, Greenwood, Fremont, and Broadview (these are just a little faster during rush hour):

- Take Hwy. 99 south until it forces you left onto 1st Ave. S. Stay in the right lane and follow directions to the 1st Ave. S Bridge (only a few blocks). After you cross the bridge, the road you are on becomes Hwy. 509. Stay on Hwy. 509 to the Sea-Tac Airport and Hwy. 518 exit. Take a left off the exit onto Hwy. 518 E, then from Hwy. 518 take the Sea-Tac exit. This exit puts you on the main road into the airport.

Airport parking options include:

- **Express meter parking**: $1/20 minutes, up to 2 hours.
- **Handicapped parking**: No charge for up to 2 hours in express meter parking; regular rates for long-term and valet parking.
- **Long-term parking**: $16/day, up to one month.
- **Valet parking**: $10 for 0-4 hours, $15 for 4-12 hours, $21 for 12-24 hours.

The following **bus routes** will take you to the airport from Downtown Seattle, and vice versa:

- **Route 194**: departures every 30 minutes throughout the day; travel time 30 minutes.
- **Route 174**: departures every 30 minutes throughout the day; travel time 40 minutes.
- **Route 184**: departures at 2:15 a.m. and 3:30 a.m. only (from the airport), and at 2:49 a.m. and 4:04 a.m. only (from Downtown); travel time 30 minutes.
- **Route 340** - daily airport service to and from downtown Bellevue. Departure times: every 20-30 minutes in both directions, Monday-Friday, every hour on Saturday and Sunday. Travel time: 60 minutes.

You also have the option of catching a shuttle. Most Downtown hotels offer shuttle service to the airport, call ahead for times and costs (it may be free if you are a hotel guest). For a door-to-door shuttle service, try one of the following:

- **Gray Line Airport Express**, 206-626-6088
- **Supershuttle**, 206-622-1424
- **VIP Airport Shuttle**, 206-277-8211
- **Yellow Express Airport Shuttle**, 206-622-3400

AMTRAK

The passenger station for Amtrak is located in Seattle's International District, near the Kingdome. Trains run south from Seattle to Portland, and on into California, and north to Canada. The Empire Builder route connects Seattle with Chicago, stopping at major cities in between.

- **Amtrak National Route Information**, 800-872-7245, www.amtrak.com
- **Amtrak - Seattle Station**, 303 S Jackson St., 206-382-4125

NATIONAL BUS SERVICES

The **Greyhound Bus Lines** terminal is located at 8th Ave. and Stewart St. in Downtown Seattle. For reservation information call the terminal directly at 206-628-5526 or Greyhound's national reservation number at 800-231-2222. Another option for bus trips to some Eastern Washington cities is **Northwestern Trailways**, call 206-728-5955 for reservations and information.

Even if you find your new home in Seattle quickly, you may need a place to stay during your first visit or visits to the city or while you're moving in. If you're lucky enough to have a friend or relative to stay with in Seattle, that's probably the most economical choice. If you're planning on staying in temporary housing for more than a couple of weeks, consider a sublet or short-term lease. Sublets are often advertised in local classifieds, particularly during the spring and summer when college students head out of town. The apartment search services listed in the **Looking for a Place to Live** chapter can assist you with finding a short-term lease for you. In addition consider the following options, which vary in expense and accommodation.

HOTELS AND MOTELS

As a port city, business hub, and tourist destination, Seattle has a large number of hotels and motels offering various levels of service and facilities. In general, the least expensive motels are those along Aurora Ave. N (Hwy. 99) north of Downtown, although these lodgings come with the security risks inherent to the high crime area of Aurora. These motels are generally not suitable for children or for adults uncomfortable with fast-paced urban settings, and for that reason are not listed here.

Rates are based on a single-bed room per night. Prices may vary, based on the season, special events, and vacancy rates. Call ahead for reservations, and make sure to ask about special discounts or business rates.

- **Alexis Hotel**, 100 1st Ave., 206-624-4844 or 800-426-7033, $125
- **Best Western Executive Inn**, 200 Taylor Ave. N, 206-448-9444, $85
- **Best Western Loyal Inn**, 2301 8th Ave., 206-682-0200, $78
- **Camlin Hotel**, 1619 9th Ave., 206-682-0100, $83
- **Cavanaugh's on Fifth Avenue**, 1415 5th Ave., 206-971-8000 or 800-

THE-INNS, $145
- **Crowne Plaza**, 1113 6ᵗʰ Ave., 206-464-1980 or 800-227-6963, $169
- **Days Inn**, 2205 7ᵗʰ Ave., 206-448-3434, $69
- **The Edgewater**, 2411 Alaskan Wy, 206-728-7000, $99
- **Four Seasons Olympic Hotel**, 411 University St., 206-621-1700 or 800-332-3442, $205
- **Hotel Monaco**, 1101 4ᵗʰ Ave., 206-621-1770, $99
- **Hotel Seattle**, 315 Seneca St., 206-623-5110, $72
- **Hotel Vintage Park**, 1100 5ᵗʰ Ave., 206-624-8000, $125
- **The Inn at the Market**, Pike Place Market, 206-443-3600, $140
- **The Inn at Virginia Mason**, 1006 Spring St., 206-583-6453 or 800-283-6453, $98
- **Mayflower Park Hotel**, 4ᵗʰ Ave. and Olive St., 206-623-8700 or 800-426-5100, $150
- **Quality Inn City Center**, 2224 8ᵗʰ Ave., 206-624-6820 or 800-437-4867, $79
- **Ramada Inn - Downtown**, 2200 5ᵗʰ Ave, 206-441-9785 or 800-228-2828, $109
- **Renaissance Madison Hotel**, 515 Madison St., 206-583-0300 or 800-468-3571 (TTY 800-833-4747), $159
- **St. Regis Hotel**, 116 Stewart St., 206-448-6366, $50
- **Sheraton Seattle Hotel and Towers**, 1400 6ᵗʰ Ave., 206-621-9000, $160
- **Silver Cloud Inn**, 5036 25ᵗʰ Ave. NE, 206-526-5200 or 800-205-6940, $93
- **The Sorrento Hotel**, 900 Madison St., 206-622-6400, $210
- **Travelodge - Downtown**, 6ᵗʰ Ave. N and John St., 206-441-7878, $69
- **Travelodge - University District**, 4725 25ᵗʰ Ave. NE, 206-525-4612, $68
- **University Inn**, 4140 Roosevelt Wy. NE, 206-632-5055, $82
- **Vance Hotel**, 620 Stewart St., 206-441-4200, $99

SHORT-TERM LEASES AND RESIDENCE HOTELS

The following hotels and leasing companies offer full suites for rent by the day, week, or month. Rooms include a kitchen or kitchenette, living room, and bedroom. Often maid service and other amenities are optional.

- **Corporate Living Network,** 888-450-0830
- **Executive Court Suites,** 300 10ᵗʰ Ave., 206-223-9300 or 800-906-6226
- **Home-Pac, Inc.,** 206-770-6616
- **Inn at Queen Anne,** 505 1ˢᵗ Ave. N, 206-282-7357
- **Oakwood Corporate Housing,** 206-861-1175
- **Plaza Park Suites,** 1011 Pike St., 206-682-8282
- **Residence Inn by Marriott,** 800 Fairview Ave., 206-624-6000
- **Short Term Suites (Dravus Court),** 15 Dravus St., 206-285-9698

BED & BREAKFAST INNS

If you're in the mood for quaint or cozy, consider a bed and breakfast. Most of Seattle's B&Bs are outside of the Downtown area, so this may also be a good way to check out prospective neighborhoods in the city.

- **Bacon Mansion,** 959 Broadway E, 206-329-1864, $84
- **Beech Tree Manor,** 1405 Queen Anne Ave. N, 206-281-7037, $89
- **Blue Willow Bed & Breakfast,** 213 W Comstock St., 206-284-4240, $80
- **Capitol Hill House,** 2215 E Prospect St., 206-322-1752, $75
- **Chambered Nautilus Bed & Breakfast,** 5005 22ⁿᵈ Ave.NE, 206-522-2536, $79
- **Chelsea Station on the Park,** 4915 Linden Ave. N, 206-547-6077 or 800-400-6077, $64
- **Dibble House,** 7301 Dibble Ave. NW, 206-783-0320, $65
- **Green Gables,** 1503 2ⁿᵈ Ave. W, 206-282-6863, $79
- **Hill House,** 1113 E John St., 206-720-7161, $90
- **La Paloma Bed & Breakfast,** 2113 13ᵗʰ Ave. S, 206-323-1283, $60
- **Mildred's Bed & Breakfast,** 1202 15ᵗʰ Ave. E, 206-325-6072, $85
- **Prince of Wales Bed & Breakfast,** 133 13ᵗʰ Ave. E, 206-325-9692, $115
- **Scandia House,** 2028 34ᵗʰ Ave. S, 206-725-7825, $100
- **Shafer-Baillie Mansion,** 907 14ᵗʰ Ave. E, 206-322-4654 or 800-922-4654, $69

HOSTELS

Hostels offer basic accommodations at low prices, but there are few restrictions that apply. Generally you'll be expected to sleep in a shared room and use a common bathroom and shower, although some have private rooms at a higher price. Some hostels require membership in an international hostelling association to get the greatest discount or even to stay in them. Others restrict the number of nights you can spend there or limit the time that you can be in the hostel during the day. The wisest course is to call in advance to make sure that you qualify (and that you'll be happy with the house rules).

- **American International Backpacker's Hostel**, 206-720-2965 or 800-600-2965
- **Continental Court Youth Hostel**, 206-241-1500
- **Hostelling International - Seattle Hostel**, 84 Union St., 206-622-5443
- **Green Tortoise Guesthouse**, 1525 2nd Ave., 206-340-1222

YMCAS/YWCAS

- **YMCA Downtown**, 909 4th Ave., 206-382-5000, men and women (at this writing, however, the Y is planning to discontinue its lodging service in the near future)
- **YWCA Downtown**, 1118 5th Ave., 206-461-4888, women only

OTHER OPTIONS

Hopefully, you'll be able to find an affordable and convenient place to stay from the listings in this chapter. For other options and to get a packet of information on accommodations in Seattle or Washington State, try either of these resources:

- **Seattle Visitor's Bureau**, 206-461-5840
- **Washington State Tourism**, 360-586-2088, www.tourism.wa.gov

After you've found a home and settled in a bit, you'll probably want to start exploring outside of Seattle. The Puget Sound area, and Western Washington in general, is a wonderful place to visit. Just a short drive away (five hours at most) you'll discover mountain peaks, lush valleys, azure lakes and streams, delightful fields of flowers, and picturesque farms. For general travel information, and a tourism packet, call the **Washington State Tourism Office** at 360-586-2088 or visit their web site at www.tourism.wa.gov.

Most of the locations listed in this chapter offer a variety of activities, lodgings, and other attractions. For information on outdoor sports and recreation destinations, specifically for hiking, fishing, skiing and the like, read the **Sports and Recreation** chapter of this book.

VASHON ISLAND, WHIDBEY ISLAND, SAN JUAN ISLANDS

Vashon Island is located in the Puget Sound just southwest of West Seattle. Small and green, with a quaint shopping district and an annual Strawberry Festival, Vashon Island is a great day trip or weekend destination. A ferry ride from Downtown Seattle or West Seattle will take you to the island. You'll probably want a car once you're there, although there is bus service on the island.

Whidbey Island, northwest of Seattle, is one of the two longest islands in the United States (Long Island and Whidbey Island trade the honor back and forth as their measurements change with erosion). Whidbey Island is most easily reached by catching a ferry from Mukilteo, but a longer route through Mount Vernon and Anacortes can save you the ferry fare. Whidbey has several picturesque towns, such as **Coupeville** and **Oak Harbor**. Make sure you try some mussels in a local seafood restaurant, and take the time to drive to **Deception Pass**, at the north end of the island. The view from the bridge is stunning, though not recommended for those afraid of heights. For a free **Island County Discovery Guide** and other tourist information, call 888-747-7777. For information on the internet, visit either of two fine web sites: www.islandweb.org/tourism.html and www.whidbey.net/islandco/.

The **San Juan Islands** are reached by ferry, either from Anacortes or Bellingham, and are worth the extra time. If possible, give yourself a long weekend or several days; the wait for the ferry alone can take several hours, especially on a holiday or summer weekend. Another option is to take a float plane from Lake Union to the San Juans, which is an exciting and beautiful way to see the Puget Sound. There are several islands in the San Juans that are worth visiting, each with breathtaking views. Stay in a quaint bed and breakfast or hotel, or check for vacation rentals on the internet or in Seattle newspapers. You'll find secluded beaches, cozy coffee shops, and charming towns. If possible, take your bike and tour the islands that way. Ferry rides between islands, especially if you're walking on or taking a bicycle, are inexpensive, but you'll want to make sure that the dock is close enough to town, or you might be in for a long haul. For more information, contact the **Orcas Island Chamber of Commerce** at 360-376-2273, **Tourist Information Services** at 360-378-6977, or visit the San Juan web site at www.sanjuanweb.com/.

Skagit Valley, located only a couple hours north of Seattle, is famous for its tulips, actually producing more tulips than the Netherlands. During the spring and summer, thousands of visitors come to the valley to see the colorful tulip fields. In addition to viewing acres of waving tulips, be sure to visit nearby **La Conner** or **Mount Vernon.** La Conner is a captivating village, with intimate cafes, homemade ice cream and candy shops, and scrumptious bakeries. A few antique malls on the edges of town attract Seattle collectors as well. Mount Vernon offers several antique malls, delicious eateries, and a local brewpub with excellent food. For more information, call the **Tulip Festival Organization** at 360-428-5959, or visit the Skagit Valley web site at www.skagit.com/.

Located on the southern tip of Vancouver Island, **Victoria, B.C.** is a direct ferry ride from the Seattle Waterfront on the Victoria Clipper. It's a small but appealing city, with a lively waterfront and beautiful gardens. **The Butchart Gardens** in particular are worth a visit. Bus tours leave for the gardens several times a day from the waterfront. Children will enjoy the wax museum with its peculiarly accurate replicas of famous and historical figures. A trip to Victoria isn't complete without high tea at the Empress Hotel, which presides over the waterfront. For visitor information call **Tourism Victoria** at 250-953-2033 or visit their web site at www.travel.victoria.bc.ca/.

A four-hour drive north of Seattle on I-5, **Vancouver, B.C.** is a cosmopolitan port city offering great shopping, including an extensive underground mall and Robson Street, which is lined with fashionable clothing boutiques, trendy cosmetics stores, and unique beauty and bath shops. Visit **Granville Island** for a bustling farmers' market during the day or live music and dancing at night. Rent bicycles and pack a picnic lunch to ride through beautiful **Stanley Park**, which overlooks the shipping activity in the bay. Music concerts and live theater performances draw many Seattle residents to Vancouver, since many tours stop at only one of the two cities. For more information about the city, try any of these three resources:

- **Tourism Vancouver**, 800-663-6000, www.tourism-vancouver. org/travelbc/
- **Discover Vancouver**, www.discovervancouver.com/index.shtml
- **Tourism British Columbia**, www.tbc.gov.bc.ca

If you're in the mood to relax and get away from the big city pace, consider a trip to the sleepy resort town of **Harrison Hot Springs, B.C.** From any point in this small town, you'll have a spectacular view of Harrison Lake and surrounding mountains. During the spring and summer, you can charter a fishing boat, take a cruise on the lake, play golf, go parasailing, play tennis, swim in the lake or the public hot springs pool, hike, water ski, windsurf, or go horseback riding. Harrison Hot Springs is just over four hours from Seattle. A stay at the Harrison Hot Springs Hotel offers a soak in private hot springs pools and complimentary high tea. While you're in town, stop by Sweet Martha Bakery and Coffee Shop for a slice of homemade pie with real whipped cream. For additional information on the town and neighboring communities call the **Harrison Hot Springs Chamber of Commerce** at 604-796-3425 or visit the local web site, www.users.uniserve.com/~ddunlop/.

Washington's own Bavarian village, **Leavenworth** is located on Hwy. 2 on the east side of the Cascade Mountains. Always popular with out-of-state tourists, Leavenworth also attracts Washington residents for outdoor activities and special events. During the summer, the town is a destination for novice rock climbers, who scale boulders along Icicle Creek. In the winter, Leavenworth offers nearby skiing at Steven's Pass as well as Christmas festivals and concerts. For more information, contact the **Leavenworth Chamber of Commerce** at 509-548-5807 or on the web at www.leavenworth.org/.

Also located east of the Cascades, **Lake Chelan** is a favorite among college students and/or water skiers. At the southern tip of the lake, the town of Lake Chelan offers crowded bars, casual restaurants, and sporting goods shops. Condominiums and motels line the lake shore, and there is public camping at nearby parks. Call ahead for reservations, though, because the area is usually packed during the summer months. For additional tourist information call 800-4-CHELAN or check out their internet site at www.lakechelan.com/.

A short ferry ride across Puget Sound, the **Olympic Peninsula** has a little something for everyone. **Poulsbo** is a small Scandinavian style village located 30 minutes east of the Bainbridge ferry terminal. Stop in for a fabulous donut at the Poulsbo Bakery, home of the original recipe for Poulsbo Bread. Just outside of town, the Thomas Kemper microbrewery offers daily tours and a tasty pub menu. **Port Townsend**, where "An Officer and A Gentleman" was filmed, has historic buildings, antique stores, unusual boutiques and kite shops. You can also catch a ferry to Whidbey Island from downtown Port Townsend. **Port Angeles**, at the northern tip of the peninsula, offers ferry service to Victoria, B.C. **Hurricane Ridge**, located only 15 minutes away from Port Angeles, is always worth a visit. The mountaintop views from the ridge are sensational, even if you only drive to the parking lot and visitors center. Nestled in the Olympic National Park, **Sol Duc Hot Springs** has cabins and a campground for visitors. Soak in the beautiful outdoor pools, take a short hike to the Sol Duc waterfall, or arrange for a massage from on-site massage therapists. Another short drive takes you to secluded **Ruby Beach,** one of the nicest sandy beaches on the Washington Coast. For more information on the Olympic Peninsula, visit the internet at www.olympus.net/. You may also call the Sol Duc Hot Springs Resort directly at 360-327-3583.

If you are interested in hiking or mountain climbing, consider a trip into the **Olympic Mountains**. Before leaving Seattle, visit a local bookstore(see the "Literary Life" section of the **Cultural Life** chapter for a list of area bookstores) for a copy of one of the many hiking guides to the Olympics. If you enjoy mountain climbing, two mountains on the peninsula are especially challenging: **The Brothers** is the twin-peaked mountain that is easily visible from Seattle, and **Mount Olympus**, while it cannot be seen from the city, is the tallest mountain in the Olympic range. To climb to the summit of either of these peaks, contact a local mountain climbing club or guide service (see the **Sports and Recreation** chapter for listings). Happily, there are many more hikes in the Olympics that are suitable for the rest of us. For information on **Olympic National Park**, call 360-452-4501 or visit the **National Park Service** web site at www.nps.gov/.

In the mood for a picturesque beach resort town and ocean view? Try either the **southwest Washington coast** or **northern Oregon coast**. **Long Beach**, at the far southwest tip of Washington State, is said to be the world's longest beach. Several annual events are held in Long Beach such as a state kite-flying festival, regional stunt kite competition, sand sculpture contest, and Fourth of July fireworks celebration. Contact the **Long Beach Peninsula Visitor's Bureau** by phone at 360-642-2400 or 800-451-2542. Across the mouth of the Columbia, the Oregon coast offers a stretch of beautiful beaches and ocean surf. **Seaside** is the most well-known destination, with affordable beach cottages and hotels and access to an expanse of white sandy beach. Other nearby towns attract fewer visitors, a plus for those in search of a private stretch of beach or a romantic getaway. If that's your preference, rent a cottage in **Gearhart** or reserve a room overlooking the ocean in **Cannon Beach**. For more information on these and other Oregon destinations, call the **Oregon Tourism Commission** at 503-986-0000 or visit their web site at www.ohwy.com/or/homepage.htm. The drive to Long Beach from Seattle is about four hours; Seattle to Seaside is four to five hours, even with Friday rush hour traffic. If possible, give yourself a long weekend, but expect more crowds if it's a holiday.

Majestic **Mount Rainier** will be a common sight to you soon after moving to Seattle. Yet despite its familiarity, the mountain is always worth a visit. During the winter, **Crystal Mountain** ski resort bustles with activity while the rest of the mountain is deserted. In early spring however, the roads begin to re-open and visitors flock to the area to hike, mountain climb, and camp. Mount Rainier is a challenging hiking or climbing destination even for experienced climbers. Some short hikes near the base of the mountain are suitable for the average recreational hiker; look in a good hiking book or trail guide for details. For anything other than a day hike on a well-marked trail be sure to research your route carefully and take an experienced outdoorsman or guide with you. If you're interested in climbing to the summit, contact a local mountain climbing club or guide service (several are listed in the **Sports and Recreation** chapter). Don't let the beauty and attraction of the Cascades and Olympics fool you; people get lost and some die every year climbing mountains in Washington. For more information, call 360-569-2211 or visit the **National Park Service** web site at www.nps.gov/.

Spend a year in Seattle and you'll be amazed by the number of events that take place here. Residents embrace the few months of sunshine and the long, wet winter months with a variety of music, food, festivals, and sporting events. Here are some of the annual highlights you won't want to miss:

JANUARY

- **Keeping the Dream Alive: Martin Luther King, Jr. Celebration** — this annual celebration is held at the Seattle Center and features a unity march, motivational speakers, music, and entertainment. Call 206-684-7200 for more information.
- **New Year's Eve at the Space Needle** — for the past several years, the Space Needle has been the location for the most lively New Year's celebration in Seattle. From the formal dinner dance at the revolving restaurant level to the casual party at the base of the needle, it has become a destination for New Year's revelers. Even if you decide to spend a quiet New Year's Eve at home — consider driving (or walking) to one of the many parks overlooking the Space Needle just before midnight. The fireworks display, which is actually set off from the top and sides of the structure, is spectacular. Call 206-443-9700 for details.

FEBRUARY

- **Chinese New Year** — this traditional Chinese festival includes a colorful parade and is held in the International District. Call 206-223-0623 for more information.

- **Fat Tuesday** — Seattle's very own Mardi Gras celebration, Fat Tuesday events take place in bars throughout Pioneer Square. Call 206-622-2563 for details.
- **Festival Sundiata** — held at the Seattle Center, this festival celebrates African and African-American culture, history, and art, with exhibits and live performances. Call 206-684-7200 for more information.

MARCH

- **Board Stiff** — a concert and snowboarding extravaganza for the Gen-X crowd, Board Stiff takes place at Snoqualmie Pass ski resort in March and is sponsored in part by local radio station KNDD "The End." Featured groups are alternative rock and punk influenced bands. In addition to loud music and exuberant fans, there is a pro-invitational snowboard competition (hence the name) and related demos and products.
- **Irish Week Festival** — a family festival to celebrate St. Patrick's Day, presenting Irish films, history, dancing, and language workshops. This event also includes a St. Patrick's Day Parade through Downtown Seattle. Call 206-684-7200 or 206-329-7224 for details.
- **Whirligig** — an educational and fun-filled family event at the Seattle Center, with activities for children 10 and under. Call 206-684-7200 for details.

APRIL

- **Seattle Cherry Blossom Festival** — a celebration of Japanese culture at the Seattle Center, this even features Japanese artists, stage performances, children's entertainment, and cultural exhibits. Call 206-723-2003 for details.
- **Skagit Valley Tulip Festival** — for two weeks in April, the Skagit Valley hosts visitors with the annual Tulip Festival. Tour brilliantly colored fields of silky tulips, set against a backdrop of Mount Baker and the Cascade Mountains. You can also enjoy local art exhibits and special events, dine in local restaurants, visit nearby antique malls in La Conner or Mount Vernon, or send bulbs in all your favorite colors to loved ones. For more information, call 360-428-5959.

MAY

- **Northwest Folklife Festival** — held every Memorial Day weekend at the Seattle Center, the Folklife Festival celebrates the folk arts communities of the Northwest. This free event offers a blend of world music and dance performance, arts and crafts exhibits, musical and artistic workshops, and films and demonstrations focusing on ethnic and folk heritage from the Northwest. There's always an abundance of fragrant and delicious foods, and usually plenty of sunshine. For more information, call 206-684-7300.
- **Opening Day** — sponsored by the Seattle Yacht Club, the first Saturday of May is the annual Opening Day celebration, which marks the first official day of the summer boating season, and has been a Seattle tradition since 1909. Pleasure boats parade through the Montlake Cut and then tie up to one another in Lake Washington. The Windermere Cup rowing race is also held on Opening Day. Even if you don't own a boat yourself, you can enjoy the spectacle of hundreds of gaudily decorated boats and the Windermere Cup race from the Montlake Bridge or from the sloping sides of the cut.
- **Seattle International Children's Festival** — a Seattle Center children's celebration, this festival features appearances by performing troupes from around the world. Call 206-684-7338 for details.
- **Seattle International Film Festival** — the Seattle International Film Festival (SIFF) hosts new, independent, and restored films in Seattle theaters for three weeks of May and June. During the festival several films are screened each day at selected theaters. SIFF is known internationally and often debuts new films or shows independently produced films well before their scheduled release dates. Some showings during the event are attended by the film-makers or screenwriters, and audience members can ask questions or offer comments on the film. For more information, call 206-324-9996.
- **Syttende Mai** — celebrating Norwegian independence day, this annual Scandinavian festival is held in the Ballard neighborhood. For details, call 206-784-9705.
- **University District Street Fair** — one weekend each May, several blocks of University Way are closed to traffic for this fair, which features arts and crafts kiosks, music and dance performances, and lots of great food. Call 206-547-4417 for more information.

JUNE

- **artsEdge** — this new event is held at the Seattle Center, and presents innovative and experimental visual and performing arts. Call 206-684-7200 for details.
- **Pioneer Square Fire Festival** — held in Pioneer Square to commemorate the 1889 Seattle Fire, this event features a parade of antique and contemporary fire trucks, as well as music, food, crafts and entertainment. For more information, call 206-622-6235.
- **Out to Lunch Concert Series** — held at venues in Downtown Seattle, this intimate concert series attracts many popular musicians. Call 206-623-0340 for details.
- **Pride Parade and Rally** — the Seattle Gay Pride Parade is a boisterous Capitol Hill event which takes place on the last weekend in June. The sidewalks along the Broadway route are always jammed with animated onlookers. Parade participants range from politicians (boring) to the Dykes on Bikes (definitely not boring). Expect the unusual and you'll be pleasantly surprised.
- **Pagdiriwang** — a celebration of Philippine culture, this festival includes music, dance, and dramatic performances. Call 206-684-7200 for details.
- **Solstice Parade** — an eclectic festival held in the Fremont neighborhood, this event celebrates the summer solstice with a boisterous parade. For information, call 206-547-7440.

JULY

- **AT&T Family Fourth** — the annual fireworks spectacular sponsored by AT&T takes place above Lake Union near Downtown. The Seattle Symphony accompanies the brilliant display from Gasworks Park, which is always crowded with people. Other viewpoints along the sides of the lake are usually full of onlookers as well. If you know anyone with a boat, convince them to head out to Lake Union to watch the fireworks from the water — truly a memorable experience.
- **Bite of Seattle** — "The Bite" takes place in mid-July at the Seattle Center, showcasing local restaurants, microbreweries, wineries, and coffee houses. Local merchants and artisans open small booths to display and sell their wares, and musicians, jugglers, and other performers provide outdoor entertainment. Call 206-684-7200 for

more information.

- **Bon Odori** — this annual festival celebrates Japanese culture, with folk dance performances, traditional foods, and a colorful parade. For details, call 206-328-0800.
- **Chinese Arts and Culture** — this Seattle Center event showcases ancient and modern Chinese opera, martial arts, and other cultural arts. Call 206-684-8582 for information.
- **Fourth of July Ivars Fireworks Display** — a fantastic show of fireworks over Elliott Bay, this Independence Day event is enjoyed from the Seattle Waterfront. For more details, call 206-587-6500.
- **SeaFair** — the SeaFair festival begins in mid-July but lasts well into August, and offers something for everyone. The Milk Carton Derby at Green Lake, which usually kicks off SeaFair, is a race of homemade boats kept afloat (or not) by milk cartons. Other events include the Annual Torchlight Parade, a performance by the Blue Angels Flying Team, and the arrival of the SeaFair Fleet, Naval and Coast Guard ships that can be toured on the Seattle Waterfront. The grand finale of this event is the SeaFair hydroplane race (and qualifying races) which take place on Lake Washington. During the races, Seward Park is packed with people and everyone with access to a boat takes to the water to watch the excitement. For more details, call 206-728-0123.

AUGUST

- **Summer Nights at the Pier** — throughout the summer months, a series of concerts is held on Piers 62 and 63 on the Waterfront. Perhaps the most intimate live music venue in Seattle, this location is also breathtakingly beautiful, with the sun setting over the Olympic Mountains, sailboats floating in the Puget Sound, and the moon rising slowly over the city skyline. The lineup of musicians is equally inspiring, with folk, jazz, and blues bands predominating. Arrive early and have a glass of wine while watching the boats in Elliott Bay. Call 206-628-0888 for details.
- **Tibet Fest** — this festival showcases Tibetan and Himalayan cultural arts, folk music, and dance. Call 206-684-7200 for information.

SEPTEMBER

- **Bumbershoot** — named after a slang term for an umbrella, Bumbershoot is a Labor Day weekend event that's been a Seattle tradition since 1971. This performing arts festival takes place at Seattle Center and showcases over 2,500 artists from all over the world. In addition to arts and crafts booths and dance performances, you'll find fortunetellers, street musicians, delicacies from local restaurants, and non-stop music concerts in multiple venues. The cost of a ticket (usually about $7) covers admittance to all of the exhibits and performances, although you'll need to stand in line to get seats for the headlining acts. Check out the Bumbershoot web site at www.bumbershoot.org/ to see some of the past musical guests at this dynamic event. For more information, call 206-281-7788.
- **Festa Italiana** — this celebration showcases Italian food, music, art, and dance, including a bocce tournament and film festival. The event is held at the Seattle Center. Call 206-684-7200 for details.
- **Fiesta Patrias** — also at the Seattle Center, this Latin American cultural festival features traditional food, music, and dance performances. Call 206-684-7200 for details.
- **The Puyallup Fair** — also known as the Western Washington Fair, this event has been held in Puyallup (PYEW-al-lup) since 1900. If you decide to "do the Puyallup," give yourself a whole day to enjoy the fair. You'll want to sample a famous onion burger, tour a cattle barn, ride the roller coaster, watch a concert, and savor fresh corn on the cob. Or perhaps you'll decide to try your skill at bungee jumping, marvel at the hypnotist's skill, visit the prize-winning vegetable exhibit, and have several hot buttery scones. Don't assume this is a little country affair, or you'll miss out on one of the best events of the year. Puyallup is near Tacoma, and is about a one and a half hour's drive from Seattle. The fair lasts for 2-3 weeks in September and is the sixth largest fair in the United States.

OCTOBER

- **Halloween Carnivals** — most Seattle Parks and Recreation Community Centers hold Halloween celebrations for children. Call 206-684-4075 for details.

- **Oktoberfest** — a beer-lover's festival inspired by the German holiday, this event is held in the Fremont neighborhood.
- **Trick or Treat at the Waterfront** — this children's event is held the weekend before Halloween at the Seattle Aquarium. Call 206-386-4320 for more information.

NOVEMBER

- **Frostbite Regatta and Head of the Lake Race** — just as the weather gets a little too cold and the wind picks up the bite of winter, two annual rowing events are held in Seattle. The Frostbite Regatta on Green Lake is a series of fairly short races, easily watched from the side of the lake with a hot cup of coffee in hand. The Head of the Lake Race, which is held on a course that includes parts of both Lake Union and Lake Washington, is a three-mile race that tests the endurance of both rowers and spectators. Make sure you bring a thermos of coffee to this one.
- **Hmong New Year Celebration** — this Laotian Hmong festival takes place at the Seattle Center and celebrates the lunar new year with art exhibits and dance performances.
- **Winterfest** — an annual holiday event, this festival features school choirs, a public ice rink, and a model train display. Call 206-684-7200 for more information.
- **Yulefest** — the Nordic Heritage Museum in Ballard celebrates the holidays during this Scandinavian event. Call 206-789-5707 for details.

DECEMBER

- **Christmas Ship Festival** — boaters in Seattle celebrate the holiday season with a festive parade of lighted boats that tour the Puget Sound, Lake Washington, and Lake Union during the weeks before Christmas. Call 206-292-8020 for more information.
- **The Nutcracker** — no Christmas in Seattle would be complete without the annual production of The Nutcracker by Pacific Northwest Ballet. With marvelous sets by Maurice Sendak, this unique production is popular with all age groups. Call 206-441-9411 for details.

AGING

- American Association of Retired Persons (AARP), 206-526-7918
- King County Aging Program, 206-296-5216
- Senior Information and Assistance, 206-448-3110
- Senior Rights Assistance, 206-448-5720

ALCOHOL AND DRUG ABUSE

- Adult Children of Alcoholics/Adult Children Anonymous, 206-783-3722
- The Al-Anon & Alateen Information Service, 206-625-0000
- Alcohol/Drug 24-Hour Help Line, 206-722-3700
- Alcoholics Anonymous, 206-587-2838
- Cocaine Anonymous, 206-467-8189
- Highline Recovery Services, 206-242-2260
- King County Alcohol and Substance Abuse Services, 206-296-7615
- King County Involuntary Treatment (alcoholism), 206-296-7612
- Nicotine Anonymous Support Network, 888-214-2140
- Salvation Army Adult Rehabilitation Center, 206-587-0503
- Valley Medical Recovery Center, 800-469-3979
- Women's Recovery Center, 206-547-1955

ANIMALS

- Animal Bites, 911
- Animal Control Service, 206-386-4254
- Humane Society, Inc (SPCA), 425-641-0080

- Pet Licenses, 206-386-4262

AUTOMOBILES

- Abandoned Vehicles (on public property), 206-684-8763
- American Automobile Association (AAA) of Washington, 206-448-5353
- Illegal Parking (on public property), 206-625-5011
- King County Vehicle/Vessel License Information, 206-296-4000 (TTY 206-296-2709)
- Municipal Court of Seattle (call for parking tickets or traffic violations), 206-684-5600
- Seattle Police Department Automobile Impound Line, 206-684-5444
- Washington State Department of Licensing, 360-902-3600

BIRTH AND DEATH RECORDS

- King County Vital Statistics, 206-296-4769
- State of Washington Birth/Death/Marriage/Divorce Certificates, 360-753-5936

CHILD ABUSE AND NEGLECT

- New Beginnings for Battered Women and their Children, (TTY/Voice) 206-522-9472
- State of Washington Child Protective Services (24 hours), 206-721-6556
- State of Washington Child Protective Services, 206-721-6500
- State of Washington Child Protective Services, 206-872-2665
- State of Washington Domestic Violence Hotline, 800-562-6025

CITY GOVERNMENT

- Chamber of Commerce, 206-389-7200
- City Attorney, 206-684-8200 (TTY 206-233-0025)
- City Auditor, 206-684-8888
- City Council, 206-684-8888 (TTY 206-233-0025)
- City Information, (TTY/Voice) 206-386-1234

- Complaints and Information, all city departments, (TTY/Voice) 206-684-8811
- Crime Prevention, 206-684-7555
- Department of Neighborhoods, 206-684-0464
- Human Rights Department, Discrimination Complaints, 206-684-4500
- Information, all city departments, (TTY/Voice) 206-386-1234
- Mayor's Office, 206-684-4000

CONSUMER COMPLAINTS AND SERVICES

- Better Business Bureau of Western Washington, 206-431-2222
- City of Seattle Consumer Affairs Office, 206-684-8484
- Federal Consumer Product Safety Commission, 800-638-2772 (TTY 800-638-8270)
- Federal Trade Commission, 206-220-6363
- State of Washington Attorney General's Office, 206-464-7744 (TTY 800-276-9883)
- State of Washington Consumer Protection Complaints and Inquiries, 206-464-6684
- State of Washington, Office of Insurance Commissioner, 800-562-6900

COUNTY GOVERNMENT

- King County Executive, 206-296-4040 (TTY 206-296-0200)
- King County Land Use Services Division, 206-296-6640
- King County Health Services, 206-296-4600
- Metropolitan King County Council, 206-296-1000 (TTY 206-296-1024)

CRIME

- Crime in Progress, 911
- City of Seattle Crime Prevention, 206-684-7555

CRISIS HOTLINE

- Crisis Clinic (24 hours), 206-461-3222 (TTY 206-461-3219)

DISABLED, SERVICES FOR THE

- ARC of King County, 206-364-1613 (TTY 206-364-7438)
- Catholic Community Services Independent Living, 206-322-3637
- Community Service Center for the Deaf and Hard of Hearing, 206-322-4996
- Community Services for the Blind and Partially Sighted, 206-525-5556
- Hearing, Speech, and Deafness Center, 206-323-5770
- Learning Disabilities Association of Washington, 206-882-0792
- Northwest Center for the Retarded, 206-285-5441
- Northwest Vocational Services, 206-324-9352
- Paralyzed Veterans of America, 206-241-1843
- Shriner's Hospital for Crippled Children, 800-432-8200
- Washington Coalition of Citizens with Disability, 206-461-4550
- Washington Protection and Advocacy System, 206-324-1521

DISCRIMINATION

- City of Seattle Office for Civil Rights, 206-684-4500 (TTY 206-684-4503)
- City of Seattle Office for Civil Rights, Hate Crimes Line, 206-233-1080
- State of Washington Human Rights Commission, 206-464-6500
- Women's Rights, 206-684-0390

DOMESTIC ABUSE

- Domestic Abuse Women's Network, 206-656-7867
- Domestic Violence Recorded Information, 206-205-5555
- National Domestic Violence Hotline, 800-799-7233 (TDD 800-787-3224)
- New Beginnings for Battered Women and their Children, (TTY/Voice) 206-522-9472
- Northwest Family Life Skills, 206-363-9601
- State of Washington Adult Protective Services, 206-587-5620
- State of Washington Child Protective Services (24 hours), 206-721-6556
- State of Washington Child Protective Services, 206-721-6500

- State of Washington Child Protective Services, 206-872-2665
- State of Washington Domestic Violence Hotline, 800-562-6025

GARBAGE

- Solid Waste Services, 206-684-7600
- Transfer Station Information, 684-8400
- Household Hazardous Waste, 206-296-4692

HEALTH AND MEDICAL CARE

- Basic Health Plan of Washington State, 800-826-2444
- Central Area Health Care Clinic, 206-296-2770
- Children's Hospital & Medical Center Resource Line, 206-526-2500
- Columbia Public Health Center, 206-296-4639
- Downtown Public Health Center, 206-296-4960
- Family Planning Hotline, 800-770-4334
- Harborview Medical Center Sexually Transmitted Disease Program, 206-737-3590
- Healthy Mothers/Healthy Babies, 206-284-7311
- Highline 24-NURSE Information Line, 206-246-8773
- Kidcare Community Health Access Programs, 206-284-0331
- King County Communicable Disease Report Line, 206-296-4782
- King County Health Services, (TTY/Voice) 206-296-4600
- King County HIV/STD Hotline, 206-205-7837
- King County HIV/AIDS Program, 206-296-4639
- King County Immunization Program, 206-296-4774
- King County Medical Society, 206-621-9393
- North Public Health Center, 206-296-4838
- Northwest Hospital MED-INFO Physician Referral Line, 206-633-4636
- Seattle Indian Health Board, 206-324-9360
- Seattle Teen Health Center, 206-938-1360
- State of Washington Department of Social and Health Services, 800-865-7801

HOUSING

- Seattle Housing Authority, 206-615-3300
- Downtown Neighborhood Alliance, 206-523-2569

- Eviction/Deposit/Mortgage Default Information, 206-634-2222
- Tenants Union, 206-723-0500
- Urban League of Metropolitan Seattle, 206-461-3792
- Central Area Motivation Program, 206-329-4111
- King County Housing Authority, 206-244-7750
- Housing Repair/Rehabilitation Programs, 206-296-7640
- Department of Housing and Urban Development, 206-220-5205

LEGAL REFERRAL

- City of Seattle, City Attorney's Office, 206-684-8200 (TTY 206-233-7206)
- King County Bar Association, Lawyer Referral and Information Service, 206-623-2551
- Legal Action Center, 206-324-6890
- Northwest Women's Law Center, 206-621-7691
- Order for Protection Order Advocacy, 206-296-9547
- Unemployment Law Project, 206-441-9178
- Volunteer Legal Services, 206-623-0281

LIBRARIES

- Seattle Public Library, 206-386-4636
- King County Library System, 800-462-9600

MARRIAGE LICENSES

- King County Marriage Licenses, 206-296-3933

PARKS

- Seattle Parks and Recreation Department, 206-684-4075

POLICE

- Emergency, 911
- King County Police Department, Non-Emergency, (TTY/Voice) 206-296-3311
- Seattle Police Department, Non-Emergency, 206-625-5011
- Seattle Police Department, East Precinct, 206-684-4300

- Seattle Police Department, North Precinct, 206-684-0850
- Seattle Police Department, South Precinct, 206-386-1850
- Seattle Police Department, West Precinct, 206-684-8917
- Washington State Patrol, Non-Emergency, 425-659-4370 (TTY 425-649-4367)

POST OFFICE

- U.S. Postal Service General Information, 800-275-8777

RAPE AND SEXUAL ASSAULT

- Seattle Rape Relief (24 hours), 206-632-7273
- Sexual Assault Center (24 hours), 206-521-1800

ROAD CONDITION INFORMATION

- State of Washington Department of Transportation Traffic Line, 206-368-4499

RECYCLING

- Seattle Recycling Information, 206-684-7600

SEATTLE PUBLIC SCHOOLS

- General Information, 206-298-7000 (TTY 206-298-7831)
- School Board, 206-298-7040
- Superintendent's Office, 206-298-7100
- Special Education Information, 206-298-7935
- Special Education Family Services, 206-298-7850
- Student Assignment Information (recorded message), 206-298-7410
- Student Assignment Services Center (North), 206-729-3370
- Student Assignment Services Center (South), 206-760-4690
- Student Enrollment Services Office, 206-298-7218

SPORTS

- Seattle Mariners (Baseball), 206-622-HITS

- Seattle Seahawks (Football), 206-827-9766
- Seattle Sounders (Soccer), 206-622-3415
- Seattle Sonics (Basketball), 206-283-DUNK
- Seattle Thunderbirds (Hockey), 206-448-PUCK
- University of Washington Huskies (all teams), 206-543-2200

STATE OF WASHINGTON

- Governor's Office, 360-753-6780 (TTY 360-753-6466)
- State of Washington General Information, 800-321-2808

STREET MAINTENANCE

- City of Seattle Street Repairs, 206-386-1225
- King County Department of Transportation, Road Services Division, 206-296-8100
- King County Department of Transportation, Road Engineer, 206-296-6530
- State of Washington Department of Transportation, Maintenance Administration, 206-440-4650

TAXES

CITY
- City of Seattle Finance Office, 206-684-8300

COUNTY
- King County Assessor's Office, 206-296-7300
- King County Real Estate Tax Line, 206-296-0923 or 206-296-3850
- King County Personal Property Tax Line, 206-296-4290 (TTY 206-296-4184)
- King County Property Tax Advisor, 206-196-5202

FEDERAL
- Internal Revenue Service, Seattle District Office, 206-442-1040 (TTY 800-829-4059)

STATE (no income tax)
- Washington State Department of Revenue, 800-647-7706

TAXIS

- Broadway Cabs, 206-622-4800
- Checker Cab, 206-762-5533
- Emerald City Taxi, 206-624-6666
- Farwest Taxi, 206-622-1717
- Graytop Cab, 206-282-8723
- Orange Cab, 206-522-8800
- Yellow Cab, 206-622-6500

TOURISM

- National Park Service, 202-208-4747
- National Park Service Campground Reservations, 800-365-2267
- Seattle Visitor's Bureau, 206-461-5840
- Washington State Department of Tourism, 360-586-2088

TRANSPORTATION

AIRPORTS
- Seattle-Tacoma International Airport, 206-431-4444
- Boeing Field, 206-296-7380

BUSES
- Community Transit, 425-778-2185 or 800-562-1375
- Everett Transit, 425-257-8803
- Greyhound Bus Lines, 800-231-2222
- Metro Transit (King County) Information, 206-553-3000
- Pierce Transit, 800-562-8109
- Seattle Personal Transit, (TTY/Voice) 206-860-8000
- Volunteer Transportation for Seniors, 206-448-5740

TRAINS
- Amtrak, 800-872-7245
- Seattle Amtrak Station, 206-382-4125

FERRIES
- Washington State Ferries Information Line, 206-464-6400 or 800-84-FERRY

RIDE SHARE PROGRAMS
- Metro Transit Ridematch, 206-625-4500 or 800-427-8249

UTILITY EMERGENCIES

- Puget Sound Energy (Natural Gas), 206-382-7858 (TTY 206-625-9607)
- Seattle City Light Power Outage Hotline (24-Hours), 206-625-4448
- Seattle City Light Electrical Emergency, 206-706-0051 (TTY 206-233-7241)
- Seattle Public Utilities, Sewer Emergency or Flooding Emergency, 206-684-7506 (North of Denny Way) or 206-386-1230 (South of Denny Way)
- Seattle Public Utilities, Storm/Slide Citizen Resource Center, 206-684-3355
- Solid Waste Services (Garbage), 206-684-7600

VOTING

- Washington State Voter Information Hotline, 800-448-4881 (TTY 800-422-8683)

WEATHER

- Weather Service Forecast and Administration, 206-526-6087

ZIP CODES

- U.S. Postal Service Information, 800-275-8777

Answering Chief Seattle *by Albert Furtwangler*
A comprehensive historical analysis of Chief Sealth's famous speech.

Deception Pass *by Earl W. Emerson*
One of several mysteries by this author that take place in or around Seattle.

A Field Guide to Seattle's Public Art *edited by Steven Huss*
This book contains five self-guided tours of Seattle's best-known public artworks, as well as essays by artists, writers, and historians.

Make No Bones *by Aaron Elkins*
One of many mystery novels by local author Elkins.

More Perfect Union *by J.A. Jance*
One in a series of mysteries featuring fictional Seattle detective J.P. Beaumont.

Rites of Passage: A Memoir of the Sixties in Seattle *by Walt Crowley*
This book blends the author's personal experiences in Seattle with an exploration of the major political events of the 1960s.

Seattle Homes: Real Estate Around the Sound *by Jim Stacey*
A quirky must-have for those looking to buy; provides detailed information about the sticky process of finding and buying a house in the Seattle area.

Seattle Past to Present *by Roger Sale*
An excellent book which traces the history of Seattle while providing unique insight into many important decisions made by local politicians and citizens.

Shaping Seattle Architecture: A Historical Guide to the Architects *by Jeffrey Karl Ochsner*
This book traces the history of Seattle's architecture through biographies of the area's best known architects. Many famous Seattle buildings and houses are profiled in this book.

Skid Road *by Murray Morgan*
> The now-famous account of early Seattle, from which the phrase "skid row" was coined.

Zagat's Seattle Restaurant Survey *edited by Tim and Nina Zagat*
> If you like to eat out or have to for work, the annual edition of this indispensable survey will help you find the right restaurant for every occasion.

AMY BELLAMY was born in Seattle. She has lived in the Ballard, Eastlake, University District, Fremont, and Capitol Hill neighborhoods. In 1991, she received a BA from the University of Washington with a major in English. Currently she works as a supervisor and technical writer for a telecommunications company. This is her first book.

READER RESPONSE FORM

We would appreciate your comments regarding this first edition of the *Newcomer's Handbook® for Seattle*. If you've found any mistakes or omissions or if you would just like to express your opinion about the guide, please let us know. We will consider any suggestions for possible inclusion in our next edition, and if we use your comments, we'll send you a *free* copy of our next edition. Send this response form to:

Reader Response Department
First Books, Inc.
3000 Market Street N.E., Suite 527
Salem, OR 97301

Comments:

_____

_____

_____

_____

_____

_____

_____

_____

_____

Name: _____

Address _____

_____

Telephone (   ) _____

3000 Market Street N.E., Suite 527
Salem, OR 97301
(503) 588-2224
www.firstbooks.com

NEWCOMER'S
ORDER FORM
HANDBOOK ®

THE ORIGINAL, ALWAYS UPDATED, ABSOLUTELY INVALUABLE GUIDES FOR PEOPLE MOVING TO A CITY!

Find out about neigborhoods, apartment and house hunting, money matters, deposits/leases, getting settled, helpful services, shopping for the home, places of worship, cultural life, sports/recreation, vounteering, green space, schools and education, transportation, temporary lodgings and useful telephone numbers!

	# COPIES		TOTAL
Newcomer's Handbook® for Atlanta	_____	x $14.95	$_____
Newcomer's Handbook® for Boston	_____	x $14.95	$_____
Newcomer's Handbook® for Chicago	_____	x $14.95	$_____
Newcomer's Handbook® for London	_____	x $17.95	$_____
Newcomer's Handbook® for Los Angeles	_____	x $14.95	$_____
Newcomer's Handbook® for Minneapolis-St. Paul	_____	x $14.95	$_____
Newcomer's Handbook® for New York City	_____	x $18.95	$_____
Newcomer's Handbook® for San Francisco	_____	x $14.95	$_____
Newcomer's Handbook® for Seattle	_____	x $14.95	$_____
Newcomer's Handbook® for Washington D.C.	_____	x $13.95	$_____
		SUBTOTAL	$_____

POSTAGE & HANDLING (*$5.00 first book, $.85 each add'l.*) $_____

TOTAL $_____

SHIP TO:

Name _____

Title _____

Company _____

Address _____

City _____State _____Zip _____

Phone Number ( ) _____

FIRST BOOKS

Send this order form and a check or money order payable to:
First Books, Inc.

First Books, Inc., Mail Order Department
3000 Market Street N.E., Suite 527, Salem, OR 97301

Allow 2 weeks for delivery

FIRST BOOKS

Visit our web site at

www.firstbooks.com

for a sample of all our books.